P9-DTX-227

THE GOLF COURSES OF
ROBERT TRENT JONES JR

THE GOLF COURSES OF
ROBERT TRENT JONES JR

GALLERY BOOKS
An imprint of W.H. Smith Publishers Inc.
112 Madison Avenue
New York, New York 10016

Published by Gallery Books
A Division of W H Smith Publishers Inc.
112 Madison Avenue
New York, New York 10016

Produced by
Brompton Books Corp.
15 Sherwood Place
Greenwich, CT 06830

ISBN 0-8317-3921-5

Printed in Hong Kong

10 9 8 7 6 5 4 3 2

Edited by John Kirk and Timothy Jacobs.
Design and cartography by Bill Yenne.
Technical consultant: Pat Sullivan, golf writer, *San
Francisco Chronicle*.

This book was developed and designed by American
Graphic Systems of San Francisco, California, a firm not
associated with Robert Trent Jones Jr or Robert Trent
Jones II International.

Editor's note:
Unless otherwise noted, distances are in yards. This is true
of the courses in Canada, most of Japan, Thailand and the
United States.

The photo of Robert Trent Jones Jr seen on page 11
appears through the courtesy of Julio Donosa,
photographer.

Photo Credits

Accu-Shot, San Diego, California: 76 (top, middle; middle), 78 (bottom, left)
The AGS Collection: 6, 11 (top)
© Fred Andrews, Keystone Ranch Golf Course: 70–71
Arrowhead Golf Club: 19 (bottom, right)
Australian Consulate General: 26 (all), 27 (middle), 64 (all), 65 (top), 88–89, 90 (all), 91 (top), 104 (top), 104–105, 106–107
Cerwin & Peck Consultants: 72
Chip Carey, Sugarloaf Golf Club: 166, 167, 168, 170–171, 172–173
City of Brooklyn Park: 44 (top), 44–45 (bottom), 46–47 (all)
Cochiti Golf Course: 31 (top)
© RE DeJauregui: 34 (all), 35 (bottom), 36–37, 98–99, 100–101 (all), 102–103
© Jerry Downs: 69 (top)
Eugene Country Club: 50 (bottom), 51 (top)
The Foster Agency—Advertising & Marketing: 82 (all), 83 (top, left)
J Flynn Associates: 48, 49 (top), 144, 146–147
Glencoe Golf and Country Club: 54–55
Intercom: 38–39
Japan Golf Association: 114
Keystone Ranch Golf Course: 68 (all)
Kiahuna Golf Club: 1, 72–73
Al Licklider: 174 (top)
Paul Logsdon: 32 (bottom), 33
Mill Creek Golf and Country Club: 94–95 (top; middle, right), 96, 97 (top)
Northern California Golf Association: 126–127, 129
Oak Hills Country Club: 115 (all), 116 (all)
Patti Cook & Associates: 84 (all), 85, 86
Pine Lake Golf Club: 118–119, 119 (top), 120–121, 122 (top), 122–123, 124–125
Princeville Makai Golf Course: 132–133, 133 (top), 134–135, 136 (top), 136–137 (bottom)
Promotion Australia Photograph by Mike Brown: 66–67 (all), 92–93
Rancho Cañada Golf Club: 74–75, 75 (middle), 76–77, 78–79
Ed Rogich—R&R Advertising: 156–157
Trent Saviers, Reno News Bureau: 80
Sentry World Golf Course: 138–139, 140–141, 142 (bottom)
Shinwa Golf Group via the Japan Golf Association: 28 (all), 29, 57 (all), 58–59, 60–61 (top), 60 (bottom)

Jay Simons, Arrowhead Golf Club: 16 (top)
Springfield Golf Club: 2–3, 9, 158–159, 159 (top, right), 160 (all), 161 (top), 162–163, 164–165
Barry Staver, Arrowhead Golf Club: 16 (bottom), 18–19 (top)
David Stoecklein, Sun Valley Golf Course: 176, 178–179, 180–181 (all)
1987 Stroke Sports Ltd via Course Guide Publications Ltd: 10–11, 40 (all), 41 (top, right), 42, 43, 108–109, 110–111 (left), 112 (bottom, right; top)
Sunriver Resort Golf Course: 174 (all)
Sun Valley Resort Golf course: 177 (top)
Waikoloa Beach Golf Club Resort Course: 182
The Waikoloa Village Association: 184–185
Wild Coast Country Club: 186–187 (bottom), 187 (top, right), 188 (all)
Norbert Wilson, Forest Meadows Resort: 52 (all), 53 (top)
Wisconsin Division of Tourism: 138 (top), 139 (all), 142 (top)
Wyoming Travel Commission: 62 (bottom)
© Bill Yenne: 4–5, 7, 12–13, 14–15, 17 (bottom), 20 (top), 20–21 (bottom), 21 (top), 22 (all), 23 (middle), 24–25 (all), 27 (bottom), 30 (bottom), 32 (top), 35 (top), 41 (bottom), 45 (middle, right), 49 (bottom), 51 (middle), 53 (middle), 56 (top), 61 (bottom), 63 (middle), 65 (middle), 69 (bottom), 73 (top), 75 (top), 76 (bottom, left), 78 (top, left), 81 (middle), 83 (top, right), 87, 91 (middle), 97 (middle), 105 (bottom, right), 113 (top), 117 (bottom), 123 (middle), 127 (top), 128 (all), 129 (middle), 130–131, 137 (top), 143 (bottom), 148–149 (all), 150, 151 (all), 152–155 (all), 157 (top), 161 (middle), 169, 175, 177 (bottom), 183, 185 (middle, right), 189, 192

**Page 1: Amid the rugged vistas of the Hawaiian island
of Kauai, the elegant and crafty arrangement of the
first hole green at Kiahuna Golf Club announces that
you've embarked on an outstanding round of golf.**
Pages 2-3: This is a view from the green of hole number
one, on the beautiful and challenging Springfield Golf
Club course, in Gifu Prefecture, Japan.
These pages: This long vista is a portrait of hole number one at The Links at Spanish Bay, a course which is
certain to become legendary. This spectacular course
is the latest, and probably the last, to be built on the
hallowed golfing ground of California's Monterey
Peninsula.

TABLE OF CONTENTS

Introduction: The World of Robert Trent Jones Jr   6

Introduction:
The World of Robert Trent Jones Jr

Robert Trent Jones Jr

When you walk onto one of his courses, you have the immediate sense of being in a special, almost transcendent setting. You realize that here is a place that not only promises an unparalleled game of golf, but the experience of a carefully crafted environment that in itself is a thing of joy. While many golf course architects—and indeed many landscape designers—impose their will upon nature with broad, crude brush strokes, Robert Trent Jones Jr works in harmony with nature in a way that is reminiscent of the Zen garden tradition that began in Japan during the Asuka Period in the sixth century. In the last two decades, he has been commissioned to work his magic in some of the most beautiful locations throughout the world. It is an artistry verging on the magical, the creation of a true artist working hand in hand with nature.

Today, the sun never sets on the world of Robert Trent Jones Jr. The evidence of his skilled hand is seen in more than 130 courses worldwide—on the continents of Africa, Asia, Australia, Europe and North America. The archipelagos of Japan and the Philippines, as well as such exotic places as Fiji, Hawaii, New Caledonia and Macau are currently adorned with splendid examples of Mr Jones' work. Even the Soviet Union bears traces of an unfinished course in which Robert Trent Jones Jr has had a role.

This book is a world tour of some of the most important creations of a man who has, with considerable ingenuity, created golf courses which demand strategy, power and valor. The courses of Robert Trent Jones Jr are also built to accomodate players of different abilities, from duffer to professional. Mr Jones' 'great risks/great rewards' philosophy gives the golfer a choice: he can attempt to carry the lake or the monstrous bunker, or he can play around them, at the cost of perhaps one stroke. Also, the use of several teeing areas at the beginning of each hole allows a course to be set up so that the average golfer is not faced with the same circumstances as the professional.

Robert Trent Jones Jr was born in Montclair, New Jersey on 24 July 1939, and is one of two sons sired by that most famous of golf course architects, Robert Trent Jones (Senior). Robert's brother, Rees Jones, is himself also a golf course architect of some note. Robert Junior is familiarly known as 'Bobby'—a nickname which was unavailable to his father (who is known to *his* friends as Trent), as the famous American golfer Robert Tyre 'Bobby' Jones was the elder Jones' contemporary.

Robert Trent Jones Jr graduated from Yale in 1961, and, feeling a yen to break away from family traditions, did postgraduate work in law at Stanford. However, he found law less to his liking than he expected, and undertook an apprenticeship to his father in the golf course architecture business.

From the Breugels to the Barrymores, artistic tradition has often passed from father to son, and this was also the case here. A brilliant father passes the baton to his brilliant son by teaching him the fundamentals of the trade, and by granting him that certain something which edged his own work into the limelight of success. So it was, but there was of course that time of parting—the young must eventually 'fly on their own.' Trent and Bobby arrived at their particular parting place in the mid 1960s, while Bobby was designing the Silverado layout for Ed Westgate. People had said that Trent's courses were getting too tough, and Bobby wanted to ease the pressure by offering more play options than his father was wont to do.

At Silverado, Westgate wanted shorter yardages than were then standard, and Bobby complied. Not only that, but he included many of the features which have since come to identify a Robert Trent Jones Jr course—the most striking of which is the incorporation of many already existing natural and cultural features of the site into the course design for enhanced dramatic effect.

Jones, Senior disagreed with Bobby's choices at Silverado, but Ed Westgate said he liked the course design—and the customer often calls the tune. Although Bobby had apprenticed on courses such as Spyglass Hill on the Monterey Peninsula, it was now time for him and his father to part ways professionally. Bobby started his own company, but the family remains as united as it ever was.

Himself an avid golfer, Robert Trent Jones Jr has participated in numerous amateur tournaments, and has contributed various articles to golfing publications throughout the country. He was also chairman of the California Parks and Recreation Commission in 1983.

His commitment to international relations has garnered him many friends—including the late Benigno Aquino, the courageous

Above: The par five, 450-meter thirteenth hole of Les Terrasses de Genève golf course, at Golf and Country Club de Bossey, France. In the late 1980s, a number of Robert Trent Jones Jr courses opened in Europe, including two in France—the renowned Les Terrasses de Genève at Golf and Country Club de Bossey; and the superb Golf de Bresson layout at Grenoble.

Les Terrasses de Genève has been proclaimed as among the 'Best Fifty Courses in Europe' by the respected British magazine *Golf World.* Measuring 6022 meters from the back tees, it is a course that calls for precision and sustained concentration. The site—a historic chateau and vineyards at the foot of Mont Salève—has been shaped into terraces, a theme that is carried through to the architecture of the greens. The first five holes are played with panoramic views (over the adjacent Swiss border) of Geneva, Lake Leman and the Jura Mountains. Holes six through eighteen thread their way through forests before culminating in a breathtaking vista of the course and lakes, the chateau and the pristine beauty of Switzerland.

The course is maintained superbly, and time will doubtless see its recognition as a classic. Also just 100 miles south of Bossey is the Golf Club de Bresson, Grenoble layout, for which the city fathers of Grenoble commissioned Mr Jones. They wanted, and got, a golf facility that will add yet more renown to this fabled sports venue.

Robert Trent Jones, Sr

The greatness of Robert Trent Jones Jr was not nurtured in a vacuum, for his father is none other than the great Robert Trent Jones Sr. The elder Jones' name is known even outside of the golfing world by dint of the impression he has made on the world of golf itself—just as, for example, baseball great Joe DiMaggio became known to people who couldn't tell a baseball bat from a tennis racquet!

Mr Jones Sr was born in England near Ince, on 20 June 1906, and came to the United States with his parents in 1911. He started out as a fine golfer hoping to make it as a pro, then felt the call to design golf courses instead: he essentially designated his own curriculum at Cornell—partaking of such school offerings as horticulture, agronomy, landscape architecture and engineering—and was without doubt the very first student to purposely undertake a curriculum that would qualify one uniquely for golf course architecture.

Shortly afterward, the architect-to-be formed a partnership with the famed Canadian course designer Stanley Thompson. The Great Depression interfered with their plans somewhat—but 'Trent,' as he is known informally, got the idea of patching into the WPA network, and built public courses with labor from that vast pool.

World War II interrupted the golf course business, and Trent got through the war years by doing patch-up work and landscape consulting for the armed forces. After the war, however, he resumed his career and began to develop his renowned strategy of making golf 'a hard par and a comfortable bogey for all classes of golfers.' The first course which he designed using this maxim was the Peachtree Course in Georgia—which was actually a redesigning job. Then came Oakland Hills—the course which elevated Robert Trent Jones Sr to a level of true greatness within his profession.

Trent lengthened most of the holes, and retrapped the fairways and greens to put a premium on accuracy. He transformed Oakland Hills into an extraordinarily challenging course, and it became legendary for the skill it demanded from those who attempted it. The prestigious US Open was held at Oakland Hills in 1951, and later in 1961 and 1985. Said the great Ben Hogan—when he finally won the 1951 Open, shooting a brilliant 67—'I've finally brought this monster to its knees.' Despite the 'monster' image which soon grew up around his courses, he was much in demand. Foremost among the reasons: it was a key element of the Jones philosophy that each hole should be tough but fair, and his long fairways and massive greens have allowed players of lesser power to enjoy an exhilarating test of golf on the same courses that also severely challenge the best pros.

Critics have said that his courses were and are too punishing, and should be toned down. Nevertheless, the record speaks: Robert Trent Jones Sr has designed or remodeled over 400 golf courses worldwide, and three courses which he redesigned and five courses which he wholly designed were included in Golf Magazine's 100 Greatest Courses in the World for 1987. In addition, his course at Mauna Kea has often been cited as one of the greatest golf courses in the world. Mauna Kea, with the famous 'water hole' which plays over the Pacific, could now be called a father and son project, because Robert Trent Jones Jr has applied his magic touch in doing some renovation there (the course is included in this book).

Among his achievements are: Spyglass Hill, on the Monterey Peninsula; Sotogrande Old Course, in Spain; the Royal Dar-Es-Salaam course in Rabat, Morocco; El Rincon in Bogota, Colombia; Firestone South in Akron, Ohio; Point O' Woods, in Benton Harbor, Michigan; and Pevero, in Sardinia, Italy. He has done renovation work on such courses as Oakland Hills, in Birmingham, Michigan; Baltusrol Lower Course in Springfield, New Jersey; and Quaker Ridge, in Scarsdale, New York.

There is probably no golf course architect who has not been influenced by Robert Trent Jones Sr's philosophy—whether it be by affinity, such as in Jack Nicklaus' methods; or whether it be by direct reaction against, as in the case of Pete Dye's modus operandi. He has authored numerous books and articles on various aspects of golf, and he has memberships in many professional organizations. He is quoted in Newsweek of 29 November 1982 as believing that 'golf has afforded me an opportunity permitted few men...to complement and sometimes to improve upon the work of the Greatest Creator of all.'

Filipino political leader who opposed the Marcos regime, and whose wife, Corazon Aquino, deposed Marcos and is now the President of the Philippines. When Benigno was jailed for his views, Bobby went to bat for him. He persuaded the San Francisco Chronicle to run an editorial about the situation, and made several trips to Washington to convince Congress to take action.

Robert Trent Jones Jr has also served on the San Francisco Commission on Foreign Relations, and, very notably, he and his wife, Clairborne, were part of the US delegation to the Helsinki Accords conference in 1975. In addition to this, he has served and continues to serve on the board of the American Society of Golf Course Architects, and belongs to various high-level golfing clubs.

Robert Trent Jones Jr has designed courses in all types of terrain. Seaside linksland is the terrain on which such original Scottish courses as the Old Course at Saint Andrews were built, and Bobby has worked on such terrain at Princeville, in Hawaii, and the Links at Spanish Bay, in Northern California. Mountainous terrain, in which the architect combats erosion by rock riprap underlying the course, has its own unique features. Such courses are usually variegated and active—as is the very beautiful Sugarloaf course in Maine. Desert terrain, with its lack of water, stunted trees, sandstorms and general resistance to 'civilization' is a challenge indeed to the golf course architect, and Jones' Cochiti Lake course in New Mexico is a fine example of an ingenious solution to these problems. Temperate conditions allow great breadth of approach, and Robert Trent Jones Jr's beautiful courses at Pine Lake in Japan and Sentry-World in Wisconsin are premier examples of courses which have been designed in temperate conditions.

A Robert Trent Jones Jr course does not hand you a good game on a silver platter; it shows you that you can gain rich rewards for testing your abilities to their limits. This is what makes Robert Trent Jones Jr a genius. He creates courses that actually call players to higher levels of play without making them miserable by precluding their own level of play.

His courses enable players of varying talents to find their challenge. But be forewarned—there is really no way that you will have an easy time of it, no matter what level you play. Mr Jones' courses combine all aspects of the game of golf, including a truly masterful sense of aesthetics. The very beautiful courses that Robert Trent Jones Jr has built for the Shinwa Golf Group in Japan—Cherry Hills, Pine Lake and Golden Valley—attest to the mastery of his artistic vision. The astonishing, flowered, SentryWorld course in Stevens Point, Wisconsin, more than amply proves that this sense of beauty is accompanied by a rare ability to create courses that

are genuinely demanding and rewarding for the golfer who—whether new to the game or an experienced player—seriously wants to enjoy a round of great golfing.

The high level of sheer beauty of his courses is a delight and a challenge in itself. While faced with carrying over the flowers at Sentry-World, one must exercise some discipline to accomplish the task—in the midst of the ocean views at the Bodega Harbour course, and with the sound of the California surf in the background at the exciting Links at Spanish Bay, one is both challenged and refreshed at the same time.

With not just a few engineering marvels under his belt—including the great Navatanee Golf Club course in Thailand, and the great Princeville Makai courses in Hawaii—Robert Trent Jones Jr has established himself as a golf course architect who can build a course anywhere you want one—and build that course to perfection.

The beautiful Springfield Golf Club course in Japan is represented by the photo *above*, which was taken looking down the eleventh hole from its lakeside green.

Navatanee, for example, was built over the span of six years on surface that had been a flooded rice paddy; the World Cup was played on this site just a very few years after water buffalo had stood knee deep in its once-flooded fields. The Princeville courses, on the other hand, were carved out of Hawaiian lava beds, and are designed to incorporate and preserve burial caves and other artifacts of ancient Hawaiian culture.

Indeed, Robert Trent Jones Jr believes that a course should reflect its natural surroundings, and should partake of—and therefore be enriched by—the indigenous culture of the area. When the late Egyptian President Anwar Sadat wanted a golf course, he called upon Robert Trent Jones Jr to transform the barren sands near the Great Pyramid of Cheops into a championship golf course.

Thinking about the challenge that lay before him, Mr Jones did his homework; he travelled, he researched Egyptian culture. Finally, in a moment of inspiration, he envisioned a course that would appear as a finely laid out championship scheme from the clubhouse level—but to air passengers flying over the site, the course would have the shape of a gigantic *ankh*, the Egyption 'Key of Life.' The base of the ankh was to point directly to the pyramids, thus rescuing them from obscurely blending into the desert sands when seen from the air.

President Sadat loved Mr Jones' brilliant idea, and the course was underway when media criticism of Egyptian domestic policy forced a work slowdown; the new course became, sadly, the symbol of what was felt to be government extravagance. When President Sadat was assassinated, the marvellous course which was a symbol of Egyptian rejuvenation was allowed to lapse—like so many treasures of mankind's artistic triumphs—under the shifting sands of the Sahara.

The Egyptian course was not Robert Trent Jones Jr's only opportunity to create unique course designs. His Mill Creek Golf and Country Club course is arguably located at least very near—if not directly within—the 'Heart' of Texas. To add fuel to the fire, Robert Trent Jones Jr designed a green which is in the heart of the course in the shape of a valentine. To seal the bargain, the Governor of Texas himself issued a proclamation declaring that heart-shaped green to literally be the *Heart of Texas*!

Neither the Texas nor the Egyptian course is by any means geographically off the beaten track for the global scope of Robert Trent Jones Jr's enterprises—a map of his courses would stretch from Canada to Australia, and from California to South Korea by way of Europe! The first golf course to be built in the Soviet Union was to be a joint project between the two most famous golf course architects in the world—Robert Trent Jones Jr and Robert Trent Jones Sr. The Russians had actually started clearing ground for the course near Moscow, when President Jimmy Carter ordered a boycott of the 1980 Olympics against Soviet policy in Afghanistan. This move put a

halt to a grand project which may well find new life within the warm breeze of Mikhail Gorbachev's *Glasnost*.

Robert Trent Jones Jr's great courses have also hosted many, many major tournaments. The World Cup Championship has been held at Navatanee, in 1975; at Princeville Makai in Hawaii, in 1978 (the same year that the World Amateur Championship was held at his Pacific Harbour Golf Course in Fiji); and at the Pondok Indah Golf Course, Jakarta Selatan, Indonesia, in 1983. Three World Cups and a World Amateur Championship hosted on one architect's courses in eight years!

The richest purse in PGA history is the boast of the Panasonic Invitational, which is played annually on the Robert Trent Jones Jr-designed Spanish Trail Country Club in Las Vegas, Nevada. The 1986 Women's Kemper Open was played at Princeville Makai; while the Asian qualifying rounds for the 1985 World Cup, and the 1987 Mitsubishi Gallant Tournament, were played at Pine Lake Golf Club in Hyogo Prefecture, Japan. The flower-bedecked SentryWorld course in Wisconsin was the site of the 1986 USGA Women's Public Links Championship and was cited in 1984 by *Golf Digest* as America's Best New Public Course of the Year.

Again, the record speaks for itself: in the American Society of Golf Architects' choice of The Best 130 Courses in the United States for *USA Today* in 1984, 18 courses were built or remodeled by Robert Trent Jones Jr—a higher percentage of courses than any other architect except Robert Trent Jones Sr, whose 35 courses on the listing attested to 'Trent's' acumen. Remember, also, that 'Bobby' has been in the business since the sixties, and his father has been in the business since the thirties—meaning, of course, that the son has made tremendous headway in a relatively brief career, and is rightfully cited as one of the greatest golf course architects in the world today.

An excellent raconteur, Robert Trent Jones Jr would probably feel quite at home in—and would be a central contributor to the friendly community atmosphere of—one of those genteel little Scottish country pubs, where the game of golf, and its apocrypha, has been discussed in depth and at great length for centuries.

Fittingly so, then, that one of the greatest golf architects of them all might feel at ease in the homeland of 'the very thing itself.' There, among the crags and heather of the Scottish braes, and on the rugged coastal lands throughout Great Britain, legends have been

born, and these legends have travelled to many a far land; they've travelled indeed, around the world—like the stories of the great Celtic Christian saints and poets Brigid, Brendan, Patrick, Cynewolf and Caedmon.

There is a strength and a glory to a fair contest; and something about the fine, sweet and canny Scottish countryside makes one think of Heaven, and how things on Earth can echo those of Heaven. So the test of spirit can be echoed in a game; and character can ring forth in one's approach to a difficult lie. Can one resist temptation, can one overcome without overreaching? Isn't there, then, a submission to something far greater, and an admittance of one's own limitations? Yes, for the very moment that one thinks he has it made, the trap has caught him once again. And that's what it is in a great golf course—that mirroring. When we thrill to a good round, it's not in self-satisfaction, but in having had a glimpse of something vaster, and altogether more grand than our mere imaginings; the very reason that the Scots courses bear epithets such as 'Royal' and 'Ancient.'

We see in Robert Trent Jones Jr a still-young architect, a man who sees the mountain and has come to it. Robert Trent Jones Jr has taken his place among the elite. What mystery

Robert Trent Jones Jr has shaped masterpieces in all sorts of terrain and locales. He has succeeded in creating distinctive golf courses the world over. Shown *below* is a portion of his Discovery Bay course, with Hong Kong's skyscrapers in the background.

is it that brings such honor? There is a strength in the touch of mastery, and Bobby Jones bears forth that touch. He quite undeniably creates some of the most beautiful and playable courses in the world. Many of his courses not only have an unmistakeable 'championship' quality about them; most are truly works of fine art.

As Dante Alighieri said centuries ago as one who glimpsed—in the *Paradise* volume of his great epic poem, *The Divine Comedy*—the source of all truly fine art:

...As one,
  Who versed in geometric lore, would fain
  Measure the circle; and, though pondering
    long
  and deeply, the beginning, which he needs,
  Finds not: even such was I, intent to scan
  The novel wonder, and trace out the form,
  How to the circle fitted, and therein
  How placed....'

The mystery remains veiled, only to be glimpsed in such rare forms as may be graced upon the Earth. Therefore, we honor our true artists; and Robert Trent Jones Jr is a true artist—a man favored to be one of the world's great golf course architects.

The World of Robert Trent Jones Jr

Eagleglen Golf Course
Anchorage, Alaska, USA

Glencoe Golf and Country
Club, (two courses)
Calgary, Alberta, Canada

(Courses in the continental USA are
detailed on the following pages)

Princeville Makai
Golf Course (27 holes)
Prince Golf Course
(18 holes)
Kauai, Hawaii, USA

(Club De Golf
Churubusco, Mexico City)

Cancun Pok-Ta-Pok
Resort Course, Quintana Roo, Mexico

Kiahuna Golf Club
(18 holes complete,
third 9 under development)
Polpu Beach, Island of Kauai,
Hawaii, USA

Kulima Golf Course,
Oahu, Hawaii, USA

Club de Golf Palma Real,
Ixtapa-Zihuatanejo,
Guerrero, Mexico

Makena Resort Golf,
(18 holes complete, second
18 under development)
Maui, Hawaii, USA

Waikoloa Beach Golf Club
Waikoloa Village Golf Club
Hawaii, USA

Mauna Kea Beach Hotel
Golf Course,
Hawaii, USA

Pacific Harbour Golf Course,
Deuba, Fiji

● Completed courses

○ Courses under development

Courses not named in boldface were simply remodelled by Robert Trent Jones, Jr

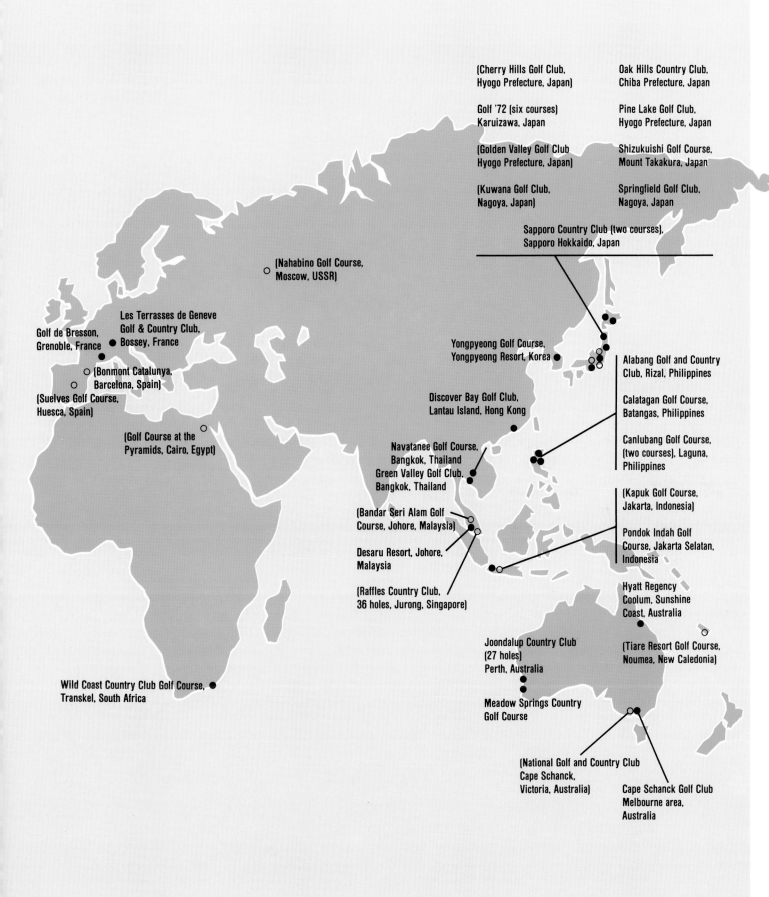

(Cherry Hills Golf Club,
Hyogo Prefecture, Japan)

Oak Hills Country Club,
Chiba Prefecture, Japan

Golf '72 (six courses)
Karuizawa, Japan

Pine Lake Golf Club,
Hyogo Prefecture, Japan

(Golden Valley Golf Club
Hyogo Prefecture, Japan)

Shizukuishi Golf Course,
Mount Takakura, Japan

(Kuwana Golf Club,
Nagoya, Japan)

Springfield Golf Club,
Nagoya, Japan

Sapporo Country Club (two courses),
Sapporo Hokkaido, Japan

(Nahabino Golf Course,
Moscow, USSR)

Les Terrasses de Geneve
Golf & Country Club,
Bossey, France

Golf de Bresson,
Grenoble, France

(Bonmont Catalunya,
Barcelona, Spain)

(Suelves Golf Course,
Huesca, Spain)

(Golf Course at the
Pyramids, Cairo, Egypt)

Yongpyeong Golf Course,
Yongpyeong Resort, Korea

Alabang Golf and Country
Club, Rizal, Philippines

Calatagan Golf Course,
Batangas, Philippines

Discover Bay Golf Club,
Lantau Island, Hong Kong

Canlubang Golf Course,
(two courses), Laguna,
Philippines

Navatanee Golf Course,
Bangkok, Thailand
Green Valley Golf Club,
Bangkok, Thailand

(Kapuk Golf Course,
Jakarta, Indonesia)

(Bandar Seri Alam Golf
Course, Johore, Malaysia)

Pondok Indah Golf
Course, Jakarta Selatan,
Indonesia

Desaru Resort, Johore,
Malaysia

Hyatt Regency
Coolum, Sunshine
Coast, Australia

(Raffles Country Club,
36 holes, Jurong, Singapore)

(Tiare Resort Golf Course,
Noumea, New Caledonia)

Joondalup Country Club
(27 holes)
Perth, Australia

Wild Coast Country Club Golf Course,
Transkel, South Africa

Meadow Springs Country
Golf Course

(National Golf and Country Club
Cape Schanck,
Victoria, Australia)

Cape Schanck Golf Club
Melbourne area,
Australia

The USA of Robert Trent Jones Jr

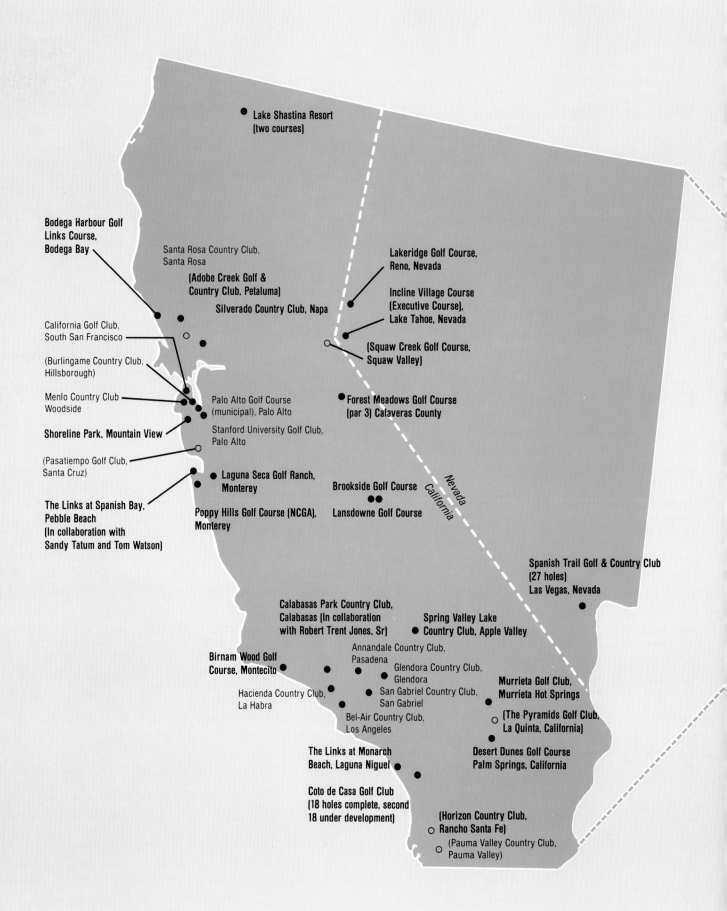

Lake Shastina Resort
(two courses)

Bodega Harbour Golf
Links Course,
Bodega Bay

Santa Rosa Country Club,
Santa Rosa

(Adobe Creek Golf &
Country Club, Petaluma)

Silverado Country Club, Napa

Lakeridge Golf Course,
Reno, Nevada

Incline Village Course
(Executive Course),
Lake Tahoe, Nevada

(Squaw Creek Golf Course,
Squaw Valley)

California Golf Club,
South San Francisco

(Burlingame Country Club,
Hillsborough)

Menlo Country Club
Woodside

Palo Alto Golf Course
(municipal), Palo Alto

Forest Meadows Golf Course
(par 3) Calaveras County

Shoreline Park, Mountain View

Stanford University Golf Club,
Palo Alto

(Pasatiempo Golf Club,
Santa Cruz)

Laguna Seca Golf Ranch,
Monterey

Brookside Golf Course

Lansdowne Golf Course

The Links at Spanish Bay,
Pebble Beach
(In collaboration with
Sandy Tatum and Tom Watson)

Poppy Hills Golf Course (NCGA),
Monterey

Nevada
California

Spanish Trail Golf & Country Club
(27 holes)
Las Vegas, Nevada

Calabasas Park Country Club,
Calabasas (In collaboration
with Robert Trent Jones, Sr)

Spring Valley Lake
Country Club, Apple Valley

Birnam Wood Golf
Course, Montecito

Annandale Country Club,
Pasadena

Glendora Country Club,
Glendora

Hacienda Country Club,
La Habra

San Gabriel Country Club,
San Gabriel

Murrieta Golf Club,
Murrieta Hot Springs

Bel-Air Country Club,
Los Angeles

(The Pyramids Golf Club,
La Quinta, California)

The Links at Monarch
Beach, Laguna Niguel

Desert Dunes Golf Course
Palm Springs, California

Coto de Casa Golf Club
(18 holes complete, second
18 under development)

(Horizon Country Club,
Rancho Santa Fe)

(Pauma Valley Country Club,
Pauma Valley)

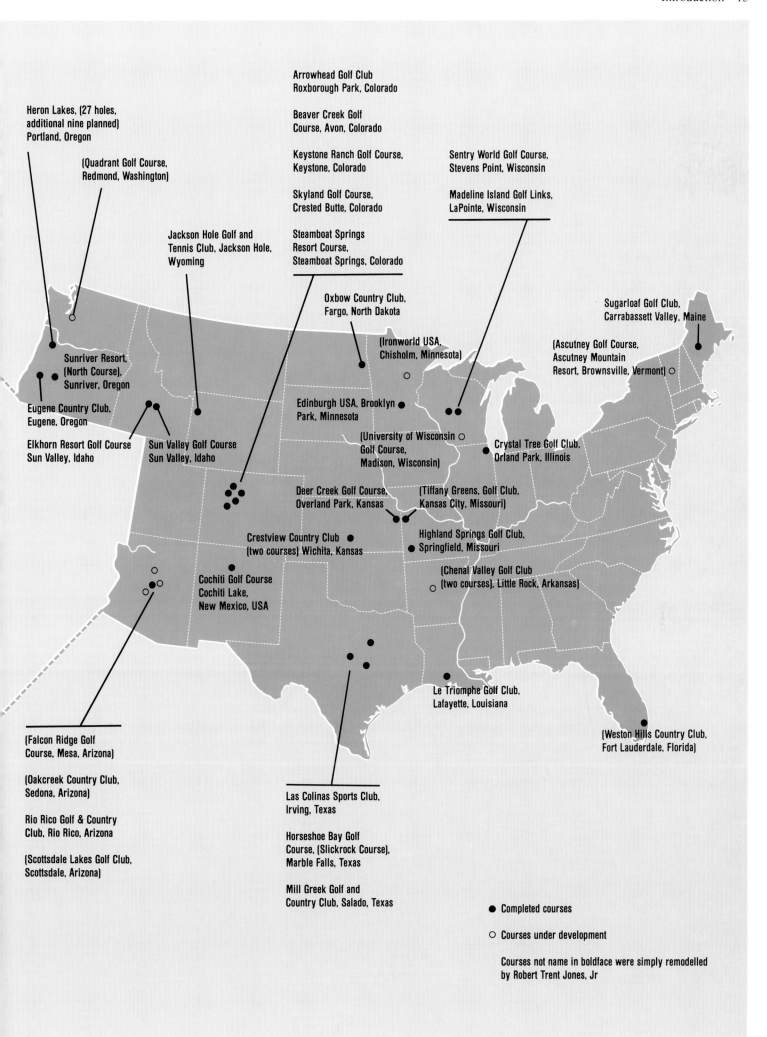

Heron Lakes, (27 holes, additional nine planned) Portland, Oregon

(Quadrant Golf Course, Redmond, Washington)

Jackson Hole Golf and Tennis Club, Jackson Hole, Wyoming

Arrowhead Golf Club Roxborough Park, Colorado

Beaver Creek Golf Course, Avon, Colorado

Keystone Ranch Golf Course, Keystone, Colorado

Skyland Golf Course, Crested Butte, Colorado

Steamboat Springs Resort Course, Steamboat Springs, Colorado

Oxbow Country Club, Fargo, North Dakota

(Ironworld USA, Chisholm, Minnesota)

Edinburgh USA, Brooklyn Park, Minnesota

(University of Wisconsin Golf Course, Madison, Wisconsin)

Sentry World Golf Course, Stevens Point, Wisconsin

Madeline Island Golf Links, LaPointe, Wisconsin

Sugarloaf Golf Club, Carrabassett Valley, Maine

(Ascutney Golf Course, Ascutney Mountain Resort, Brownsville, Vermont)

Sunriver Resort, (North Course), Sunriver, Oregon

Eugene Country Club, Eugene, Oregon

Elkhorn Resort Golf Course Sun Valley, Idaho

Sun Valley Golf Course Sun Valley, Idaho

Crystal Tree Golf Club, Orland Park, Illinois

Deer Creek Golf Course, Overland Park, Kansas

(Tiffany Greens, Golf Club, Kansas City, Missouri)

Crestview Country Club (two courses) Wichita, Kansas

Highland Springs Golf Club, Springfield, Missouri

Cochiti Golf Course Cochiti Lake, New Mexico, USA

(Chenal Valley Golf Club (two courses), Little Rock, Arkansas)

(Falcon Ridge Golf Course, Mesa, Arizona)

(Oakcreek Country Club, Sedona, Arizona)

Rio Rico Golf & Country Club, Rio Rico, Arizona

(Scottsdale Lakes Golf Club, Scottsdale, Arizona)

Las Colinas Sports Club, Irving, Texas

Horseshoe Bay Golf Course, (Slickrock Course), Marble Falls, Texas

Mill Greek Golf and Country Club, Salado, Texas

Le Triomphe Golf Club, Lafayette, Louisiana

(Weston Hills Country Club, Fort Lauderdale, Florida)

● Completed courses

○ Courses under development

Courses not name in boldface were simply remodelled by Robert Trent Jones, Jr

Arrowhead Golf Club

Roxborough Park, Colorado USA

Located in the foothills of the Rocky Mountains, on the outskirts of Denver, the very beautiful Arrowhead Golf Club course exists amidst some of the most striking and unique natural scenery to be found anywhere. Huge sandstone plinths jut up from the bed rock, through the fertile soil, and create a stunning accent and contrast to the wooded, rollings hillsides. It is a location that causes one to pause, and wonder from whence it came.

Robert Trent Jones Jr's course design melds into and uses this awesome beauty to great effect, creating a course in which there are no unmemorable holes. The setting is, in the words of *New Yorker* golf commentator Herbert Warren Wind, 'splendid and spectacular.'

Redolent of Old West history, the course interweaves such epochal echoes as the 'Jackson Photo Site,' on the dogleg of the fifteenth hole, where a famous Old West photographer had set up his camera to record the handsome and monumental sandstone formation there—one of his photographs includes part of the

The dramatic Jackson Photo Site on the fifteenth hole, *above,* **and a serene lake,** *below.*

wagon train (the 'Hayden Expedition') with which he was travelling.

Originally intended for the exclusive use of the residents of nearby Roxborough Park, the course was created in the early 1970s, the hand of design genius Robert Trent Jones Jr guiding the development of this golfing dream. Then, in mid-decade, the beautiful but still fledgling course was left in a state of neglect, a victim of the 1974 real estate market collapse. Luckily, Bob Waggoner (then of Meadow Hills Golf Course in Aurora, Colorado) had stumbled upon the Roxborough course that same year, while on a 'Sunday drive' in the hills. He was struck by the majesty of the setting, and by the course's cunning design.

After some years of wrestling with various legal and financial entanglements which surrounded his attempts to build a coalition to buy the abandoned course, Waggoner linked arms with Chuck Harrison, who was highly experienced in Denver's financial world. In 1978, the battle was nearly won—legal arran-

gements had been made, and the process of renewing the course was underway. Efforts were so personal, and so dedicated, that a common phenomenon was that of hauling rocks in and out of the area in the trunk of one's car!

The course was then owned by Arrowhead Golf Associates—a limited partnership of Harrison and Waggoner (as general partners) and 33 limited partners. Following this, a group of major western financiers bought the interests of Arrowhead Golf Associates. Bob Waggoner spearheaded the improvements made by these lovers of golf.

Hole one is a straight 431 yards from the regular tee. It's advisable here to keep the ball to the right, as the fairway rolls to the left, toward a rock formation and the water hazard which helps to guard the green. The green wraps around the water in a dogleg, and is additionally guarded on the approach by two sand traps. Hole one shares its green with hole seventeen.

The second hole rolls to the right, and a bunker guards the green to the left. There are no easy decisions on this course! At hole three, rock formations back the green, and two fat bunkers front it on either side. This par 3 hole is more visual hazard than anything else, and it looks shorter than it is: wear your golfing glasses or you're in trouble.

Hole four, at 413 yards, seems shorter than it actually is. Get near the green and everything becomes even more interesting in a hurry; there's one lake that it's all too easy to roll into, a brief hiatus at the end of the fairway, and across a patch of rough, another lake that plays vacuum cleaner with mis-hit shots to the green which lies beyond it, on its own little island amid the rough (and of course, keeping the green happy out there in Robinson Crusoe land is a nice little sand trap). Play cool, calculate and you will have an exhilarating hole of golf!

The fifth hole is a par five loaded with action. Tee shots have to cross a patch of rough, with a distracting lake on the right, and must make it between the two more lakes that guard

the mouth of the fairway; furthermore, a huge rock on the right lies in the line of flight, and the fairway is angled so that shots passing into the rough here face the massive rock's wall-like back which of course obstructs one's passage toward the green. Failing acquaintance with the rock, the golfer faces the rock's 'friend' across the elbow of this fairway—a very large and voracious sand trap. Make it around the right-tending bend, and you face Goliath himself, an oblong green surrounded with bunkers. Sensational.

Hole six is a par four with three bunkers set strategically around the green, so that the unthinking shot will earn you more chances to practice your swing on this one. An interestingly asymmetrical two-legged bunker approximately one third of the way down the fairway is set to swallow errant shots. A mariner's dilemma awaits you at the seventh hole. Also a par four, this hole is all clear until you hit the halfway mark on the fairway. At this point a pincer—composed of a fairly deep bunker on the left and a broad lake on the right—could make you lose your confidence. The fairway runs downhill, into the lake, so be ready. The green's tricky too, so check its tilt.

Hole eight has a massive rock formation to the left, which tends to grab your attention: wait until you've finished the hole, then stare at nature's grandiosity. If you don't, there is so much sand en route to, and surrounding, the green, that you could wind up contemplating desert flora and fauna before you sink your shot. The ninth hole is extraordinarily beautiful, and the championship tee is set back on a spit of land which has a rock wall to its right, demanding a very controlled long shot down the narrow left hand side of the fairway. A big green with two large bunkers and a rolling fairway seem to complete the setup, until you look to your right at the large lake there.

Arrowhead's tipsheet warns you about the tenth hole. Three bunkers lie to the right on the fairway, and the green has two bunkers, one of which is cited as the one bunker on the whole course that you should be most careful of. Hole eleven features a green which is tilted away from the tees—sort of a feeder to the stand of scrub oak behind the hole. Two big bunkers front the green. This is a par three, with massive rocks for scenery (and upon which to ponder your plight if you hit into the oaks).

Hole	1	2	3	4	5	6	7	8	9	Out	
Back	453	532	199	436	349	454	393	412	207	3435	
Middle	431	505	188	413	333	416	354	383	177	3200	
Forward	387	501	142	377	309	384	310	311	111	2832	
Par Back/Middle	4	5	3	4	4	4	4	4	3	35	
Par Forward	4	5	3	5	4	4	4	4	3	36	
Hole	10	11	12	13	14	15	16	17	18	In	Total
Back	418	153	415	174	364	398	578	204	543	3247	6682
Middle	398	141	399	174	356	361	549	177	494	3049	6249
Forward	380	121	378	130	247	314	519	146	454	2689	5521
Par Back/Middle	4	3	4	3	4	4	5	3	5	35	70
Par Forward	4	3	5	3	4	4	5	3	5	36	72

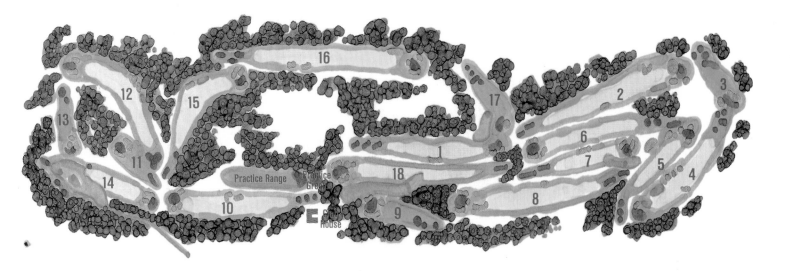

The twelfth is a long, slow dogleg left, with three bunkers in its elbow, and a ditch running most of the length of the fairway to the left. Scrub oak compounds the dangers, and the green itself is tricky, with bunkers left and right to help you aim your shot, and hope you've hit it right.

Hole thirteen has been called 'the most beautiful hole in the West.' This visual wonder combines optical intensity with a big drop from tee to green that demands your attention—you could find yourself dancing with less than delight as your ball sinks in the lake just beyond the green. Two big bunkers front the green of this very interesting hole, which begins from the tees in a small valley formed by several of the aforementioned sandstone rock formations.

Hole fourteen is also really beautiful, and has a variety of tee placements, including one ladies' tee in the middle of a lake! The championship tee fires from a sandstone alleyway, and men's tees have three locations. Wherever you are, the lake is a factor in teeing off, as is the rock just on its opposite shore which will surely be pestilence to shots from at least two men's, one ladies' and the championship tee. Once over this hurdle, a threatening grove of trees to the fairway's left could seem to magnetize your ball to them, and the green is shallow and slippery with two bunkers guarding its left front.

The fifteenth is the 'Jackson Photo Site' hole mentioned at the beginning of this article. A massive 187-foot high sandstone formation inrupts on the crook of its dogleg-right fairway. Opposite this, a pair of hungry bunkers lie in wait, and if you elude these hazards, the green is very tricky, with bunkers on three sides. Hole sixteen is 549 yards from the men's tees, and is a par five. You go uphill and down on this one, and there are six bunkers total, with three devoted entirely to the green. A stand of scrub oak behind the green *looks* farther away than your ball is likely to find it. Beware the trees.

Hole seventeen shares its green with hole number one. This fact alone makes for some visual distortion, as the green is massive—but then again, but not all of it's yours to play for this particular hole. A largish bunker just beyond the green makes things difficult. Just on the green's inside bend, two lakes could also make things wet. The eighteenth hole is a par five that hits you with everything. You tee off directly at a lake and the rock that fronts it. Hold up short and there's a tree to the right of the rock, and then you're on the home stretch, but the contoured fairway tries to roll you into the lake. Another tree to the left, a rock to the

The photo *above* faces us toward the green on hole eighteen, with the unmistakable Jackson Photo Site in the background. *At right*, we look out over the tees of hole thirteen, 'the most beautiful hole in the West.'

right, and then a 93- by 100-foot green protected by four bunkers and a stand of scrub oak behind.

Besides the beauty of this course, there is sheer subtlety of design; Mr Jones has wrapped these holes around the beauties already extant at the Roxborough site. The sandstone is massive, monumental and resonant of the tremendously powerful landscape of its Rocky Mountains location. At the end of the day at Arrowhead, you may want to stay around for a while—and watch the subtly glowing sandstone change and change again as the sun goes down...and stay awhile longer, to visit with the deer who come out when day is gone.

Bodega Harbour Golf Links

Bodega Bay, California USA

This Robert Trent Jones Jr course is the centerpiece of a planned community just off California's picturesque State Route 1, approximately one mile south of the town of Bodega Bay.

The tantalizing first nine was finished in 1976, but the golf community had to wait another 11 years before the second nine was brought into being. Since its completion in September of 1987, this 18 hole golf course is one of the most talked about and respected courses in Northern California—a ruggedly beautiful area that has much of which to boast in the realm of golfing.

This course is located in the vicinity of various important shorebird sanctuaries and conservation areas, including Sea Ranch North and South, Stewarts Point, Salt Point, Timber Cove (also Fort Ross—an important historical site of early Russian colonists), the Muniz-Jenner Highcliffs, Duncans Mills, Pacific View/Russian River South, Bodega

Golf at Bodega Harbour starts with the sign *shown above*. Putters get a workout, *opposite*, on marshland hole seventeen. *Below:* The fifteenth green.

Bay and Valley Ford. Therefore, golfers may well be blessed with closeup views of ospreys, herons and other indigenous California shorebirds on and near the course site.

Most of both nines are built on a bluff overlooking the bay, but the new nine—which now forms holes one through nine—plays up to and climbs the highest hill in the area for a spectacular view of the Pacific ocean and the rugged surrounding countryside. Then down across the bluffs and back toward the clubhouse, for a connection with the second—and older—nine.

This set of holes—now ten through eighteen—descends to a tidewater marsh, where the arena of play on holes sixteen, seventeen and eighteen is truly a test of golf in a spectacular arena, with greens set down upon the marshland which figures so prominently in the playing of these holes.

At the first hole, you tee off across a deep ravine for a breathtaking start to your round of

golf. Widely variegated tees provide golfing pleasure for a wide range of talents on this dogleg right, which has sand traps exactly where they will sharpen your play most. The green itself has traps left, left rear and right front.

Succeeding holes are intermingled with sites for pleasant, well-planned dwellings on the gently undulating coastal hills. The second hole features a welter of traps close to the driving line, and a green bunkered left, right and rear. Hole three has you teeing off to a green protected heavily left and right, with pot bunkers preceding these—straight up the middle and stop on a dime! Golfers at the fourth hole tee off over a brace of bunkers to a landing site which is also well bunkered, playing on to a contoured green with a bunker right.

Hole five is a zigzag—left and right and left again—the first turn bent around bunkers, the second backed and opposed with bunkers on the wide fairway. The green is bunkered left, right front and right, ensuring your attention to the last 'zag.' These holes climb the hills and grant you a truly 'top of the world' view. Golfers at hole number six tee off to a contoured green bunkered on both sides and behind; not too hard or too soft here! The view is superb.

The seventh's tees face a rather tricky green with a heavy bunker to the left and a smaller bunker at right front. Hole number eight has two massive, staggered bunkers which form a 'needle's eye' which you must thread en route

Bodega Harbour can be seen beyond the bird sanctuary, as a backdrop to the view *at left* of hole sixteen. *Below* is a glimpse over the back tees at the green, on hole seventeen. Bodega Harbour is to our left here.

to a green which is bunkered at right front. Hole nine has a bunker at fairway left which may serve to keep your shot right—into the maw of the 'X' bunker there. From that point, staggered bunkers guard the green at front, and a lone bunker catches overflow from the rear. The tenth is a delayed dogleg right, with bunkers right to keep you tending left toward trouble. The green is broad but shallow—a good carry, and a very good landing, are needed here.

The eleventh breaks toward the left at the 'hinge' formed by massive bunker emplacements right and left. The green is thus basically surrounded with bunkers. Hole number twelve's tees face a triangular green, which is

set point first, with bunkers right and left, guarding its flanks. Hole thirteen forms a delayed dogleg right on a contoured fairway, the turn coming at a place which is guarded by two bunkers left and one right. The oblong green has bunkers left and right. The fourteenth hole drives straight toward a green which is bunkered directly in front and at right and left. Hole fifteen tends slightly to the right at a point guarded by two opposing bunkers. The triangular green is massively bunkered in front, and waxes toward the rear, with a bunker on either flank.

The final three holes of this fine 18 are down the cliff, below the ocean-facing clubhouse. These holes are immediately adjacent

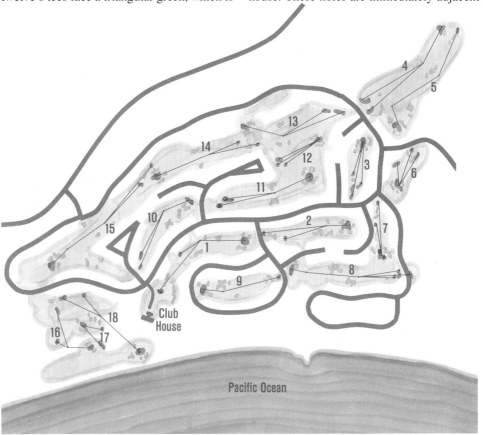

Hole	1	2	3	4	5	6	7	8	9	Out	
Blue	407	334	203	407	491	155	216	487	327	3027	
White	389	308	175	371	448	136	172	451	301	2751	
Red	283	251	135	305	415	88	128	397	270	2272	
Mens Par	4	4	3	4	5	3	3	5	4	35	
Ladies Par	4	4	3	4	5	3	3	5	4	35	
Hole	**10**	**11**	**12**	**13**	**14**	**15**	**16**	**17**	**18**	**In**	**Total**
Blue	332	399	186	413	443	510	291	152	467	3193	6220
White	292	363	158	377	400	476	271	137	405	2879	5630
Red	267	346	117	353	355	458	164	88	326	2474	4746
Mens Par	4	4	3	4	4	5	4	3	4	35	70
Ladies Par	4	4	3	4	4	5	3	3	5	35	70

to a bird refuge, and outstanding hazards here are patches of marshland, which are—as can be expected—included in play (players cross the soft ground on a plank bridge).

The sixteenth features widely variegated tee settings, with the back tees forming a right angle with the fairway, and the front tees coming almost straight on. The green is protected right and left, and just downhill is the sort of rough that will literally swallow your ball.

Hole seventeen again has a variegated tee setup, and rests just down a small cliff from the eighteenth's tees. You tee off to a green which has a huge bunker all along its left, and a small but important pot bunker to catch over-powered shots behind. The Pacific Ocean is, as it is from much of this course, in full view downhill to the left.

The finale, hole eighteen, descends toward the Pacific Ocean—a real beauty, with the point of landing for most tee shots on the fairway very well guarded at right by a covey of

Looking out over hole sixteen from just above hole eighteen, the waters of the Pacific Ocean and Bodega Bay mingle to bedazzle the eye in the photo *above*. Seen *at right* is the green of hole eighteen, which lies just a few yards from the Pacific Ocean.

bunkers. The green, some distance away, is protected directly in front by a lengthwise, peanut-shaped bunker, and has bunkers at right, left rear and rear. Hedges and a small cliff drop are all that separate you from the ocean! A gem.

The hill holes are like a tiara for this majestic course, but the sixteenth, seventeenth and eighteenth holes are the true crown jewels here, with their spectacular ocean views and 'back-to-nature' motif. Robert Trent Jones Jr always designs his courses to incorporate artistically the natural assets of any given course locale; at the very top of his profession, and a brilliant artist by any standard, he continues to create memorable golfing experiences for aficionados of the game worldwide.

Cape Schanck Golf Course

Cape Schanck, Australia

Stretching over 580.7 acres of Australian coastal bushland, the spectacular Cape Schanck Golf Club course lies just 49.7 miles from Melbourne, and adjacent to the National Golf Course of Australia, which is discussed later in this book; Robert Trent Jones Jr has used the recurring themes of ocean, bushland and rolling dunes to create these two 18 hole golf courses that can only be described as 'magnificent.' Both of these courses are of extremely high level, and are open to the public. The Cape Schanck Golf Club's undulating fairways lead to smooth, fast greens, and play is arranged around several tee settings to suit a variety of golfing talents.

In addition to its own excellent 18 hole course, Cape Schanck has a 'betting hole,' which is a very challenging par three, at which golfers can truly settle the question of who plays better—if that question has not yet been answered after 18 holes of golf on the course that is considered to be Australia's finest public golf course. Following is a hole-by-hole description.

Hole one is a dogleg right with bunkers positioned to catch overflights, and a hillside and a bunker left leading to the green approach, which has one bunker pinching in tight from the left. The second hole starts off over two incursing bunkers on the fairway's right. The fairway then cuts right, and another bunker right and a pinching bunker left make the green approach a matter of attention. Hole number three (a par three) starts off over a road to a large green with two bunkers right and one large bunker at left.

The fourth hole has an irregular fairway which tapers suddenly at its end to a narrow green approach which is protected on the left with a hefty bunker. Par three hole five has large bunkers en route to a green which is

amply protected on three sides by mounds and rough. Hole number six starts off from the right to a large fairway which is protected right, and has a bunker on the left of, and directly in the center of the approach to a long, narrow green.

Hole seven, a tough par three, starts off over the edge of a lake—most shots will go directly for the green, foregoing the small fairway. The green has trees right, bunkers at rear and left rear, and of course, a lake at left and left front. Hole number eight carries over the opposite edge of the same lake en route to a large fairway having a massive bunker on its left, and several very tricky bunkers set in a notch at right—opposite these is a corona of pot

bunkers on the left. The green bends to the right around a large bunker, and is protected at left rear by another bunker.

The ninth hole plays to a dogleg right with a bunker protecting the green approach; additionally, trees protect the green's right and a pot bunker protects the left rear. The tenth plays to a delayed dogleg left with two bunkers left and a huge bunker on the right of its 'shank.' These bunkers immediately precede the green which has trees at its left, right and rear. Hole number eleven starts off over foliage and through the trees to a left-tending fairway which has bunkers in its inner curve. The green cuts sharply left, with bunkers on its inner and outer sides.

Hole number twelve plays long to a contoured fairway having a green approach which is threatened from the left by a huge sunken bunker, while a similar setup applies to hole thirteen. This time, the fairway is squeezed from the right by two bunkers with a little 'bulge' of fairway in between. The green itself heads into a small bunker. The fourteenth is a par three that looks simple, but elevation is involved here; be sharp with this kidney-shaped green, or it's in the rough you go!

Hole number fifteen's very serpentine fairway hides a massive bunker which lies directly in line with most tee shots. The narrow, undulating approach leads to a green which is protected left and right with bunkers. The tees on sixteen form a 'Y,' with the back tees shooting through the trees to an abbreviated fairway/green setup, having a bunker at its nexus, and a bunker just behind the green. A great par three. Just beyond this are the tees for hole seventeen. Tee shots must carry over a gulley to a double dogleg right, which has non-obvious bunkers just where they'll create the most interest—if you know what we mean!

Hole	1	2	3	4	5	6	7	8	9	Out	
Championship	347	517	193	330	150	339	168	485	355	2884	
Mens	327	489	172	316	141	310	143	454	345	2697	
Ladies	309	477	152	275	130	278	128	416	310	2475	
Par	4	5	3	4	3	4	3	5	4	35	
Hole	10	11	12	13	14	15	16	17	18	In	Total
Championship	276	339	344	335	158	364	144	465	306	2731	5615
Mens	257	327	334	328	153	357	140	455	290	2641	5338
Ladies	245	313	321	308	136	323	114	422	261	2443	4918
Par	4	4	4	4	3	4	3	5	4	35	70

Distances in Meters

The green has a massive bunker on its right.

The eighteenth hole's tees must cope with trees hanging over from the right, a bunker lying directly where over-powered tee shots can find it, and a fairway which fades, near the green, around a right-lying bunker. A bunker at left also protects the green approach, and the green itself is surrounded by sloping ground. This all adds up to a superb test of golf.

This course offers golfers of all abilities a challenging round of golf. The vistas of Bass Strait are breathtaking, the golfing superb, and a cannily designed sprinkler system and full course maintenance crew keep this marvellous course in top condition year round.

The Cape Schanck Golf Club has a fully modern driving range, practice putting and chipping green, full range of rental equipment and an excellent, completely stocked golf shop. The course's locker room and shower facilities are equipped with every convenience, and Cape Schanck's ultramodern club lounge, bistro and restaurant give the finest service and provide the best à la carte cuisine on the peninsula.

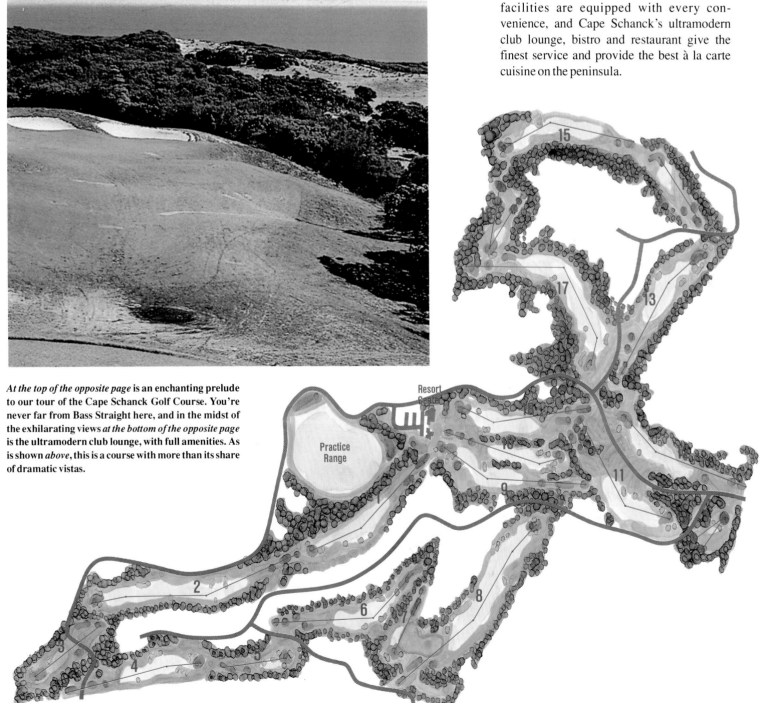

At the top of the opposite page is an enchanting prelude to our tour of the Cape Schanck Golf Course. You're never far from Bass Straight here, and in the midst of the exhilarating views *at the bottom of the opposite page* is the ultramodern club lounge, with full amenities. As is shown *above*, this is a course with more than its share of dramatic vistas.

Cherry Hills Golf Club

Hyogo Prefecture, Japan

This splendid course is set in Japan, and is one of three Shinwa Golf Group courses which have been designed by Robert Trent Jones Jr—the other two being the astonishing Pine Lake Golf Club course and the exquisite Golden Valley Golf Club course. Designed with a sense of mystery, gentleness and elegance, this course also has a commanding view of the Sea of Harima and Awaji Island. The course's location is classically Japanese, and could well be the subject of any number of delicate Japanese watercolors.

Mr Jones Jr sets out to incorporate the serenity found in the European countryside with the crisp, classic Japanese sense of beauty, accomplishing a lyricism and subtlety of expression rarely found in any landscape. Here, too, at Cherry Hills Golf Club is found a brilliant course design of the highest level, adorned with horticultural arrangements—and a quality of play—that are nothing short of memorable.

The 27 hole course at Cherry Hills demands every trick from the golfer's 'bag,' and yet is enjoyable—due to its multiple tee setup—for golfers of a wide range of capabilities. The openness of its terrain, with multiple ponds and streams, hearkens back to a purer time, and evokes a sense of quietude and reflection. The floral boldness that points out, and yet mysteriously melds with, the warmth of the setting reminds one that this course was created by the same artistic genius who conceived and built the legendary SentryWorld course in Wisconsin, half a world away.

Above, **Mr Jones energetically directs Cherry Hills' construction. Cherry Hills subtly echoes the flora of Mr Jones great Wisconsin course, SentryWorld** *(below).*

Here, in the mysterious East, this strikingly lovely course also offers a full test of golfing ability. It is an international masterpiece of nuance, subtlety and grand sweeping vistas which complement the extremely high level of enjoyment which is offered to golfers of all levels who play at Cherry Hills. With a choice of East, West and South nines, our hole-by-hole description of this fine course begins with the East nine, as follows.

The golfer at hole one has to play the contoured fairway, with bunker right midway down, and a bunker left at the mouth of the green. Roll has to be accounted for, and there are plants behind and rough to either side of the green. For the short second hole, the golfer starts off across an amphitheater-like bowl (with a stream running through it) to a green/fairway compound which has the lozenge-shaped fairway (with the stream to its right) tucked over to the right of the green, rather like an auxiliary item. With an ample bunker at the juncture of the fairway and green, and another set to the green's left, the golfer has plenty to deal with here.

Long hole number three, with its well-contoured fairway, rounds to the left, with a slight ridge and bunkers to either side of its 'turn.' Then you head for the green, which approach is pinched by bunkers either side. The green itself has foliage right and left. Also, running in and around the verdure that lines the fairway on the right is a little stream that could easily be a home for errant balls. It should be added that, as with all of these holes, the level of beauty here is stunning. Hole four is a shallow dogleg right that demands a tee-off across a stream which could, unless it's on the money, land you in foliage left, on the 'knee' of the fairway. Then it's straight down the contouring to a green with rough on the left and behind, and a bunker on the right.

You work uphill on hole five, a slight but appreciable rise from tee to green which describes a bend to the left. Your tee shot could overreach, and with the help of contouring, find the bunker at the dogleg's knee. A little too cautious and it's nature on the right. You overcome this, and a large bunker guards the green approach left, while a shallow depression guards the green on its right. Hole six demands a straight shot to a sunken green which is cunningly set between two bunkers front and one behind. Very interesting.

The seventh hole is a shallow dogleg left which climbs steeply over its 500 yards from tee to green. Tee shots must cross a road and a stream, and must avoid a bunker set in the left of the fairway, just where shots aiming to cut the distance may land. Beyond this bunker, a deceptive little spit of land lends hope to those who would cut the inside corner on the curve—beyond this, all too soon for the unwary, is rough and plants. Escape this and there are bunkers—two right and two left—waiting behind the various undulations of the

fairway. The green itself is bunkered left front and right rear, with a hillside and greenery beyond.

Hole number eight plays to a rolling fairway which has greenery to its left and right, plus a bunker to its right. The fairway then curves to the left, with three menacing bunkers set left of, and more plants and a road set right of, the green, which is also bunkered right rear. Hole nine starts off across a road to a dogleg left, the whole of which seems to pivot on a massive bunker lying in the amphitheater formed by the fairway's bend. Then it's a shot to a green which has three lobes and a bunker in the crux of each side. The splendor of the trees behind and the massive bunkers toward the fairway may you give pause before you make the shot.

After this, you may perhaps decide to play the South nine or the West nine for a truly full day of golf. Either option offers its particular charms—the subtle brilliance of the South nine is a favorite of many—but then the overtly lacustrine sheen of the boldly beautiful West nine has its admirers, too. Perhaps we will begin an imaginary round of golf anew—leading off with the mysterious and masterful South nine:

Hole one plays down a steep incline on a fairway with a bunker right and a stream to the left. The green breaks to the left and its right neck and face are protected with a long bunker; trees behind, and the stream downhill to the left, add to the challenge here. The second hole starts off downhill across a lake to a green which is bunkered at rear and at left rear; a stream meanders to the left and an incline lies to the right. Hole three plays uphill along a deep set stream to the left. The fairway curves into and narrows toward the stream. A carry will get you to the green, which is bunkered at rear and at left, and has the stream at front and right.

The fourth commences over a lake to an irregular, well-contoured fairway, which serpentines at its end and hides a bunker at right in one of its folds. A stream from the lake is a companion for much of the fairway's right side. The green approach is protected right and left, with the right bunker riding up on the face of the green; behind are trees and greenery. Hole five plays downhill over a very serpentine fairway dotted with declines and bunkers in its folds, and surrounded by forest. A dangerous place to slice! First left, then right, then left again—a carry would save some grief, but you'd best be on the mark. The green is shaped appropriately like a snake's head, and has massive bunkers all along its 'jaws.' This serpent is just about to disappear into the trees at the green's rear.

The sixth hole starts off uphill along a gentle serpentine to the left, again with bunkers hidden in its folds. Trees help to guard

the inner curve, and the last rightward curve aims toward a lake which is glimpsed at this point through the trees. Your ball could become aquatic here. The green cuts sharply left, and is protected under its 'chin' with an exten-

Delicately beautiful as a floral arrangement, the lake view on the South nine, shown *above*, refreshes the spirit and challenges the golfer's attention.

sive bunker, while at the 'back of its neck' lies yet another adequate bunker. Here, there is the incipient danger of getting lost in the trees which surround this hole. The seventh plays uphill along a radical left curve around a rough. On the inner curve near the tees is a very extensive bunker which could keep you out of trouble. Across a small jetty of land, on the same side of the fairway, is another extensive bunker which rides up under the green as it completes the curve to the left. Another left-lying bunker finishes the protection there. All along the outer curve—the right hand side—are trees and greenery in which one may get lost if one is not careful.

Hole eight starts off across the other end of the rough which made hole seven so interesting. A tiny fairway leads to a green approach pinched in by an incursing bunker at right, and the triangular green fronts the lake with its longest side and has yet another bunker, at right rear. To the direct rear are trees and bushes. The ninth plays downhill to a highly contoured, gentle left curve having a large slanting bunker to the right, in opposition to a lake which rides two-thirds of the fairway's left. Shots sliced right may catch the bunker on that side near fairway's end, and the green itself wraps left around the end of the lake and is protected on all other sides with bunkers.

You may want a respite before going on to the West nine. Rest a moment, take in the verdant surroundings, the quiet lake at your feet.

East											
Hole	**1**	**2**	**3**	**4**	**5**	**6**	**7**	**8**	**9**	**Total**	
Blue	380	205	525	425	450	180	500	370	405	3440	
White	355	185	500	395	420	155	460	350	380	3200	
Red	335	155	410	345	335	95	415	300	360	2750	
Par	4	3	5	4	4	3	5	4	4	36	
West											
Hole	**1**	**2**	**3**	**4**	**5**	**6**	**7**	**8**	**9**	**Total**	
Blue	410	565	415	180	450	350	195	320	525	3410	
White	380	530	395	160	420	330	175	295	500	3185	
Red	340	470	300	145	320	295	125	250	445	2690	
Par	4	5	4	3	4	4	3	4	5	36	
South											
Hole	**1**	**2**	**3**	**4**	**5**	**6**	**7**	**8**	**9**	**Total**	
Blue	410	185	420	450	565	405	395	165	520	3515	
White	390	160	395	415	510	390	350	130	485	3225	
Red	335	125	350	375	465	315	320	120	420	2825	
Par	4	3	4	4	5	4	4	3	5	36	

Through the trees, a glimpse of the practice range reminds you that this is no ordinary golf course; you are playing a visual gem, and a tough, meditative challenge on a level which is not simply a nice round of golf—this course quietly exhilarates, and subtly demands your very best, whatever your talent may be. Seldom before have you been so richly rewarded for your efforts.

The first hole of the West nine has a serpentine fairway with a huge bunker right, leading up to a contoured green having a large bunker left, and a small bunker at right. Hole two plays down a fairway which cuts radically to the left, and then slowly meanders to the right, having a huge bunker on this latter side, and having another bunker early on, placed just so to catch errant tee shots to the left. The green is canted to the right, and has a massive bunker guarding that exposed face, and a small bunker on the left of its rather pinched chin— to catch overpowered shots. Hole number three starts off across a gulley which contains a lake to a contoured fairway, and then carries another lake to the green, which rises dramatically toward the rear and has a large bunker on its right.

The course map *below* shows at a glance that the golfer truly has his choice of challenge at Cherry Hills. With East, South and West nines to choose from, one could find nearly limitless golfing adventure here. Note the lakes on the West nine.

Trees surround the green on the fourth hole, which starts off with the tip of the lake we met at hole three just to the right—don't slice! The fairway is tiny, and the green has three lobes, one of which faces the tees and has fair-sized bunkers on either side. Hole five plays slightly uphill. Beware the bunker at midway right of the fairway. The green bends to the left, and is protected on its hidden right side with a small bunker, on its exposed left side with a massive bunker, and at left rear with a small bunker. A grove of trees and a slope at right rear complete the enclosure!

The sixth is tree-lined at right, and bunker-lined at left! The approach to the green descends dramatically, and is pinched with bunkers at either side. That rear bunker has surely caught its share of over-powered balls. Through the trees beyond the bunkers at right you may glimpse the almost otherworldly valley of lakes which runs between the sixth and the third and fourth holes. Hole seven crosses a gulley to a small fairway and green combination. This curves to the left and is protected on both of its arcs from fairway to green with concomitantly big bunkers. Close behind the green is a grove of trees and bushes.

The eighth starts off over a valley containing a lake with another lake very close on the right. From the valley, the land rises gradually to the green. The fairway tends to the left, and the green heads into a corner full of trees, with the additional protection of a huge bunker along the fairway and green at left, and a small bunker at right. Trees and water everywhere!

Hole number nine is the grand finale for the West nine, and a grand, grand finale for any eighteen holes of golf. You tee off on a gradual rise to a gently serpentine fairway which tends left, then right. For the first half, there are trees right and a lake beyond them; and trees left and a lake beyond them. The rise then begins in earnest, and bunkers all along the right and all along the left accompany a sudden hook to the right, with the green atop the rise—and trees, greenery and the maintenance area and a parking lot beyond. From here, you can look back down the length of the hole, and through (and over) the greenery to what would now be your opposite facing right side. Here, you can see some of the lakes that in effect frame the tees of this and the eighth hole; look to the left, and you'll see another valley of lakes, separating this and the sixth and seventh holes.

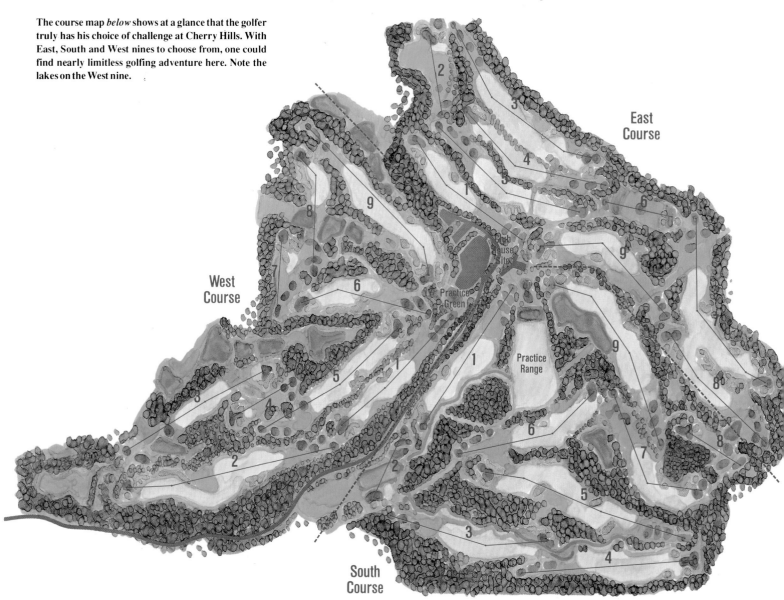

Cochiti Golf Course

Cochiti Lake, New Mexico USA

This course, which opened in 1981 and which has been honored by *Golf Digest* as one of the top 75 public courses in the United States, is an oasis in the arid New Mexican hills. Robert Trent Jones Jr has used his craft to work that same desert aridity into several of the traps in this beautiful course. Located just 40 miles southwest of Santa Fe, this fine golf course is easily accessible.

Situated near Cochiti Lake (which verges on the historic Santa Ana Indian Reservation), Mr Jones' design rhymes with that liquid jewel by means of its several water hazards—miniature 'lakes' which contrast and balance their greens and fairways just as Cochiti Lake itself does its desert setting. Here and there, hummocks of desert land erupt from the smooth green of the course to provide roughs.

Not only has *Golf Digest* designated Cochiti Golf Course as one of the top 75 public courses in the US, the American Society of Golf Course Architects has declared Cochiti to be one of the best designed 130 courses in the United States. Following is a hole-by-hole description of this exciting desert course.

Hole one's serpentine fairway has a large bunker to its left. The green here is literally surrounded with bunkers. The second hole has two bunkers in a left-lying fairway pocket, and the green is separated from the fairway by a deep arroyo. The green additionally has a bunker at rear, with a lake beyond this. Hole number three's dogleg right bends around the same lake, and the green here has bunkers at right, left and directly in front!

Hole number four starts off over the edge of the lake to an irregularly-shaped green having a large bunker at its upper left. The fifth plays along a narrow fairway which arcs right and has bunkers in all its most treacherous spots. The five-lobed green has four bunkers out in front in a narrowing 'gunsight' pattern. The fairway of hole six fades away from left-lying bunkers which eat up most of the approach to the green. Set obliquely to the right, the green calls golfers to a carry over at least one of these bunkers.

The seventh hole tees off to a rounded green having comparatively large bunkers covering nearly all of its side area! Hole eight is a dogleg right which is cut off from the green by an arroyo. Carry over this, and the three bunkers which front the green, and the playing

A fine and graceful course has emerged from the New Mexico hills. The photo *above* shows that, with proper planning, the desert can indeed be made to bloom.

fun has only begun. Hole number nine is a sweet, stunning test of golf. You tee off to a severe dogleg right which has a lake and bunkers just off its 'knee,' and then the contoured green faces you; the bunker at its left rear seems to be trying to tell you something!

The tenth has a drumstick-shaped fairway which widens toward the moment of truth—meaning, in this case, a water carry to the green which has a premonitive bunker at its left front in addition to all that water! The left-canted green of hole eleven challenges tee

shots with its bunkers on either side and championship putting surface. The twelfth plays as a dogleg right, with a tri-lobed green having bunkers just behind its side lobes—a fine test of accuracy.

Hole number thirteen is a long serpentine which lazily curves right, then suddenly strikes to the left, with the green as its 'head.' Bunkers on its outer curves may keep you to its narrow width, and the bunkers at the front, left and right of the green keep the challenge alive. Hole fourteen plays back the other way, with a bunker on its left-curving fairway's inner curve, and bunkers at the left, right and rear of its green. The fifteenth plays to a fairway which hooks to the right at the approach

Hole	1	2	3	4	5	6	7	8	9	Out	
Blue	517	393	360	185	522	375	120	365	415	3252	
White	482	370	340	167	485	342	113	345	395	3039	
Red	430	345	306	114	446	315	100	340	360	2756	
Par	5	4	4	3	5	4	3	4	4	36	
Hole	10	11	12	13	14	15	16	17	18	In	Total
Blue	314	140	415	530	440	299	183	503	375	3199	6451
White	284	120	380	490	411	274	163	485	350	2957	5996
Red	215	110	280	470	386	249	148	463	215	2536	5292
Par	4	3	4	5	4	4	3	5	4	36	72

to the green. The green has bunkers on both sides and in front.

The sixteenth hole features a long tee carry to a smallish, contoured green having bunkers on either side, and hole seventeen plays down a straight, tapering fairway with a bunker on its left side and 'gunsight' bunkers—two right, one left—prefacing the green. Of course, the green will be a test of your putting skill. The eighteenth hole is, fittingly, the great water hole of this great golf course. You tee off over the edge of the same water which we encountered at hole ten, but at this point, it has grown to be a lake! From here, a severe dogleg right faces you with opposing bunkers very near the likely landing spot. Then, if you dare, you can carry over the edge of a second lake (which we encountered at hole nine) to a green which juts toward the water, and has its 'landlocked' side protected by a huge right-lying bunker.

Cochiti Golf Course is a delight for golfers, and a test of all facets of a golfer's game. It is a desert triumph for Robert Trent Jones Jr.

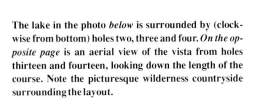

The lake in the photo *below* is surrounded by (clockwise from bottom) holes two, three and four. *On the opposite page* is an aerial view of the vista from holes thirteen and fourteen, looking down the length of the course. Note the picturesque wilderness countryside surrounding the layout.

Coto de Caza Golf Club

Orange County, California USA

Gnarled oaks, dating back two centuries or more, and a copse of ancient willow trees adorn Coto de Caza. Actually, these ancient trees became a very significant part of Mr Jones' palette in the designing of this course. The Trabuco Canyon countryside—where the course is located—is extremely beautiful, and there was the opportunity in this rolling landscape to build a unique course. As Mr Jones stated in an article (written by Robert D Thomas) on the course in the January/February 1987 issue of *Fore* magazine, 'I was attracted by both the trees and the terrain...The trees both provide and shelter a hazard, and their shadows add a unique perspective to the course.'

Opened in 1987, Coto was the first championship course to be built in Orange County for 20 years. An additional 18 hole course is scheduled to be constructed by 1990. Like many of Jones' courses, the greens are large at Coto, but are not unfairly difficult, neither are they easy—as Jones explains in the aforemen-

The hillside of the second hole forms a perfect composition with tree and sky, *above*. The bunker on the fifth's fairway is the intimidating image *below*. *On the opposite page*, a view across bunkers of the fourteenth.

tioned article: 'You have to understand what severity means in greens...In all the great courses of the world—Augusta, Pine Valley, Oakland Hills, all the way back to St Andrews—greens are meant to defend a target just like bunkers, water, rough, trees or anything else.

'On great courses, it's not enough just to hit the green; you have to hit the target, which is the flagstick. Coto's greens...are not as difficult as Poppy Hills—the courses are entirely different. But Coto's greens are not easy, either.'

In the same article, Mr Jones goes on to say '...This is a thinking player's course...and straight drives are the key when playing it. Landing spots have been incorporated at varying lengths so that all golfers will be rewarded if they use their heads.'

Coto de Caza is a par 72 course with tees at 7086 yards, 6665 yards, 6018 yards and 5362 yards—a challenging course for most golfing capabilities; as Mr Jones says in *Fore*

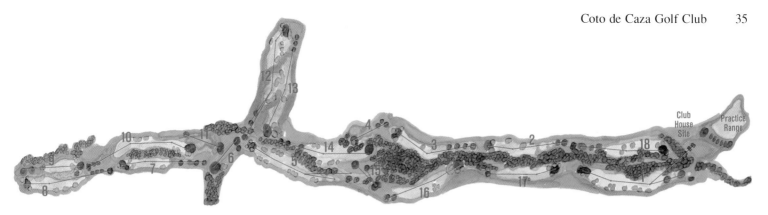

Hole	1	2	3	4	5	6	7	8	9	Out	
Gold	597	364	422	198	540	199	407	432	310	3469	
Blue	576	331	390	179	522	177	371	419	282	3247	
White	483	310	344	159	450	155	351	382	245	2879	
Red	429	288	308	135	426	143	284	336	239	2588	
Par	5	4	4	3	5	3	4	4	4	36	
Hole	10	11	12	13	14	15	16	17	18	In	Total
Gold	538	193	554	462	470	152	403	431	414	3617	7086
Blue	514	183	532	439	438	130	382	403	397	3418	6665
White	486	165	489	413	399	97	356	371	363	3139	6018
Red	440	115	455	361	370	87	296	333	317	2774	5362
Par	5	3	5	4	4	3	4	4	4	36	72

magazine, 'I wanted to design a course that, for lack of a better word, was clearly masculine...By that, I mean a championship-style course that is difficult, but fair....'

Many of the course's bunkers surround the eighth and ninth holes, and more than 100 bunkers help to defend the entire course. An overall characteristic is the requirement of making long, accurate drives and careful approach shots. The first hole is a dogleg right, par five uphill challenge of 595 yards; the seventeenth and eighteenth holes were described in *Fore* magazine by former US Open champion Johnny Miller as, '...the most demanding driving holes I've ever seen.' Mr Miller has also stated 'It doesn't get any better than this!' in reference to Coto de Caza—a quote that is used proudly in the club's membership package.

The three large windmills which are Coto de Caza's 'unofficial symbols' are not only decorative, but very useful to golfers checking their wind direction. Water hazards, also quite lovely, are the two lakes on the course, one of which is a full two and one-half acres. This lake makes the tee shot for the eleventh hole necessarily a long carry. Here is a brief hole-by-hole description:

Hole one is terrific and entails teeing off over a ravine; women's and regular tees must carry over rough. The rolling fairway is bordered by a plethora of bunkers left, and a wooded ravine right. The green is double bunkered left. Three bunkers on the right, with the last of these snuggled up to the green on its right face, make the second hole interesting. To the left, a stand of oaks impends near the fairway. The green is protected also on its left face. Hole three is a dogleg right, so you could be in trouble if you hit too hard, and the green is massively bunkered right and left, with another bunker behind.

On hole four, you tee off a long (165 yards) flight over water to a diagonally placed green backed by a bunker and a stand of oaks. Pretty exciting! Concentrate especially on this one. Hole five starts off from the longer tees at a dogleg right, and from the shorter tees, a slightly less acute approach to the fairway. The longer tees also have to carry over a ravine with a stream in it. It's a long drive down the slender, well-bunkered fairway, with what amounts to a pyrotechnic display of bunkers

toward the end, which will swallow up the errant long shot. The green itself is bunkered behind. The sixth hole is a blast across the nether regions to a green that looks tiny indeed, enclosed as it is in a cul de sac of oaks. Adding to the excitement is a bunker at left front, just under your line of flight.

Hole seven is a narrow fairway with inclined bunkers blocking the approach to a well-guarded green. The mouth of the fairway of the eighth hole is impinged upon by a huge bunker with an oak in it on the right, and three well-placed bunkers on the left. Drive toward a green with three bunkers at right front, right and right rear, and a bunker at left front. Hole

number nine's tee shots pass a tree at left, and approach a small green which is bunkered directly in front, at left, and at right by the previously mentioned massive bunker. Good luck on this one.

Hole ten curves to the right in a crescent which is guarded on its inside by trees, and on the apex of its curve by two bunkers and a stand of trees. The green is protected right by two bunkers, one in advance of the green itself, and one on its side. On the left of the green is a lake, and you know what that means.

Hole eleven has one of the windmills to its left—which is actually considered to be essential to the playing of this hole whose fairway consists of a broad lake. The tiered green is also impetus to concentration. The twelfth shares a mass of fairway with the thirteenth. Your tee shot could, however, find its way into the large bunker in its flight path. From here, it's a shot across rough to the secondary fairway leading up to the green. This fairway is shaped like an exaggeration of the outline of Italy and is bunkered in every nook and cranny of its perimeter where errant shots might stray. The green itself is guarded by two bunkers left and one large bunker right, with rough behind.

Hole thirteen has one of the best valley views on the course. A rolling fairway, with two bunkers where they will be most effective, leads up to a green with one bunker on the left. The fourteenth demands a tee shot that clears one bunker left, and three right, with the third here in dead line with any likely tee shot. You've got to think! From here on, it's a rolling fairway that leads to a green, the left of which approach is impinged upon by trees, and the right rear of which is also arboreally interesting. Hole fifteen shoots the gap between two oak trees to a green that tilts back to front, as if to dump your ball into the stream which you have just carried over. Incredible action for such a short hole!

The sixteenth is a long drive past three bunkers on midway right of the fairway. The maw-like bunker in front of the elevated green is not the end of travails here; for bunkers right and rough left are also to be considered with this green. Hole seventeen is a slight curve to the left, with an oak tree standing in the near-middle of the fairway like an unwary jaywalker. Get past this, and the green is practically outlined with bunkers!

Tee shots on the eighteenth hole must clear three small bunkers left. An inruption of greenery that forces the fairway into an extreme, narrow arc to the left will pose a problem or two. The green itself is guarded right and left with bunkers, and from behind by trees. It is a marvellous hole, and a triumphant end to your great round of golf at Coto de Caza.

'Coto de Caza' is Portuguese for 'Preserve of the Hunt,' which reminds us, as we consider the design of this course, that this area once was an exclusive hunting preserve for Portuguese gentry. History, in a way, repeats itself—for, in addition to the course, Coto de Caza also includes a huge development project of some 6000 homes in a planned community slated to occupy the verdant canyons of the area east of Mission Viejo and south of El Toro, California—and most of the member-,ships in the golf club will be reserved for property owners.

Altogether, the undulating terrain, large greens and yawning bunkers make this a challenging and extremely beautiful course: it offers 18 of the finest holes of golf anywhere.

Seen *below* is a line of bunkers on the perimeter of the twelfth hole. Note the steep face of the second bunker here. Combined with undulating terrain and large greens, bunkers like these keep the pressure on and the challenge keen.

With the rugged hills of Trabuco Canyon in the background, a lady golfer prepares to sink a putt on the lakeside green of hole ten. In Orange County, California, Coto de Caza—'The Preserve of the Hunt'—also means great golfing.

Discovery Bay Golf Club

Lantau Island, Hong Kong

The Discovery Bay course, situated on Lantau Island, has breathtaking views over Hong Kong Harbor. Just nine months after its opening, this superb Robert Trent Jones Jr golf course hosted the Hong Kong Amateur Championship—the first time ever that the Royal Hong Kong Golf Club's fine courses at Fanling did not host this important tournament.

There are many challenges at Discovery Bay, and among these are the many vertical angles of play—slanting lies, holes downhill, or steeply uphill—which call for canniness and precision. Such variegation is in part due to the fact that Mr Jones had to transform a steeply mountainous hillside into a championship golf course.

The course is a rolling, razorback-ridged plateau among the mountaintops of Lantau Island, and its rugged, sparse beauty reminds one of the courtyard of a mountain king. This is in part the product of moving over 5.2 million cubic feet of earth from the peaks to the valleys of the area that became the course.

The Discovery Bay course is situated some 754.6 feet above sea level—a fact that causes some golfers to bewail the wind, which varies from week to week. And its mountainside emplacement could easily result in lost balls for some golfers, according to Malcolm Grubb in his article on the course in the

Like a mountain castle, the Discovery Bay clubhouse oversees its domain in the photo *above*. Seen in the view *below*, the beautiful eighth hole, with its reflecting lake, makes you feel you're on top of the world.

Strokesaver booklet on the Discovery Bay Golf Club.

But this is in keeping with Robert Trent Jones Jr's philosophy of building courses that make the golfer think. As with many of the courses he's designed, the Discovery Bay course demands control, strategy and the intelligent use of power—the golfer who drives

the ball while sacrificing accuracy is in for trouble.

The first hole, for instance, features an angled fairway and an elevated green; to the right is a ravine, which spells doom for the golfer who slices to the right. Elevated greens and tees are yet another Robert Trent Jones Jr trademark—one of the many ways in which his courses both challenge the golfer, and take advantage of the rare and beautiful vistas which are part of many of this architect's course locales. Throughout the Discovery Bay course, downhill playing and uphill playing present challenges, the mountainside venue calls for strategy and the changes in elevation call for a conscious approach to perspective—no 'first glancing' here.

The first seven holes are the most difficult; the final 11 have promise of offering the golfer a chance to 'even the score'— especially the last three: the tenth's horseshoe green with its central bunker is a putting challenge. The eleventh through the fifteenth holes are fairly straightforward, and the sixteenth, seventeenth and eighteenth are all opportunities for birdies, being pleasurable yet challenging holes. Following is a hole-by-hole description of this exciting course.

Hole number one plays as a dogleg right, with tee shots carrying over a stream to a serpentine fairway having a rock and a water

drain on its left early on, and a ravine to the right. The oblong, obliquely-set green is protected by bunkers at left front and right. From this and the several succeeding opening holes can be had an intense and exquisite panorama of the rugged, rocky, mist-mottled peaks which rise up around this site. The second hole carries over a stream and plays with water to the left up to the mid section of the green. The three-bunkered green should be a putting challenge, and the water a pleasure and a good foil. Hole three plays to a fairway which curves right, then hooks left with the green around the tip of a lake. The fairway bunker at right will cause some calculation, and lots of water to the left tempts a carry to the green—beware that bunker behind the green!

At hole four, two fairway bunkers which angle across the foot of the fairway are sure to make your tee shot a thoughtful one. A bunker smack dab in the middle of the green approach adds interest here. The fairway of hole five connects to that of hole four. Fairway bunkers also come into play early on here. In addition, the fairway is sliced across by a lake which must be carried to the green. The green has one ominous bunker at left. A challenging, and rewarding, hole. The tees of hole six share a lake with hole three. The very long fairway has trees right and a bunker left early on, then bunkers pinching the fairway from right and left. The green is surrounded by some four bunkers—one of which is directly in front!

Hole seven has a narrow fairway, and the green, which wraps left behind a bunker, is heavily bunkered on its rounded right side. Hole number eight is short and sweet; its abbreviated fairway has a lake to its right, and the green wraps around behind this lake, so that Robert Trent Jones Jr's 'great risks, great rewards' philosophy comes into play. Tee shots to the green must carry over water here; to the fairway, not so—but caution could cost you the thrill of carrying over the lake, and maybe shaving a stroke from your score. Any way you play it, beware the big bunker behind the green!

The ninth hole plays as a dogleg left, with two big bunkers on its outer 'knee.' This hole plays, as most of the holes on this course do, on a hillside, with uphill on one side, downhill on the other and a distinct incline to the playing surface. The green is well bunkered. The mountainous terrain of this course makes

Hole	1	2	3	4	5	6	7	8	9	Out	
Championship	382	146	394	450	374	486	379	160	367	3138	
Regular	350	128	358	390	340	450	357	133	335	2841	
Front	325	108	332	342	290	386	350	114	304	2551	
Par	4	3	4	5	4	5	4	3	4	36	
Hole	10	11	12	13	14	15	16	17	18	In	Total
Championship	506	422	346	171	366	324	338	136	480	3089	6227
Regular	488	395	328	138	350	308	314	120	444	2885	5726
Front	446	340	306	106	286	274	282	112	412	2564	5115
Par	5	4	4	3	4	4	4	3	5	36	72

Distances in meters

Seen *above*, the rugged and enchanting ninth hole at Discovery Bay has all the challenge you could want—and its fresh mountain air will invigorate you.

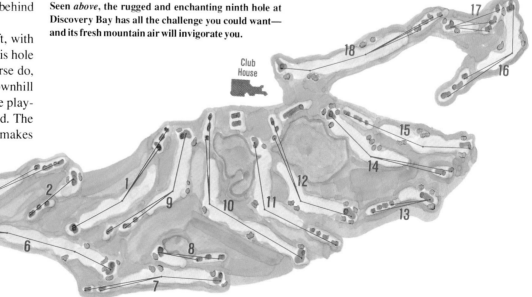

number nine a great hole for testing your sense of perspective, and the concomitant accuracy of your shots.

Hole ten is the longest on the course, at 553 yards from the back tee. You tee off with the tip of a lake (which also figures in play for hole eleven) to your left. The fairway is an extremely long, narrow, undulating dogleg right with a lot of 'shin.' A bunker awaits overpowered tee shots at the 'knee,' and another bunker hides on the right, toward the green. It's a great driving hole. The eleventh is a dogleg right with a bunkered 'knee.' A lake cuts across the green approach, and a bunker lies just opposite, so you must carry over water to the green, on the left of which is a lot of water.

The twelfth hole starts off over a lake, then bends left, with trees just inside the bend, and a bunker cater-cornered to them, which calls you to a good deal of accuracy here. Surrounding the green are numerous bunkers. Hole thirteen starts off to a short fairway/green combination, with an extremely well-bunkered green. The fourteenth hole plays to a serpentine fairway that truly makes for a great round of golf. The fairway hooks right around a cluster of bunkers on the right, then recurves around a left-lying lake, bulges left and swings out around a large bunker at left which actually fronts the green. On all sides of the green are bunkers, and with the lake to the left, you're talking hazards galore here.

Hole fifteen starts off to a fairway which curves gently to the left. An early bunker on the right and three cater-corner bunkers on the left make for a 'gunsight' coming into one of the most crucial curves of this fairway. The green is bunkered at left and on its right approach; it is a large green, and offers a true and gratifying test of your putting finesse. The sixteenth hole is straight forward with bunkers at both sides of the fairway and a two-tiered green having bunkers and slopes on either side.

The seventeenth's back tees carry over a ravine to the right to a short fairway and a contoured green which has bunkers directly in front and behind. The eighteenth hole has opposing bunkers early on—and on the latter part of of the fairway, two bunkers at left keep your attention focussed on the green, which is curved over to the right. Well-protected, this green is the satisfying conclusion to a hole which demands strength, accuracy and acumen—and this hole itself is the grand finale for a round of golf which asks the golfer to test his skills for great rewards; the old Hong Kong golfing hand as well as the golfing tourist will find this to be a course with both challenge and inspiration built into it.

In the foreground at right are the opening holes of a golfing adventure. The course at Discovery Bay melds a brilliant layout into a monumental setting.

Edinburgh USA

Brooklyn Park, Minnesota USA

Edinburgh USA is a municipal golf course operated by the Parks and Recreation Department of the City of Brooklyn Park, a northern suburb of the 'Twin Cities' of Minneapolis and St Paul. This is a course in which the public is treated to facilities and course design, service and a clubhouse which can only be termed superb.

Not only designed by one of the world's foremost golf course architects, this exquisite course is also equipped with a magnificent clubhouse, which features three restaurants, one of which features the cuisine selections of the award-winning D'Amico & Partners. This impressive edifice is designed to replicate a graceful Scottish country manor and is equipped to provide golf, business and social amenities that equal those of the finest clubs in the land.

Above is a typically tree-lined fairway at Edinburgh USA. Edinburgh's striking Scottish manor-style clubhouse, shown *below*, provides full amenities for golfers.

The course features 100-year old trees and 12 acres of water, as well as one of the world's largest putting surfaces in the triple green that combines holes nine, eighteen and the course's practice putting green.

Located in a residential community on the upper Mississippi River, Edinburgh USA offers the general public a wonderful golf facility. This residential community—known as The Highlands of Edinburgh—is a development of homes featuring designs by award-winning designers.

In a hole-by-hole description of this fine course, it may be noticed that hole one is a dogleg left on the fairway shared with holes two and nine. Careless shots can all too easily find the bunker lying right, at the 'elbow,' and over-cautious shots will find the three bunkers lying left, opposite the elbow. The rather ser-

pentine fairway approaches an 'L'-shaped green which is surrounded by bunkers.

The second hole combines a wide variety of tee positions with a short fairway and a heavily-bunkered approach to the green, while hole three is an excellent trial of golfing skills. Tee-off heads you straight for the lake or the bunkers—three of which lie left, on the apex of this gentle dogleg right, and the last of which makes an hourglass of the fairway. The lake lies right, and impinges on the fairway all the way to the green, which is trickily bunkered left, protected by a lake right, and canted so that bunkers or lake could be real problems.

The fourth hole is a dogleg right, long in the 'shin.' Avoiding the lake on the right of the 'knee' could land you in the two bunkers at the 'kneecap' or worse still, in the second lake which *worries at* the fairway from the left beyond the bunkers. This lake interacts with the fairway in a series of serpentines, the second of which brings the fairway to the green—on the right side of which are three bunkers hungrily waiting for the shot that overreacts to the lake on the left.

Hole number five features trees left on the tee-off, and two bunkers set boldly in the center of the fairway. Shots to the right of these risk landing in the lake which rides the

fairway's right. The green is set beyond a fairway bottleneck constructed of bunkers left and lake right; in back are rough and trees. Hole six is around the tip of the same lake that plagued (and made beautiful) the previous hole. A very short fairway, and a shot at the green around a horn of the lake. The green is protected at left rear with a small bunker that catches too-straight shots, and at rear by a broad bunker.

The seventh starts off to a serpentine fairway with a lake to the immediate left halfway down the fairway, and all the way along the tees. The fairway has two groups of bunkers, on the first righthand bend, and on the right again, as the fairway curves into the green,

which itself is backed by greenery. Hole number eight's fairway is one with its tees, and bends around a sizable lake, an inlet of which separates the fairway from the green, which itself is surrounded on three sides by water. A pleasure, I'm sure.

Hole nine ajoins its fairway to that of hole one, and shares a green with hole eighteen. It's a narrow tee shot to the left of a right-impinging bunker, and to the right of another encroaching bunker on the left—these two being set close together. Then down the fairway to a trouble spot having bunkers right, left and center! The right bunker sweeps around fully protecting the right of the green, and the left side of the green is protected by another

Hole	1	2	3	4	5	6	7	8	9	Out	
Championship	510	193	408	514	335	195	424	165	520	3264	
Club	492	176	393	484	315	178	404	150	508	3100	
Intermediate	474	133	360	448	282	141	369	125	486	2818	
Forward	440	93	304	425	258	124	341	101	449	2535	
Par	5	3	4	5	4	3	4	3	5	36	
Hole	10	11	12	13	14	15	16	17	18	In	Total
Championship	335	435	550	414	203	544	165	394	397	3437	6701
Club	313	415	515	390	185	528	145	374	370	3235	6335
Intermediate	267	404	479	372	164	482	118	343	352	2981	5799
Forward	242	376	438	347	123	446	106	317	325	2750	5255
Par	4	4	5	4	3	5	3	4	4	36	72

bunker and trees. There is also another bunker at right rear.

The tenth has a fairway which is split by rough, which encourages shots directly at a left-lying bunker on its second half, which is cater-cornered to a right bunker a little further toward the green; this bunker also cuts slightly in front of the green. Overcorrections for this could land in either of the two bunkers behind the narrow, obliquely-set green. Hole number eleven has a fairly straightforward fairway. Teeing off requires a carry across the arm of a lake which impinges on fairway access. The rolling fairway may take you near another lake arm which reaches toward the fairway at about midway—as if to literally grab the ball. The green approach is pinched with two bunkers and the green is surrounded by trees.

The twelfth is a long, gradual serpentine to the right, with an obliquely set green; three bunkers cut into the green approach from the left, and there are trees at left and behind, and a bunker at right rear. Hole thirteen is a slight bend left, with a gaping bunker to the right, where your tee shot is likely to land. The green is triangular, with bunkers set into its sides, and trees left and right most of the way. The fourteenth hole's fairway is just twice the size of its smallish green; the green itself is bunkered on each of its three sides.

Hole fifteen has a quick, tricky dog leg to the right, which could lead the unwary to trouble in the bunker revealed so suddenly by this bend. Afterward it's a drive straight into the very teeth of three bunkers which lie left, the last of which severely pinches the fairway, and on the right, two bunkers keep up the sand quotient. The green is a square with indented sides, with rough to the rear.

The sixteenth commences across a massive bunker to a green having a bunker at right, and trees right and behind. Hole number seventeen starts off to a fairway which is completely surrounded by a lake, and then it's a shot across the widest part of the lake to a smallish, triangular green having two sides to the lake and rough at rear. The eighteenth is a slight bend left which starts off into the jaws of a gaping bunker on the elbow of the bend, at right. Over corrections could land you in the rough at left. Then it's straight down the fairway to a green approach having a bunker at right, and at rear—across the broad but shallow green (which connects to that of hole nine)—a very large bunker, and at left, rough, with a considerable amount of green trailing away to the left rear.

With their interestingly contoured surfaces, the eighteen holes of the Edinburgh USA Golf Course compose a great municipal course, unparalleled for its playing qualities.

The golfers *at upper right* are on the lakeside seventeenth green. *At right* are some of the rolling fairways and massive bunkers that await you at Edinburgh USA.

Elkhorn Resort Golf Course

Sun Valley, Idaho USA

This splendid golf course partakes of the atmosphere of Idaho's Sawtooth, Boulder and Pioneer Mountains, where Ernest Hemingway found some of his greatest inspiration. Located in Sun Valley, the Elkhorn Resort Golf Course is considered by *Golf Digest* to be 'the best in the State of Idaho, and one of the top 130 in the nation.'

Sun Valley Resort has been dubbed 'America's favorite year-round playground.' Seasonal activities include skiing on Mount Baldy (which is said by experts to be one of the finest skiing mountains in the world), tennis, horseback riding, fishing, swimming, hiking, white-water rafting and other activities.

Elkhorn Resort plaza features meandering paths through picturesque gardens, excellent restaurants and fine shops. This deluxe resort came under the guidance of Amfac Resorts in June of 1987. Committed to excellence, Elkhorn boasts a brand-new $4.5 million refurbishment, elevating all guest facilities to an even higher state of luxury.

The prime interest here is, of course, Elkhorn's championship golf course, which was collaboratively designed by Robert Trent Jones Jr and Robert Trent Jones Sr. The course is arrayed around a series of streams, lakes and sand traps, and generally follows the road which runs from Sun Valley to US 93.

Holes one through four, and eight and nine surround Elkhorn Village, where most of the resort's visitor amenities are located, including Elkhorn's fully equipped golf shop.

Holes one through eight run the gamut of low brush and strategically placed bunkers. Undulating vistas enrapture the senses at every turn, especially as you reach the fifth hole, where an unexpected stunning view, as you edge over a rise, can take your breath away. Most of these holes are confined in their own framework of low brush, and the occasional juniper and Scotch pine add further interest. Water is the nemesis of holes nine through eighteen, and challenges the talents of every level of player. A stream becomes involved with hole nine just to the left of the green, and follows the tenth hole all the way up on that hole's right, only to form a pond directly in front of the green of short hole eleven!

The twelfth hole starts off across another stream, and culminates in a green which has stream on two sides of it; hole number thirteen has the stream as a companion—first on the right, then, crossing it, on the left—for the entirety of that hole's length. The fourteenth starts off beside the stream, and its green is confined by same on its right side.

The stream follows hole fifteen entirely on that fairway's right, and just the opposite for the sixteenth, which plays to the other side of the stream. Hole seventeen is a dogleg left which roughly follows the inner curve of the stream, and the par five eighteenth has the stream on *its* right, and brush on its right.

Altogether it's an interesting course, set in a stunning location. Great golfing is to be had here.

At Elkhorn, the Idaho mountain scenery seems to be everywhere, as the photo *at left* suggests. *Above right*, we have a view of the course, along the valley.

Hole	1	2	3	4	5	6	7	8	9	Out	
Championship	405	438	224	427	644	154	417	450	592	3751	
Mens	387	371	202	392	605	137	361	422	566	3443	
Ladies	367	300	172	291	569	100	337	395	521	3052	
Par	4	4	3	4	5	3	4	4	5	36	
Hole	**10**	**11**	**12**	**13**	**14**	**15**	**16**	**17**	**18**	**In**	**Total**
Championship	386	159	423	519	167	367	351	434	544	3350	7101
Mens	350	135	392	488	128	341	332	388	527	3081	6524
Ladies	293	78	350	461	117	302	311	333	503	2649	5701
Par	4	3	4	5	3	4	4	4	5	36	72

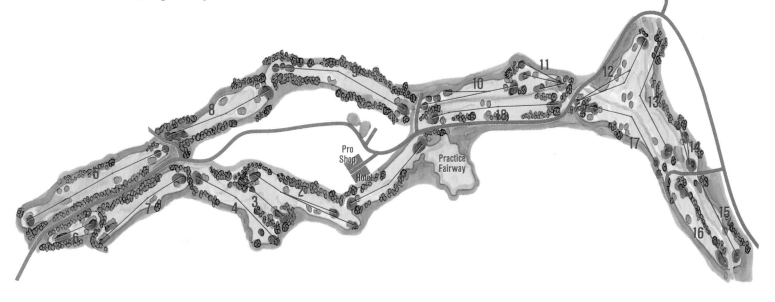

Eugene Country Club

Eugene, Oregon USA

The Eugene Golf Club course was originally built in 1923 by Chandler Egan, and was completely remodeled in 1967 by Robert Trent Jones Jr and Robert Trent Jones Sr. The course was reversed; Jones Sr had never done that before, or since. The members of the country club played the course even during its remodeling, and when the process was completed, as part of the grand opening, the course was played the old way one day and the new way the next day.

An extremely well 'treed' course, the Eugene Country Club is replete with stately evergreens, maples, oaks, ornamentals and 60 varieties of trees in all. It was included among the great golf courses of the United States in a survey taken by the American Society of Golf Course Architects in 1987.

The Eugene Country Club course has a European feel, with its nooks and crannies, and is highly attractive.

To begin our hole-by-hole description of this fine course, it should be said that all the fairways are rolling, producing a variety of lies. Hole number one has a wide fairway, with bunkers right and left, leading to a green protected right and left with bunkers. Intermittent trees keep it visually interesting, and the green backs up to the tees for hole two—which hole is straightforward to a large, heavily protected green having bunkers right front, left front and at rear. Lots of trees here. The third is shaped a bit like a caveman's club, with the fairway widening to the green from the tees. Two bunkers left at midway could cause some consternation—look sharp! The

green is round, protected left front and right rear. Again, lots of trees and shrubbery to get mixed up in.

Hole four has an intrusive bunker at right on the fairway, as well as a largish, well-protected green. All along the right is a lake. Hole number five plays slightly downhill, and gives you a chance to carry over a stream which feeds the aforementioned lake. The green here has three bunkers behind to define the target. The sixth tees off to a long fairway which features a turn to the right, and then a carry across a stream to a green which is bunkered at rear.

The seventh is a short hole, which carries across the aforementioned stream to a green which is well-bunkered behind, with lots of verdure backing up the bunkers! Hole number

eight climbs a slight bit, has a fairway bunker at right and a green which has a small bunker rear and two large bunkers at front. The ninth is a slight dogleg right that plays through pear and apple trees! The rolling green is bunkered right and left.

Hole ten, a slight uphill with bunkers left and a very well bunkered green with shrubbery behind, builds you up for hole eleven—featuring a curve to the right which has you playing straight at a stand of trees if you're not thinking. The entrance to the green involves a lake inlet which intrudes half way, and the shallow green itself is backed by cunningly set bunkers at rear. A small stream awaits any shot over the green.

The twelfth plays around a curve of the small lake which intruded on hole eleven, and additionally has trees and shrubs left. Its green is bunkered behind and at right. Hole thirteen is a classic par five, with a tight driving area, bunkered left, and a large grove of oak trees on the right. The second shot plays between fir trees on the right, and huge maples on the left. Hole number fourteen is a dogleg right, with shrubbery on the left of the green. The fifteenth is the most difficult par four on the course. Adding to the challenge here, a deep bunker protects the front of the elevated green, and trees await errant shots in the 'elbow' of the fairway.

Hole number sixteen features a drive to a tilted green with bunkers front and back, and water to its right and left. Hole number seventeen requires a faded tee shot to the right half of the fairway—a huge tree protects the opposite side. The eighteenth hole is a slight dogleg right with a green which is bunkered left and right: a satisfying close for a meditative and very interesting round of golf, which bears the unmistakeable signatures of Robert Trent Jones Jr *and* Sr.

Built on a great location, and refurbished with a true sense of mastery, the Eugene Country Club is an outstanding inland golf course.

The photo *on the opposite page* shows the clever, verdant setting of the elevated green at hole number one. *Above*, the eleventh green is at the far left and the twelfth green is at the right, with a pond flowing between.

Hole	1	2	3	4	5	6	7	8	9	Out	
Blue	395	215	390	408	185	545	200	485	450	3273	
White	380	200	373	390	140	515	140	478	388	3004	
Red	360	155	354	323	125	485	120	410	369	2701	
Yellow	355	145	349	313	85	482	105	400	364	2598	
Par	4	3	4	4	3	5	3	5	4	35	
Hole	10	11	12	13	14	15	16	17	18	In	Total
Blue	401	400	183	525	383	410	492	347	433	3574	6847
White	383	362	168	518	367	385	474	331	414	3402	6406
Red	360	345	125	457	337	357	443	279	392	3095	5796
Yellow	355	300	115	445	332	352	438	274	348	2959	5557
Par	4	4	3	5	4	4	5	4	4	37	72

Forest Meadows Golf Course

Murphys, California USA

Robert Trent Jones Jr started this 18 hole, par 60 executive golf course from scratch in 1972. The course was completed in 1973 and was opened in 1974. It is located on State Highway 4 near Bear Valley Ski Resort at an elevation of 3500 feet, in the 'pine and snow country.' Very beautiful, with stands of pine and cedar everywhere, the course is set at the top of the Stanislaus River Canyon, and its spectacular views are breathtaking.

Forest Meadows Golf Course is famous for its excellent physical condition, and is renowned as 'the best course in 100 miles.' It is open to the public year-round, except for times of heavy snow in the winter. A brief hole-by-hole description of this fine course follows:

Hole one gives golfers an opportunity to ford a stream—twice, as water crosses the fairway and also cuts in front of the green, which is protected by large wraparound bunkers left and right. A very short second hole has a tiny fairway and its green is protected front and rear. The third starts off

across a lake to a fairway which describes a dogleg left, most of which is the green itself—large and protected with a bunker at rear. Hole number four is a dogleg right with a bunker in its 'knee,' and a green with bunkers obliquely set at left front and right rear.

The fifth starts off across a stream to a short, fat fairway and a large green protected with a bunker at left rear. Hole number six again starts off across a stream, to a short fairway and large green which is protected with three bunkers at left front. The seventh virtually tees off to the green, which is protected at left and right front with bunkers. The eighth tees face a porkchop-shaped fairway and green combination, with the green protected cunningly at left rear—just where overreaching shots will be swallowed up.

Hole nine starts off to a dogleg right fairway, the most part of which is green that is protected heavily left with a large bunker, and at rear and at right with bunkers. The tenth is a straightforward lob to a fairway protected at first with a bunker right, and then the green, which has two crescent-shaped bunkers—one behind the other—on its left front. Hole eleven's tees play to a short fairway with a shallow green which is protected heavily at right and left front.

Holes twelve through fifteen give executive golfers lots of putting practice, with their virtually nonexistent fairways and dominant greens. The twelfth is similar to, but with an even more abbreviated fairway than, hole eleven, the green being set obliquely with bunkers at far right and left front. Hole thirteen is an interesting short hole; it starts off with a hop to an abbreviated fairway—or directly to the very accessible green which is protected at right front with a comparatively large, intrusive bunker, and at left rear. The bunkers are set so that shots to this obliquely-set triangle green can all too easily find them.

Hole number fourteen again features the dominant 'green in the fairway' design, the green here being set with bunkers left and at right front. Hole fifteen is a long shot to a large green protected at left front. The sixteenth starts off to a full-sized fairway, and thence to a green protected at right front with a large bunker and at left front and rear with small bunkers. Hole seventeen starts off across a wide stream to a tricky green protected at right rear by a voracious crescent bunker. The eighteenth completes this round of golf by teeing off down a long fairway, to cross a small lake to a slanting green protected by a bunker at extreme left.

Perhaps the most beautiful hole of this very beautiful course is number fifteen. A 200 yard par three, it is perched at the rim of the Stanislaus Canyon—from which one can see the snow-capped peaks of the Sierra Nevada range, 200 miles distant.

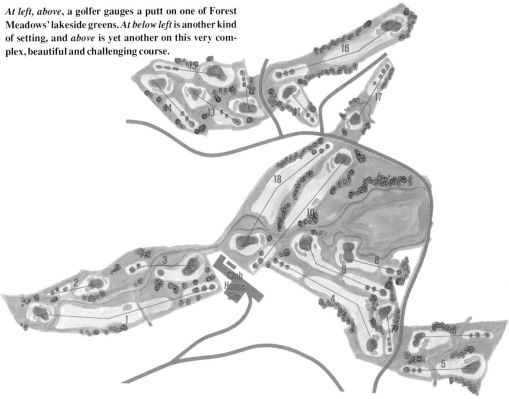

At left, above, a golfer gauges a putt on one of Forest Meadows' lakeside greens. *At below left* is another kind of setting, and *above* is yet another on this very complex, beautiful and challenging course.

Hole	1	2	3	4	5	6	7	8	9	Out	
Championship	522	145	181	355	204	163	133	178	211	2093	
White	500	126	167	333	195	136	112	167	188	1924	
Red	480	110	147	303	178	129	112	158	170	1787	
Par	5	3	3	4	3	3	3	3	3	30	
Hole	10	11	12	13	14	15	16	17	18	In	Total
Championship	353	128	109	133	103	199	373	158	355	1911	4004
White	333	107	93	123	98	175	347	141	324	1741	3665
Red	318	101	81	111	83	168	327	128	311	1628	3415
Par	4	3	3	3	3	3	4	3	4	30	60

The Glencoe Golf & Country Club

Calgary, Alberta, Canada

The Glencoe Golf & Country Club contains two full 18-hole courses—the longer, more demanding Glen Forest Course, and the shorter, more gentle Glen Meadows course. The Glen Forest course is designed in the great Scottish tradition.

Both courses are the product of the outstanding creativity of Robert Trent Jones Jr. Opened on 1 July 1984, the course which was to be the Glen Forest course played 16 holes in its unfinished condition. Facilities were several trailers which did service as a pro shop, clubhouse and maintenance facility.

The 16 holes had grown to 18 by August of 1984, and the second 18 holes (now officially known as the Glen Meadows Course), were under construction. By 1 July 1985, the first nine holes of the Glen Meadows course opened, followed by its second nine on 15 August 1985.

The clubhouse was, in turn, finished on 1 April 1986 and the entire course (clubhouse included!) celebrated this milestone with an official opening ceremony on 1 July 1986. Work continues to bring the maintenance facilities and other service areas to a permanent building status.

The Glen Forest and Glen Meadow courses are historically the first Robert Trent Jones Jr, golf courses in Canada, marking a real milestone for Canadian golfers. Hills, dales, pine forests and open meadows make the Glen Forest 18 a joy and a challenge. With great alacrity and a canniness that evokes nothing if not Scotland, Mr Jones has laid this lowland course out for the delectition and challenging of golfers of any ability. A hole-by-hole description of the Glen Forest course follows.

Hole one is a long shot to the fairway that risks embedding itself in the big bunker that lies in its line of flight, and halfway down the fairway, a stream meanders across for distrac-

tion and perchance to swallow your ball. From there two-thirds of the way down the fairway, two bunkers right threaten to pull you in, and the triangular green with its base turned toward you is protected more than amply with one bunker to a side, and one bunker on its right front.

The second hole two is also very lively! The tees and the fairway, while not connected, form an acute dogleg right, with lots of territory to cover between tees and fairway, including the stream which follows its right side full length. *Where* you touch down on the fairway had better be between those bunkers at left and the stream, or you'll be playing 'catch up.' The green itself is blocked directly by a bunker, and is protected at right and left rear by two bunkers, and by the stream at right. Hole number three is an oblique dogleg left, with likely landing spots very near the voracious bunker set in the fairway's 'knee.' Then,

Glencoe was the site of the 1989 Canadian Professional Championships. *Below* is a photograph of the par three seventh hole on Glencoe's Glen Forest Course. Compare this image with the course map on page 56 of this text.

it's across a depression to the green, which is protected at right rear by respectable-looking bunkers.

Hole four starts off across a stream and the head of a lake which follows the fairway full-length on the left. Also, coming into the fairway at about halfway from the right is another lake. The green is pinched between a largish bunker at right and the lake at left, which impinges upon the approach, and embraces the green on its entire left side. Contouring makes this a bit more hazardous, and, well, you've got to like water here! The fifth is a tasty shot from the tees across a small inlet of one of the aforesaid lakes. A small fairway tempts shots directly to the green, but that green is effectively water-guarded on three of its sides, including that rather impinged-upon approach. If you miss the water, which lies to the right, and ahead (if you overshoot the green), there is a bunker just to the left.

Hole six is a long fairway, pinched a bit one-third to one-half of the way to the green by two large bunkers, and the green itself lies amidst a veritable explosion of bunkers. A change of

pace from water to ground, but sure to be very interesting. The seventh is, at 229 yards, a hole that is short in distance but long on hazard. The entire right side of the fairway is one long bunker, which impinges upon any straight approach to the green. The green itself is bunkered left rear, and, *of course,* at right front.

Hole number eight is a long drive down a straight fairway that is lined with trees down both sides and is pinched left with rough at the two-thirds point, and is pinched right a bit further on by a big bunker, which leads to a green which is surrounded by bunkers. Hole nine is a dogleg right. The hole has a meandering stream to the left. Tee shots hazard a big bunker in the crook of the fairway, and two well-placed bunkers just beyond the 'elbow' of the fairway. The approach to the irregularly-shaped green has a big bunker to the left.

Hole number ten has a fairway which is parallel that of hole number six, but is separated from it by a huge bunker. A shot from the championship tee has to cross a stream—which threads through and around the tees—twice, while the other tees have just one leg of the stream to cross. A bunker, down the right side of the fairway, creates a hazard. In turn, the green approach is pinched by bunkers right, and the stream left. It can be fun.

The eleventh features lots of water and a straight, narrow, tree-lined fairway. Tee shots must carry over the inlet of a lake. Near the head of the first half of fairway, a bunker left makes things interesting, and just after this, the stream which splits the fairway has to be overcome. Beyond this, the serpentine second half of fairway leads to an obliquely set green, well protected on the right of its approach by a massive bunker.

The twelfth is a long, tree-lined, dogleg right featuring a long tee approach to the fairway, which could find the rough but for one's finesse. Then it's an approach to the green which is ambushed left by a bunker, and at the very mouth of the green, Scylla and Charybdis await in the forms of two big bunkers. The green could be a bit of a Circe, besides! Hole number thirteen has a short fairway, similar to the middle holes of Mr Jones' Forest Meadows course in California. Tee shots reach for an extremely well bunkered and narrow green. Hole fourteen is a long dogleg left, with tee shots landing in opposition, hopefully, to the bunker in the fairway's 'elbow.' Then it's a blast across a no-man's land of bunkers which form an unbroken trench across the last third of the fairway. In turn, the green is surrounded by bunkers, with an additional bunker on the left approach.

Hole number fifteen is a gem. Tee shots overfly the inlet of a lake, confronting a pair of bunkers on the left of the dogleg right fairway.

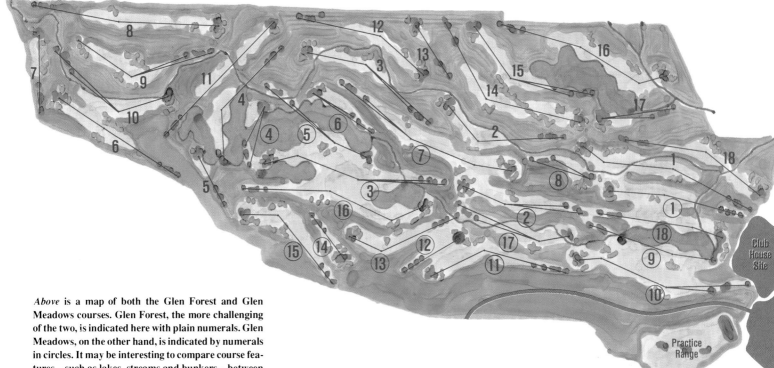

Above is a map of both the Glen Forest and Glen Meadows courses. Glen Forest, the more challenging of the two, is indicated here with plain numerals. Glen Meadows, on the other hand, is indicated by numerals in circles. It may be interesting to compare course features—such as lakes, streams and bunkers—between the two.

The approach to the obliquely-set green is pinched at left by a large, inset bunker. The sixteenth beautifully features a lake which provides a complement to the serpentine fairway on the right, and a bunker left early enough on to give tee shots pause, and at left, again, at a rather crucial juncture—where a short dogleg left begins at a wide stream, across which lies the green, with bunkers left and right behind. A bunker at the right, on the dogleg's 'elbow,' assures that your attention is addressed to the problem at hand.

Hole seventeen could give fits to the unattentive golfer. It is a clever hole, the perfect penultimate hole for the brilliant preceding 16 holes. The championship tee carries over the whole lake, with the other tees carrying only the lake inlet. A very short fairway will lure most tee shots to the green, which has lake right, and bunkers at left. A beauty! The eighteenth hole is a truly grand dogleg right. Tee shots confront a pair of bunkers on the fairway's elbow, and trees and a stream down the right side. Green approach shots must cross the stream, and then must cope with a green whose mouth is pinched extremely on the left by a cluster of bunkers—and the green itself wraps around behind these same, with a bunker at left and slightly to the rear, to add excitement.

This 18 hole golf course provides a practically novellic sense of adventure, and in keeping with a slightly more leisurely sense of good literature and art, Mr Jones has also designed the second 18 of Glencoe's 36 holes, the Glen Meadow 18, a fine golf course by anybody's standards.

The future is bright for this new facility, and its 36 holes of golf can only improve with age.

GLENCOE (Glen Meadows Course)

Hole	1	2	3	4	5	6	7	8	9	Out	
Blue	397	371	531	159	365	185	562	176	372	3118	
White	370	346	496	127	340	170	532	146	332	2859	
Red	330	309	455	99	270	121	473	108	267	2432	
Par	4	4	5	3	4	3	5	3	4	35	
Hole	10	11	12	13	14	15	16	17	18	In	Total
Blue	500	416	190	358	168	355	534	338	365	3224	6342
White	437	376	165	312	143	329	498	298	334	2892	5751
Red	404	332	134	273	120	274	462	265	285	2549	4981
Par	5	4	3	4	3	4	5	4	4	36	71

GLENCOE (Glen Forest Course)

Hole	1	2	3	4	5	6	7	8	9	Out	
Blue	551	373	428	413	168	398	229	533	430	3523	
White	510	338	399	380	139	357	183	497	401	3204	
Red	464	303	365	346	108	323	133	468	368	2878	
Par	5	4	4	4	3	4	3	5	4	36	
Hole	10	11	12	13	14	15	16	17	18	In	Total
Blue	407	438	419	161	518	411	552	209	439	3554	7077
White	363	407	385	132	457	377	518	176	385	3200	6404
Red	323	379	333	107	434	337	489	128	367	2897	5775
Par	4	4	4	3	5	4	5	3	4	36	72

Golden Valley Golf Club

Hyogo Prefecture, Japan

This is another course which Robert Trent Jones Jr has designed for the Shinwa Golf Group of Japan. An absolutely beautiful course, it is set in a stunning location, among meadows, babbling mountain streams, low, rolling mountains and pristine hill country beauty. Robert Trent Jones Jr has taken this magnificent natural wonder and lifted it into the realm of the legendary.

The clubhouse design echoes classic Japanese architecture with the airiness inherent in that tradition. Accomodations are of course full and superb and, again, the course is truly a wonder.

South Pond on hole eighteen would qualify as a good-sized lake in anybody's book, and the green hillsides absolutely reverberate that odd sense of tranquility and adventure which only the finest mountain environments offer. It is a feeling that calls one to take up the challenge, and to fully encounter the exquisite realm of creation. This then, is the fabulous design and setting for a truly masterful golf course, and such is the Golden Valley Golf Club.

In the photo *above*, Robert Trent Jones Jr and course officials confer on construction plans. The first green is to the left of the rock-walled stream *below*.

Robert Trent Jones Jr has greatly added to this challenge, and has fulfilled the sense of this locale as only a master could. This course offers the tranquil, meditative essenses of mountain streams and beautiful lakes in their full measure—such features call one to come to their level, which is one of the keenest chal-

lenges known to man—to approach God's creation as one somehow worthy of partaking, just what Hemingway had tried to get to in his writing! The struggle, the wrestling, the triumphs and defeats that take all that a man has to give; it is the stuff of epic, it is the stuff of life.

Mr Jones' reading of Albert Camus may have something to do with it, yet there is something altogether transcendent in this course, in this setting. In weaving the natural challenges cited above—the tranquility that brings the heroic into the fabric of this majestic course—Mr Jones has called upon that which has for centuries has brought men to consider that inward call to action, the quietude that evokes the spiritual—that is, the sense of something altogether greater than oneself, but yet that in which one participates. And the participation here is in the golfer's submission to the spirit of his game; the sacrifice, the necessary forgiveness, the hope, the faith and the gladness that one has a chance at that which is beyond one's own perceived abilities.

Endowed with such wonder and the hearty hill-country topography of Hyogo Prefecture, the Golden Valley Golf Club course is a challenge and a great delight. Following is a hole-by-hole description; in general, fairways roll excitingly, and greens provide a feeling of greatness to the finish of each hole. Some of the holes on this course have been modified somewhat from Mr Jones' original design, and where any extensive modifications have been made, they are noted.

Hole one is the second longest hole of the course, at 532 yards from the championship tee—which carries to the fairway over an arm of a rock-lined stream. Tee shots have a chance of rolling across the fairway directly into a brace of well-placed bunkers. The fairway is then parallel to the stream, and is inrupted by same near its foot, close to the green. Shots carry over this stretch of water as well, and the vestige of fairway on the green side, and the green itself, are protected by bunkers at rear. The approach to the green is pinched by a bunker at right front, which only adds to the opening of a great 18 holes of golf, as—bunker or not—unwary golfers could well wind up in the stream, which lines the green's right edge. A wonderful hole, and a visual knockout.

Hole number two describes a dogleg left, with shots having to cross the stream toward the end of a long flight from the tees. With trees and a bunker directly ahead, and the stream just behind, landing sites on this rolling green add challenge; and immediately after this, the fairway lies with stream left, and the green itself is protected by bunkers on its pinched right approach, with the stream winding by at left—and trees behind. The view back from the green toward the fairway is a vista of seemingly endless mountains guarding the rolling valley floor.

The third starts off near the edge of a lake, with the championship tee getting the largest slice of the lake. The short fairway is heavily contoured and has a bunker right, and the green has the lake on its left. Hole four starts off to a serpentine fairway having the stream on its left, and featuring, just at the fairway's first major undulation, a downhill drop to the lake. The fairway then describes a major curve to the left, and as this 'neck' connects with the green, two bunkers provide a bow on the left of the green's 'chin.' In addition to this adornment, the green has the stream to its left, as does the entire length of this hole from, the tees onward.

Hole number five starts out slightly straighter than did the fourth, and features the by-now familiar stream on the left. It has been changed entirely from its original configuration, which itself featured a subtler usage of bunkers. Just where most tee shots will find their landing, the fairway has trees and stream

Above is the hole one fairway, facing toward the green.

left and two hills set at a diagonal toward the tees—at right. Make it between these and you are skirting the right edge of the fairway, brushing limbs with the trees there. Now, in another reconfiguring, it's a hop across a winding stream to the last quarter of fairway, and the inverted-triangle green, which has bunkers set decoratively and dangerously in each of its sides, and, as an added threat, has the stream downhill to its right.

The sixth takes you up the other side of the stream, though this hole plays opposite the previous holes, and therefore, the stream is still to your left. The contoured fairway leads to a pinched green approach just where two bunkers inrupt from either side. It's downhill to the stream at left or the trees at right. Hole seven starts off to a fairway which turns right, then left as it wraps around one side of the same lake which we met at holes two and

three. Tee shots here could err straight ahead into the lake, or could overcompensate and find the hillock, which lies in the 'knee' of the fairway. The lake always near at hand on the left, the fairway extends straight, then hooks left, with three bunkers guarding its 'elbow,' to a green—which heads into the lake—with bunkers at right rear and, left front, and of course the lake at left.

Hole number eight has been reworked extensively, with replacing of tees and reshaping of green and fairway. A bunker lies almost directly in the flight path of tee shots to the green, 90 yards away. This is the shortest hole of the course at 176 yards. The ninth is a dogleg right, with trees guarding tee shots from the left, and also to the left of the 'thigh' of the fairway; at its knee, a sloping bank to the stream guards the outer curve. The fairway then serpentines left, and as it then recurves right, a steep bank streamward and a hefty bunker emplacement guard the approach to

the green from the left. From here, the clubhouse is in view across a gulley and a road lined with trees.

Hole ten lies on the other side of the clubhouse, and contours around, and plays into, a hillside. Play is straight from the tees, and likely landing spots are guarded with bunkers to the right of the fairway. Farther on, the highly contoured fairway will make the downhill bunkers left and the uphill bunker right, which guard the mouth of the green, especially hard to avoid. The green itself is headed into a hillside.

The eleventh is the longest hole of the course, at 558 yards. The tees are elevated and play downhill to a contoured fairway which is limned by a stream on its right, and then on its left, from the halfway point where the stream crosses over the fairway. The stream widens shortly after this to the arm of a lake, which cuts into the fairway, pinching the approach to the green. This green has water to its left and at

its head, bunkers to its right, and rough and trees at its right rear.

Hole twelve has a serpentine fairway that hooks left—leaving the *inattentive* golfer to cope with the four hillocks which lie just beyond this bend, then comes back right to narrow toward the obliquely set, oblong green which is protected on its approach with bunkers right and left. At left rear is a stream, at rear are trees, and at right rear is rough.

The thirteenth has a stream to its left. Tee shots drive toward a fairway which is defended to the right and left of its 'hook to the left' by bunkers. Another hook toward the green end takes you right, and just inside this curve is another bunker. At the mouth of the green, bunkers inrupt from the left and right. At right rear, it's trees, while left rear is downhill to the stream. The bunkering of this hole has been reworked since the original.

Hole number fourteen no longer starts off across a stream as it once did. Its winding fair-

way has also been 'gentled down,' and is protected by three bunkers which inrupt from the left, near where the stream flows by. Tee shots risk overflying the bend in the fairway—and finding these bunkers, or the stream itself. On the right of the green's mouth are two bunkers, one of which gets assistance from a bunker left in pinching this approach. The stream lies to the left of the green. The fifteenth now starts off across a single stream instead of, as originally planned, two branches of a stream to an abbreviated fairway/green setup, to the right of which is the stream, and to the left of which is a massive, all-too-easily found bunker.

Hole sixteen plays with the stream always close at hand, downhill to the left, and, as reconfigured, starts off across a convolution of same. The fairway has also been straightened a good deal, and no longer does a massive bunker lying at its two-thirds point threaten shots. Instead, a tiny, decorative

bunker follows on the stream side of things, the left, after the golfer's initial encounter with a hillock on the same side, earlier on. The approach to the lozenge-shaped green is pinched by bunkers on either side. The green itself is flanked by two large bunkers on its left side, and heads into the stream.

The seventeenth hole no longer starts off across the stream, but now starts off across a convolution of the stream, keeping same to its left. The fairway/green combination features a green which is larger than the diminutive fairway. There is a small bunker at the green's right, and the green also has water at left and immediately ahead.

Hole number eighteen is a gem with water as several of its major facets. Tee off across the mouth of a lake—to an isolated section of fairway which has trees and a cluster of three bunkers at its left, and the lake close at hand to its right. From here, it's another water hop, across an even wider arm of the lake known as 'South Pond,' to the second half of the fairway, which curves to the right and has bunkers placed strategically on the outside of the curve—where errant shots are likely to find them. The fairway curves around an inlet of the lake, and thus is rather wetly protected on its right. In addition, the reconfigured green has bunkers right front and rear, and left front and rear, and trees left, to guard it. The green also features a pinched approach and trees left. All water here is close at hand and downhill, so that one had better truly think about his shots; this hole requires everything—power, finesse and the ability to *appreciate* outstanding golf.

This is a magnificent course, rippling and refreshing as a mountain breeze on the course's beautiful South Pond. Its design is the product of one of the world's greatest creators of haiku in green: Robert Trent Jones Jr.

Hole	1	2	3	4	5	6	7	8	9	Out	
Champion	532	439	214	371	397	435	514	176	375	3453	
Regular	498	416	198	336	375	407	478	154	327	3189	
Front	473	388	158	323	346	378	422	127	296	2911	
Ladies	357	306	93	237	321	348	396	98	266	2422	
Par	5	4	3	4	4	4	5	3	4	36	
Hole	10	11	12	13	14	15	16	17	18	In	Total
Champion	427	558	360	469	393	223	436	155	540	3561	7014
Regular	405	540	327	450	366	199	408	132	518	3345	6534
Front	390	521	276	413	373	170	389	109	516	3157	6068
Ladies	341	453	231	383	299	136	293	99	466	2701	5123
Par	4	5	4	4	4	3	4	3	5	36	72

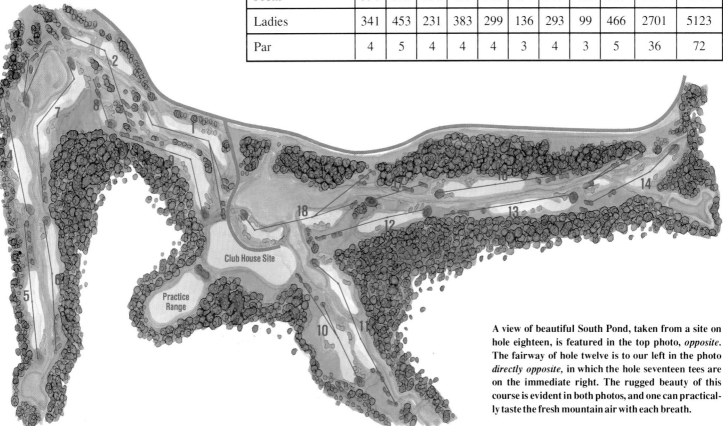

A view of beautiful South Pond, taken from a site on hole eighteen, is featured in the top photo, *opposite*. The fairway of hole twelve is to our left in the photo *directly opposite*, in which the hole seventeen tees are on the immediate right. The rugged beauty of this course is evident in both photos, and one can practically taste the fresh mountain air with each breath.

Jackson Hole Golf & Tennis Club

Jackson Hole, Wyoming USA

Its greens and bunkers completely redesigned by Robert Trent Jones Jr, this course was originally designed—in 1961–1962—by Bob Baldock, the still-active course designer who currently resides in Sacramento, California.

The Grand Teton Lodge Company bought the course on 26 April 1967. Mr Jones started his redesign work in June of 1967, and completed same in the summer of 1971. All greens were back in play in the summer of 1972. The course has been designated one of the best designed 130 courses in America by the American Society of Golf Course Architects, who used, as criteria, natural beauty, design aesthetics, drama and subtlety, and fairness and playability. The scenic mountain grandeur of the Teton Range provides this setting for the par 72 championship course, which measures 7168 yards from the blue tees, 6783 yards from the white tees, and 5949 yards from the ladies' tees. As of the actual publication of this

writing, the Jackson Hole Golf Course will have hosted the 1988 USGA Public Links Amateur Championship.

In addition to this, Jackson Hole Golf Course has hosted five Wyoming State Amateur championships. Course facilities include the Strutting Grouse Restaurant, which is open for Sunday brunch, lunch and dinner; a fully equipped pro shop, a practice fairway and putting green and six tennis courts. Following is a brief hole-by-hole description of this magnificent course.

Hole one starts off to a right-tending fairway, with severe contouring. A lake, lying left, precurses the green, which wears a halo of water and has two bunkers—left and right—at front. This one gets you ready! The second hole starts off along a long, narrow fairway with water all along its right, and three bunkers at even intervals at right, too. A stream cuts across the foot of the fairway and forms a lake which guards both fairway and

green on the left. The green has bunkers left and rear, and water on both sides.

Hole number three starts off over a stream to a virtual island. The small fairway and green have a lake left, which wraps around to the right, just beyond the green. A bunker on the green's right completes the scenario.

The fourth's tees are backed up into a lake—water on three sides, you must carry rough to the front, to a contoured fairway which is split by a stream. On 'the other side,' the green is set among slopes and has a small bunker at left front and a large bunker at right. Hole five starts off to a dogleg left with a bunker on its 'inner knee,' and a stream at its outer curve. The green is bunkered at left and right front and right rear, and the stream rides to the right. Hole number six has a small fairway and an even smaller green, having bunkers left, right and behind.

At hole number seven, the back tee carries over a stream to a long, narrow fairway pinched at the middle by opposing bunkers. The green is small, and is bunkered at right and left rear. The eighth plays to a dogleg right fairway with opposing bunkers at its bend. Before the stream carry to the green, opposing bunkers pinch the fairway. The green is bunkered at right front and left rear, and is set among slopes. Hole nine starts off over the branching of a stream to a fairway having an early bunker at right. The stream is a consistent part of play to the left, and the green is bunkered at left front, with slopes all around, and of course, the stream at left.

The tenth hole has a stream all along its right hand side, and starts off along a long, narrow fairway to a green which has bunkers at left and right front and the stream at right. Hole number eleven starts off with the Gros Ventre River all along its left, and must carry a tributary of this river. The green is oblong and heads into the river—with bunkers at right front and at rear. Hole twelve plays to a fairway which is pinched and thrown to the right by a bunker mid-way. The green features a very heavy bunker at right front, slopes, and bunkers on its left and rear which are set to catch cuts or overpowered balls.

Hole number thirteen features tees which are set in a 'Y' configuration—and with good reason, too! The lakes and stream setup here would challenge any golfer. The far tees carry down the left side of a stream and over a lake to a green which fronts on one lake, has another lake to its right and is bunkered rear. Put water wings on your ball for this one! The fourteenth starts off with a lake and a stream at its left, and carries over the stream to a fairway having two bunkers right where they'll make you really consider that tee shot. Opposing these bunkers are a lake and stream all along the fairway's right. The green is fronted by bunkers left and right, and of course has the

stream to its right. Hole fifteen starts off straight down a fairway having a single grass bunker at midway right. The green has bunkers left and right on its narrow chin, and blooms out behind these, with a slope at rear.

Hole number sixteen starts off to a fairway which cuts suddenly to the left—as its end almost encloses a bunker which dominates the front of the green, which has two bunkers at rear. Hole seventeen starts off to a dogleg left having opposing bunkers at its 'knee.' The green is fronted by two bunkers which widen toward the fairway, so it's 'shoot the chute' to the green. Beyond the green's broad back, however, is a slope for the overeager to reckon with.

Famed entertainer Milton Berle confers with an associate on the seventeenth hole, in the upper photo *on the facing page*. As is evidenced by the lower photo *on the facing page*, Wyoming's magnificent Grand Tetons provide the backdrop for rounds of golf at Jackson Hole.

The grand eighteenth hole curves to the right, and has a cluster of bunkers at its vital bend. The mass of bunkers right may make you tend left—straight on toward the lake waiting a little further on, there. Then it's across some contouring to a pinched green approach which is rife with bunkers, and an oblong, obliquely-set green, protected with one bunker front and three bunkers at right rear, just where your pin-point precision shot must split the difference. A great end to 18 sensational holes of golf.

Our hats are off to Bob Baldock, but most of all to the genius of Robert Trent Jones Jr, whose redesign work on the greens and tees of this course have truly made it 'a cut above.'

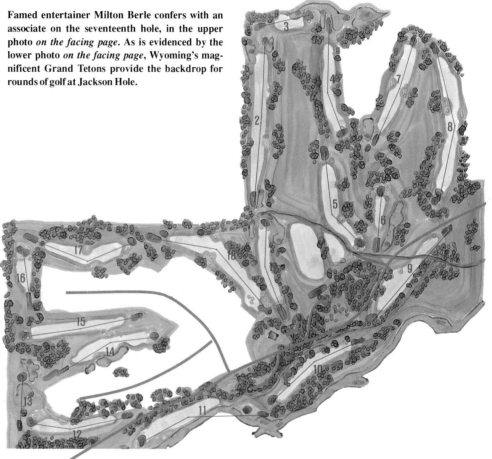

Hole	1	2	3	4	5	6	7	8	9	Out	
Blue	351	581	203	433	394	220	429	593	439	3643	
White	337	556	176	410	379	195	393	574	418	3438	
Red	323	456	109	352	364	160	378	490	384	3016	
Mens & Ladies Par	4	5	3	4	4	3	4	5	4	36	
Hole	10	11	12	13	14	15	16	17	18	In	Total
Blue	408	530	364	169	438	449	203	412	552	3525	7168
White	389	527	333	150	408	434	188	388	528	3045	6783
Red	332	464	301	93	378	418	173	358	503	3020	6036
Mens Par	4	5	4	3	4	4	3	4	5	36	72
Ladies Par	4	5	4	3	4	5	3	4	5	37	73

Joondalup Country Club

Connolly Shire, Western Australia

B uilt by Robert Trent Jones Jr, the Joondalup Country Club golf course is acclaimed by many experts to be the finest golf course in Western Australia, and one of the best in the nation. It is located in undulating brush and dune country within the City of Wanneroo, Connolly Shire, 15.5 miles northwest of Perth, and just 1.2 miles inland from the Indian Ocean. This 6275 meter, par 72 course was commenced in 1984, along with the building of a residential development which will include a resort hotel, a community house, retirement housing, a primary school, a shopping center and 1200 allotment parcels for homes.

This golf course is one of several Robert Trent Jones Jr golf courses in Australia. These include the beautiful Meadow Springs course (which is also located in Western Australia),

the great National Golf Club course and the Cape Schanck Golf Club course—both of which are situated on Cape Schanck, near Australia's eastern coast. Joondalup's undulating fairways and hidden bunkers promise many fine rounds of golfing pleasure for golfers in all categories of experience and talent. Golfers start out playing away from the clubhouse, and end their round playing back toward the clubhouse. Following is a hole-by-hole description.

Tree-bedecked hole number one is a dogleg left with opposing bunkers at its 'knee.' The green lies a distance beyond, with its right face hidden behind a series of bunkers. Hole two starts off to a fairway which goes left, then right, with heavy bunkering along its right, indented, side. The green approach is bunkered right and left, with the heaviest bunkering at

Joondalup hosted the Western Australia Open and the PGA Championship in 1987. *Facing page, above:* Going for the pin on hole number three. *Facing page, below:* Action on the first green. *Above:* Teeing off on the second hole.

left. In evidence here are steep drops into a quarry along one side of the fairway, which also come into play.

The third hole is spectacular—it starts off across a canyon with steep, rocky sides. Tees are arranged along the rim of the chasm opposite the green, which is bunkered at front and left. The bunkers here are definitely nothing to ignore! Hole four describes a long, mild 'S' with a gigantic bunker protecting the full face of the green. The fifth features an elevation to one side and proceeds toward a green which has a tree dead ahead, beyond the rearmost bunker, which bunker is all but hidden from view.

Hole number six fades, then straightens, with the green hooking to the right behind a large bunker, after a series of bunkers right which are staggered cleverly in balance. The seventh, a par three, carries over a bunker to a fairway-green combination which curves left around a host of bunkers, while the eighth plays down a long, serpentine fairway with opposing, pinching bunkers at the first curve, and a staggered balance of bunkers left and right later on.

The fairway of hole nine requires an accurate tee shot to avoid fairway bunkers which are ready to catch the unwary. The green is framed with two bunkers. Hole number ten starts off to a dogleg right, and a long accurate shot is needed—to a green hidden behind two

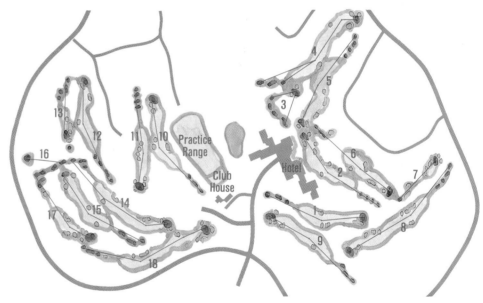

Hole	1	2	3	4	5	6	7	8	9	Out	
Championship	368	375	130	460	384	363	197	483	390	3150	
Mens	346	346	121	435	366	328	165	458	369	2934	
Ladies	297	302	86	387	320	235	134	424	339	2524	
Par	4	4	3	5	4	4	3	5	4	36	
Hole	10	11	12	13	14	15	16	17	18	In	Total
Championship	404	337	365	210	471	395	129	310	504	3125	6275
Mens	375	318	359	192	429	351	114	287	476	2901	5835
Ladies	347	304	285	106	381	314	87	223	407	2454	4978
Par	4	4	4	3	5	4	3	4	5	36	72

Distances in meters

bunkers left. The eleventh is a short par four and is a 'sleeper.' A wayward tee shot produces an easy double bogey. Accuracy is the key to a sloping green pinched with three rolling bunkers.

Beyond the ravine which splits the fairway of hole 12 is a bunker at left, which will catch uncontrolled carries. Big bunkers right and left guard the green approach. The thirteenth, another par three, brings the golfer along the wall of a quarry and any birdie here is a birdie earned, indeed. Hole fourteen has 'gunsight' bunkers early on its fairway, and the green has a protecting bunker at front left and a large tree which must be negotiated before reaching the putting surface.

The fifteenth plays to a crescent fairway tending to the right, and a very pinched green approach with huge bunkers, while the sixteenth starts off across no man's land to a small green with a bunker at right rear. Hole number seventeen carries over a good stretch of typical Australian bushland en route to the fairway, which then cuts left and is bunkered all around, with a huge bunker directly in the green approach.

The eighteenth is bunkered strategically along its left, with hill sides to the right, and intricate bunkering around the green; a powerful hole to play, and a great ending to a very fine 18 holes of golf—which have been brought to you courtesy of the talents of the very talented Robert Trent Jones Jr.

Action at the fifth tee is shown *at left*, and the second green appears in the photo at *above left*. The third hole 'canyon' can indeed be carried, as is shown *immediately above*, and at the *top* of this page.

Keystone Ranch Golf Course

Keystone, Colorado USA

Of this course, Robert Trent Jones Jr said, in a publicity release from Keystone Ranch:

'This course is beautiful, different, challenging and tough; it never will let the golfer capture it, but he will have fun trying. The Keystone Ranch course will be appreciated by experts and enjoyed by intermediates, if they can shoot at least 85. Beginners will be totally frustrated: they will complain about the meadowland and their lost golf balls. The expert will think this course is superior. He will have fun figuring out all the angles, but he will never tire of it. This is a small course in yards, but a long course in playability. At this altitude (9300 feet), the ball goes 10 percent farther, and the player will feel exhilarated from his hit. I have not stressed length in this course; I

have stressed accuracy and strategy. It, therefore, is a superior course for strategic reasons. An expert is not one who necessarily scores better every time. He is a person who has played all his life and who knows the difference between a Rembrandt and a copy.'

A Rembrandt it is, indeed—its 7090 yards having been carved out of the green, rolling

meadows of a majestic mountain valley. The Keystone course is a real beauty, with greens that could easily have been the graceful product of hillside runoff, and whose verdant textures seem to embody sunlight just as the front lawn of an old western homestead might have. Yet these same exquisitely naturalistic greens were actually crafted by the hand of one of the finest golf course architects in the entire world—Robert Trent Jones Jr, the Rembrandt of golf course designers.

The history of the Keystone Ranch itself goes back to the 1800s. Luke Smith, who spent his childhood on the ranch site, bought three ranches which had been homesteads on the property. He and his family used the old ranch for a summer place. Mr Smith's Denver-based Quick-Way Truck Shovel Company

grew, and as it did, so the ranch house was added on to. In 1938, as a wedding gift for his daughter, Bernadine Reynolds, Luke Smith built the large fireplace in the ranch house living room.

While Mr Smith did business in Denver, *Mrs* Smith was in the business of raising Hereford cattle—so the place was more than a vacation ranch, it was a real working ranch. In addition, it served Luke's business interests. He often invited business contacts for stays at his ranch, and over the years, two former Colorado governors, among other notables, came to visit. In 1955, then-president of the United States and avid amateur golfer Dwight D Eisenhower was invited to visit. This was precluded, sadly, by President Eisenhower's suffering a heart attack—from which he, fortunately, recovered.

In 1957, the Smith-Reynolds ranch—as it was known due to Bernadine's marriage—was sold to the Montana Petroleum Company. The MPC in turn sold it to the Ralston Purina Company and Keystone Resort partnership, in 1977. At this time, development on the golf course and 74 private homes began on 325 acres of the total 506 acre site.

Surrounded by 12,000-foot peaks which are snowcapped almost year-round, the outstanding visual qualities of this course are, of course, not the only attractions here. Built on the classic linksland pattern of the early Scottish courses, some of the holes of this course have no fairways, some descend a narrow, rolling valley, and others play out onto open meadows from the woods. The increase given each golfer's shots by the high altitude will make even the youngest feel younger still!

The first hole has the golfer standing at an elevated tee, from which his shot is down the narrow tree-lined fairway. It is birdie or bogey time here. Hole two is also straight, its green being visible from the tee, yet the third leaves the woods behind and doglegs right to high ground. The fourth hole is the first linksland

Refreshing as a mountain breeze is the cool vista shown at *above left*, and *at left*, Colorado sunshine creates a nimbus of flying sand for a golfer's stroke to the green. *At the top of this page*, an experienced golfer putts amid green mountain scenery.

Hole	1	2	3	4	5	6	7	8	9	Out	
Blue	528	433	429	412	190	564	207	422	368	3553	
White	508	408	406	391	169	527	174	391	318	3292	
Par	5	4	4	4	3	5	3	4	4	36	
Hole	10	11	12	13	14	15	16	17	18	In	Total
Blue	463	351	171	552	172	403	422	414	589	3537	7090
White	421	313	143	529	138	375	392	402	516	3229	6521
Par	4	4	3	5	3	4	4	4	5	36	72

hole, a dogleg left that hops a stream, with a green having bunkers front and rear, while hole number five's green lies beyond a small waterfall from the tees, accessible by a shot across meadowland. Hole six features extensive bunkering, especially to the right of the green, and plays back into the meadow.

Hole seven has sagebrush to the right and a two-acre pond to the left—also, a massive bunker lurks to the right of the green.

Hole eight is phenomenal for the amount of bunkering placed directly between the golfer and the green, and the ninth requires a carry across a limb of a nine-acre lake to a green which is extremely well bunkered, its mouth open only to the lake, which is ever-present on your right here.

The tenth hole is a long drive uphill to a large green, with three bunkers placed strategically between tees and green, in contrast to hole number eleven, which is a short drive uphill to an elevated green. The fairway features massive bunkering on the right of its second half, and the green is protected front, left and right. The twelfth is a shot to a green amidst the trees, with bunkers left and right of its chin.

Hole number thirteen roller-coasters to a tough green surrounded on three sides with bunkers, and hole fourteen drops extremely toward the green, which itself is well protected left and right. Hole fifteen features a cluster of three staggered bunkers on the fairway, and its obliquely-set green is protected on three sides with bunkers—the only open side faces to left rear.

The sixteenth funnels into an extremely well-trapped fairway, and its triangular green is set point-forward with bunkers on its left and right sides. Hole seventeen features a large obstruction between the back tees and the foremost tee, and has a tricky green bunkered at front and at right. This hole can be played in many different ways. The eighteenth hole here is a fitting capper to a demanding and thoroughly enjoyable afternoon of golf—in Mr Jones' words from the *Keystone Ranch Bulletin* of June/July 1980: 'This hole borders the lake. It is like Beethoven's Fifth. Hole seventeen builds you up and hole eighteen hits you.' With lots of water play, a plethora of bunkers and a stunning lakefront view, hole eighteen is indeed a master stroke for a course that is a master *work*.

The course's pro shop and the esteemed Keystone Ranch Restaurant are housed in Luke Smith's large and historic ranch house. Mr Jones' course architecture incorporates surroundings and history into the esthetics and design of the course, and the ranch house follows suit, giving the Keystone Resort a wonderfully Old West feel.

At left: **An endless Rocky Mountain vista at Keystone.**

Kiahuna Golf Club

Poipu Beach, Kauai, Hawaii USA

Located at Poipu, on the sparkling South coast of Kauai, this is a par 70, 6353 yard, 18 hole championship course. The marvellous ocean and mountain views availed to users of the course are but a few of its attractions. The generous fairways which are evident here are the product of extensive landscaping, which involved grading the course's lava bed and then covering that with over 500,000 cubic yards of topsoil. Robert Trent Jones Jr has 'signed' this course with well-contoured greens and rolling landscape. In addition to this, Mr Jones has made every effort to preserve the heritage of this site, retaining, in the course design, many of the historic Hawaiian temples and artifacts which were originally part of the location.

The first hole here features a lake to the left of the tees, a bunker at fairway right, and a stone wall impinging on the fairway from the left. The green is open to the front, but is otherwise surrounded by bunkers and trees.

Hole number two is a dogleg left, again featuring a stone wall on the fairway, and a green nearly surrounded with bunkers; hole three involves a creek-jumper to a challenging green. The fourth hole features trees and the

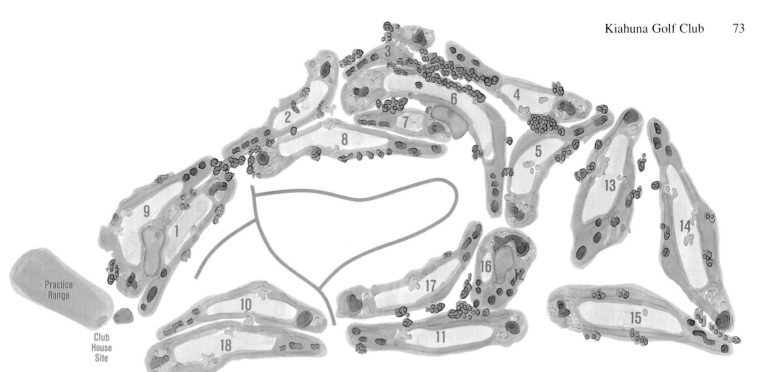

Hole	1	2	3	4	5	6	7	8	9	Out	
Championship	346	329	187	355	380	530	178	441	379	3125	
Mens	305	302	163	334	320	496	125	384	354	2783	
Ladies	264	246	85	265	270	458	99	344	330	2361	
Par	4	4	3	4	4	4	3	3	4	33	
Hole	**10**	**11**	**12**	**13**	**14**	**15**	**16**	**17**	**18**	**In**	**Total**
Championship	363	405	168	355	510	438	178	415	396	3228	6353
Mens	308	379	138	307	473	387	145	367	344	2848	5631
Ladies	286	335	104	263	442	324	124	328	304	2510	4871
Par	4	4	4	4	5	4	3	4	4	36	69

unseen but very much felt defense of a crosswind. Bunkers crossing the fairway are a feature of the fifth, which also has a well-bunkered green.

Hole six is a par five, sharp dogleg left with a lake, a stone wall, trees and a large, massively bunkered green. Straight par three hole seven has a green protected left and right and a lake dead ahead. At the eighth hole, we encounter the crosswind again; the situation is complicated by an elevated green which is bunkered all across its front and has a grove of trees behind. Hole number nine is a par four dogleg left, which normally plays into a strong headwind.

The tenth's bunkers at fairway left and right lead to a tricky green having bunkers behind. A long, tricky par four eleventh hole features a massive bunker at the tee end of the fairway, and an obliquely-set green having bunkers front and rear, just where errant shots are likely to find a home. Hole number twelve is a classic Scottish-style hole, with a very tricky water hazard, while hole thirteen is a straight par four with a huge, hungry bunker at fairway left, and the fourteenth features a veritable lit-

ter of fairway bunkers leading up to a well-bunkered green.

Hole number fifteen has the crosswind again—shots to the left run close to trees, and the green is elevated and has four bunkers. The sixteenth features a deadly water hazard and extremely changeable wind; hole seventeen is a dogleg right with a bunker on the inner 'knee'—shots to the green must pass between two well-shaped bunkers. The eighteenth hole has a fairway which teeters figuratively between two staggered bunkers set at driving distance, and a between-two-bunkers shot at the narrow green.

Generally, the wind is a strong factor here—the course has been designed to incorporate it as much as any other physical obstacle, and golfers will find themselves playing into, out of, or across wind. All in all, this is a course that asks the golfer to think, to strategize and to play with a sense of finesse, and is an enjoyable, extremely playable course.

The contoured and rolling surfaces of this course are in evidence on the *facing page*. The very rugged mountains of central Kauai are visible in the background.

Laguna Seca Golf Ranch

Monterey County, California USA

Called 'The Sunshine Course'—by comparison with its fellow courses just a few miles to the west, on the often fog-shrouded coast of the Monterey Peninsula—Laguna Seca is a rugged 18 holes of golf. Robert Trent Jones Sr began work on this course, and then gave the work over into the capable hands of his then-assistant, Robert Trent Jones Jr. This course is said to play like a mellow yet exciting combination of both of the master architects' styles. As he loves to do when it is possible, Robert Trent Jones Jr has melded his course into its native countryside: he has designed a course that weaves through copses of oaks, winding uphill and down.

The course, as is intimated above, rests in the Monterey Peninsula's best weather area, with usually sunny, warm days predominating. This is a 6075 yard championship course, also measuring 5632 yards and 5233 yards from the men's and ladies' tees, respectively.

The first hole is a fairly straight par four to a well-bunkered green—watch the bunkers also situated at the apex of the tree-lined fairway here; par three hole two is a straight shot up the middle to a dangerous, massively bunkered green; the very long, par five hole three features a tree-lined fairway leading to an extremely well-protected bunker-feeding green—shots from the tee must additionally

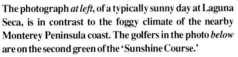

The photograph *at left*, of a typically sunny day at Laguna Seca, is in contrast to the foggy climate of the nearby Monterey Peninsula coast. The golfers in the photo *below* are on the second green of the 'Sunshine Course.'

be straight and true through some trickily placed oaks.

The fourth hole is a little more open, but still surrounded by woods, and there are two bunkers placed just where you'd put your first drive if you didn't think well enough of the shot. From there it's accuracy again, between the bunkers and onto the green. Long, dogleg left hole five features a long, dicey shot between the trees to the narrow fairway—long, but not as long as hole three, this hole culminates in a green which is protected by three bunkers and a cul de sac of trees.

Hole	1	2	3	4	5	6	7	8	9	Out	
Championship	343	151	500	379	504	328	363	157	404	3129	
Regular	334	138	484	363	480	313	331	136	388	2967	
Ladies	302	134	479	369	474	280	305	99	374	2816	
Mens Par	4	3	5	4	5	4	4	3	4	36	
Ladies Par	4	3	5	4	5	4	4	3	5	37	
Hole	10	11	12	13	14	15	16	17	18	In	Total
Championship	420	333	173	540	154	552	393	127	341	3033	6162
Regular	400	285	161	512	134	510	373	107	309	2791	5758
Ladies	341	245	117	481	117	410	265	94	300	5186	5186
Mens Par	4	4	3	5	3	5	4	3	4	35	71
Ladies Par	4	4	3	5	3	5	4	3	4	35	72

The sixth hole is another dogleg left, tree-lined, with water and bunkers heading the green. The championship tee at hole seven has to contend with trees impinging to the right, and a potential tour of the rough as a by-product of overcompensation on this—then it's a tour down the fairway, which curves to the left and is bordered with trees, to an obliquely set green which is protected by two bunkers. Hole eight (see detail map at right) has a large water hazard edged with trees hooking into the fairway en route to a wide green; the ninth is a straight, tree-lined par four—excepting the ladies' rating of par five—with a bunker slyly set, just where it will make you most consider your shot, at a slight offset to the green.

The tenth is a moderately long, lazy curve to the right, lined with woods. It has a quicksand pit—off to the left before the green—but this is surrounded by a barrier of trees, which in turn serve to 'shove' the approach to the green off to the right, where of course, a bunker awaits the unwary. Hole eleven (see detail map at right) is largely tree-lined, and describes a delayed dogleg to the right—the elbow of its boomerang-shaped fairway leads toward a bunker. The approach to the green is obstructed on the left by trees, and the open right hand side is clear to one of the green's four protecting bunkers.

The twelfth is simply a beautifully, artistically layed out par three hole. With the championship tee firing straight down the middle into the nose of its arrowhead-shaped fairway, and with the men's and ladies' tees coming in from the left and right, respectively, this hole broadens toward the green—an irregular ellipsoid set obliquely, protected by two bunkers. Hole thirteen is a very long par five 'banana' curving to the left, with trees marching roughly at a diagonal across the foot of the green, beyond which—and just where the average shot through the trees would land—are two bunkers. These obstacles may serve to prepare the canny golfer for the green itself, which is protected by four bunkers,

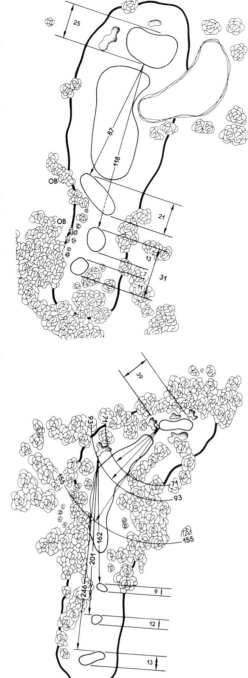

At right is the eighth green, and *below* is the eleventh hole at Laguna Seca. See, for comparison, the maps of both *above* and the text references to same on this page. Note the pond on the eighth.

The extensive bunkering around the green on hole seventeen is very evident here (*above*). The layout of this green and its defense is both intimidating and beautiful! The tees at hole seventeen are exciting in themselves, as is seen *at right*. These photos harmonize with the map and text references *below*.

three of which are staggered directly in front of the green, and one of which is set behind to catch overshots.

The golfer at hole fourteen faces a par three challenge with five bunkers surrounding the green. Hole fifteen is a water hole; its first challenge is a verdure-surrounded little pond just in line with the first shot onto the fairway. The second challenge is a lofting shot over another tree-studded pond which cuts the fairway in two—which, if overshot, will leave you in the rough; and the third challenge is a very tricky shot over another verdant watercourse which is set close to the comparatively shallow green, necessitating a shot that has considerable loft to it very close to the edge of the green—needless to say, a bunker awaits over-powered shots.

Hole number sixteen is a dogleg right, the tee shot having to clear a verdant water hazard onto an irregularly shaped green with a bunker in the line of flight, and a very well protected green. The seventeenth is a par three hole with five very strategically placed bunkers surrounding the green (see detail map at right). The eighteenth hole comprises a 336-yard bend (from the back tee) to the right, with trees planted here and there. Four bunkers guard the green—three in front, one at back.

This course was—as are all those touched by the hand of Robert Trent Jones Jr—designed to meld serenely into its surroundings, forming an ecological whole with the countryside. Its contours are most pleasing, and will afford golfers both challenge and a great deal of pleasure.

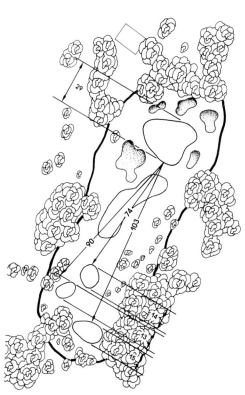

Lakeridge Golf Course

Reno, Nevada USA

Rock outcroppings, streams and lakes artfully combine to create a unique golfing experience near the heart of one of Nevada's largest cities and entertainment centers. The spectacular fifteenth hole provides great aesthetic pleasure, and yet the overall competitiveness of this course more than complements the outstanding visual effects of this course.

This course was recommended as one of *Golf Digest's* 'Places to Play' in February 1987. It is, indeed, an excellent place to play. Following is a hole-by-hole description of this marvellous course. Bear in mind that these holes are surrounded by native Nevada flora—and things can get a bit prickly if you go out of bounds!

Hole one is a dogleg right that bends around two bunkers, and carries a stream to a

Seen *below* is the spectacular green of Lakeridge hole number fifteen. This green is in the midst of a lake. In the background is part of the city of Reno, Nevada.

precision-bunkered green—*ie*, accuracy is all important here! The second hole tests your sense of distance and ability to modulate strength: you tee off across a pond to a shallow green bunkered behind and to the right, with a stream to its left. Hole three is a dogleg right, with bunkers just after the 'knee,' and a right-lying bunker stretching smack-dab into the approach! A bunker left will keep your shots on target, and the stream at right will provide some distraction. Dogleg right hole four has

bunkers lying in the probable landing area. From this little trap, you face a green with another directly bunkered approach. The shallow green will allow overpowered shots to be swallowed by the bunkers behind it.

The fifth breaks right at a pivot formed by two bunkers and a lake. The diagonally-set green is bunkered oppositionally on its exposed and rear flanks; you could even wind up in the rough at right rear. Hole number six plays across a lake to a triangular green which presents its narrow apex to you, flanked by two huge bunkers. A stream, no doubt full of lost balls, babbles along behind. Hole seven seems at first to be a pretty straightforward drive down the fairway to a green protected by two bunkers right and one left—which form pincers on the approach. Eagle eye, be with me now!

The eighth's back tees carry over a pond to a fairway which has an incidental-seeming bunker lying right early on—which no doubt has caught many a flubbed tee shot. Then you carry a three-lobed pond and a stream beyond that to a torus-shaped green which fronts on the stream and cradles a bunker behind: for many, it will be sand or water—or, for the very unfortunate, both in succession! Hole number nine is a dogleg left which breaks at bunkers left and heads for a green which essentially fills a cul-de-sac of bunkers. Perhaps it's no mere coincidence that the putting greens are near this hole.

Hole ten features a long carry—longitudinally down a stream—from the back tees to a fairway having bunkers just left of where the 'money' shot will come to rest. Be sharp here! Then it's a carry across another stream to an obliquely-set green. This green has a literal flock of bunkers on its exposed flank, as if it were some sort of a big, green ewe sheltering its lambs. Beware, though— these 'lambs' eat golf balls, and the 'strays' opposite them are sure to devour any 'excess.'

The eleventh plays down a fairway which forces your shots to the left—into the teeth of a large number of small bunkers on the green approach there. Between these and a bunker that lies right is, in fact, an approach to the green that will require your good judgement and shot control. Hole number twelve has two ponds—one apiece for front and back tees to carry to a triangular green whose apex faces you, and whose three sides are well bunkered. Sand and water again! Hole thirteen is a dogleg left which breaks around two bunkers left—these form an alley in cooperation with two right-lying bunkers farther on. This leads you to the broad, shallow green bunkered right and left—which creates, in its setup, an air of expectancy, which air is built upon with hole fourteen.

The fourteenth starts off across a stream, obliquely, and must avoid two bunkers lying near a reasonable 'landing spot' to the left. A stream and a pond lie to the right. A shot to the shallow, oblong green must avoid the bunker which lies in the approach. This is but the second wave in the building excitement that leads to the very striking fifteenth hole, which is one of the most spectacular human achievements in the state of Nevada—a state with more than its fair share of the spectacular. Here, you tee off from a rocky ridge that is 120 feet above a green that is set on an island in Lake Stanley. A babbling stream at your feet will distract you; the panorama of the beautiful lake, the buildings of the Lake Ridge development and the city of Reno will only add to the distraction—and then you realize that you're immediately faced with a difficult shot to a small-seeming green which lies far below you and is bunkered massively at front and at rear. Away we go!

Hole number sixteen brings us back down to Earth, with its straightforward opposing fairway bunkers and obliquely-set green having bunkers at right front and at left. Ac-

curacy and judgement of distance is important on the large, smooth, well-bunkered fairway of this hole. The same is true of the course, overall. Hole seventeen is a dogleg right, which breaks at two opposing bunkers. The 'sharpshooting match' gets more intense as you face that green approach with its 'pincer movement' bunkers. The eighteenth plays to a left-arching fairway having a bunker at left, early on—to create interest for those hoping to shave strokes off their score. Play is toward a stream lying all along the right. The green heads left, with a bunker on the approach at right to catch miscalculated shots, and bunkers on the left and right of the green itself. Dead ahead is the clubhouse.

The holes from the thirteenth on form a sequence which describes a crescendo and a decrescendo; the former being the fifteenth, and the latter being the satisfying, restorative sixteenth through eighteenth holes. The course is a symphony in green, created by that maestro among golf course composers, Robert Trent Jones Jr.

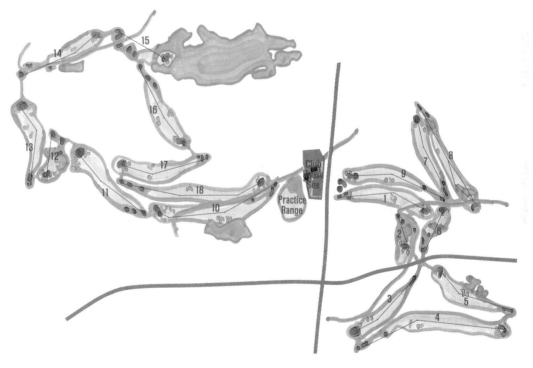

Hole	1	2	3	4	5	6	7	8	9	Out	
Championship	410	166	329	599	344	213	381	536	417	3395	
Tournament	365	151	310	569	317	181	359	487	403	3142	
Forward	326	95	284	480	284	131	303	393	348	2644	
Par	4	3	4	5	4	3	4	5	4	36	
Hole	10	11	12	13	14	15	16	17	18	In	Total
Championship	473	381	197	360	340	239	449	358	525	3322	6717
Tournament	458	351	157	331	300	226	383	329	507	3042	6184
Forward	360	314	129	307	250	156	273	293	433	2515	5159
Par	4	4	3	4	4	3	4	4	5	35	71

Le Triomphe Golf Club

Lafayette, Louisiana USA

This is an 18 hole championship course which has been designed with two unique major considerations; the course reflects, with its mighty oaks and blossoming fruit trees, the southern Louisiana environment—while having been designed around and through the housing development which forms the other 'partner' in the Le Triomphe community.

One enters the residential community and golf club within view of the Arc de Triomphe, a copy of its namesake in Paris. The course clubhouse, Chateau de Triomphe, overlooks the course and is a splendid country mansion in the French 18th century style, which hearkens back to the influence of the region's

Seen *above* is Le Triomphe's 'Arc de Triomphe,' and *below* are the number one fairway (at right) and number eighteen fairway (at left and also *facing page*).

early French-speaking settlers. In addition to the course, there are also four tennis courts, a pool, playgrounds, parks, bike paths and jogging trails.

The course has practice putting and chipping greens, a driving range, extremely attractive surroundings and the innovatively thought-out holes which one would expect of a Bobby Jones course. Lakes and or a watercourse accompany holes one, three, seven, eight, twelve, thirteen, fifteen, sixteen and eighteen. Each hole carries a colorful name.

The course—which reminds one a bit of Normandy—features rolling fairways and greens for a splendid, bucolic test of golfing ability. One starts out and comes to rest near

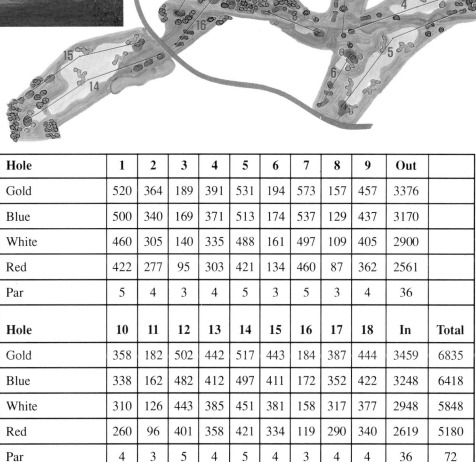

the clubhouse: holes one and eighteen form a joint complex of fairways, and lie head to foot.

Hole one, which is called *Firefly*, itself backs up to a practice green and starts off to a fairway having a large bunker immediately to the right. Tees are also lined on their right by a lake. It's then a long, undulating fairway to the green, at which point the fairway cuts right, leaving shots exposed to the care of a huge bunker there at the mouth of the green, which is backed by rough and a line of trees.

Some of the more outstanding holes from this point are number three (*Prayer*), which features a diagonal tee shot across a stream; number four (*Escape*), which features a similar, but longer tee shot, and a much longer and peril-fraught fairway; and the very well-bunkered, very long and serpentine hole five (*Bottomnotch*)—which also starts off across a stream.

Hole seven (*Needle's Eye*) features no less than three lakes—one left and one right of the fairway, and one curving around the green—two huge and three smaller, but cleverly placed bunkers, and trees. The eighth hole (*Arc's Shadow*) starts off across a lake to a murderously bunkered green which is also fronted by the lake; hole ten (*Camelback*) features a virtual flak attack of bunkers. Hole eleven (*Beach*) is practically swallowed by a bunker; and the twelfth hole (*Bleeder*) undulates in complement to a lake on its whole left side.

Hole number thirteen (*Gator's Jaw*) forms a rightward arc around a lake and then has to carry over a stream to a tree-backed green; holes fourteen (*Outback*) and fifteen (*Longfel-

Hole	1	2	3	4	5	6	7	8	9	Out	
Gold	520	364	189	391	531	194	573	157	457	3376	
Blue	500	340	169	371	513	174	537	129	437	3170	
White	460	305	140	335	488	161	497	109	405	2900	
Red	422	277	95	303	421	134	460	87	362	2561	
Par	5	4	3	4	5	3	5	3	4	36	
Hole	10	11	12	13	14	15	16	17	18	In	Total
Gold	358	182	502	442	517	443	184	387	444	3459	6835
Blue	338	162	482	412	497	411	172	352	422	3248	6418
White	310	126	443	385	451	381	158	317	377	2948	5848
Red	260	96	401	358	421	334	119	290	340	2619	5180
Par	4	3	5	4	5	4	3	4	4	36	72

low) feature some very fancy bunker placements, and a lake close by the tees of hole fourteen. The sixteenth (*Big Sir*) carries over a stream en route to a small green. The championship tee of hole seventeen (*Slot*) lies in a cul de sac of trees, and the entire hole is lined on its right with a thick column of trees, and is well-serpentined and extremely well-bunkered left and behind the green.

The eighteenth hole (*Triumph*) pivots right on the 'hinge' of an oblong lake, which axis thrusts unwary shots toward a stand of trees lying among the fairway's undulations to the right. The green itself is well-bunkered left towards the clubhouse, and is indeed a triumphant conclusion to a stunning round of golf—provided via the genius and artistry of the brilliant Robert Trent Jones Jr.

Westin Mauna Kea Beach Hotel Golf Course

Kamuela, Hawaii USA

The praise that has been heaped upon this course is practically overwhelming. Some call this course a miracle, some call it a monster—but any way you consider such comments, they add up to the fact that this is a demanding and unforgettable golf course.

Mauna Kea was once again ranked among 'America's 100 Greatest' and 'Hawaii's Finest' by *Golf Digest* in November of 1987, and was also rated ninth in aesthetics by the magazine. *Golf Digest's* distinguished review team's criteria were the following: shot values, resistance to scoring, design balance, memorability, aesthetics, conditioning and tradition. A popular course with the likes of Tom Watson, Jack Nicklaus, Chi Chi Rodriguez and Bob Rosburg, this beautiful

Seen in the photo *above* is snowcapped Mauna Kea. *Below* is an aerial shot of hole eleven. The green *at right* is the famous third, Mauna Kea's 'water hole.'

course, which serves as a practice haven for Isao Aoki, was included in the 'Twelve Magnificent Golf Courses of the World' calendar by Paul Gleason.

Robert Trent Jones Jr had the honor of doing some major reworking on this, one of the most revered and famous golf courses in the world. The Westin Mauna Kea's course was named for the nearby snowcapped volcano, Mauna Kea—which literally means 'white mountain' in Hawaiian—and was built in 1964 by Robert Trent Jones Sr; in 1974, his brilliant son was called in to re-tune parts of the course.

The elder Jones, who has designed more than 300 golf courses around the world—16 of them considered among 'America's 100

greatest'—applied the full range of his considerable knowledge to overcome the extreme difficulties which the site imposed. The course was conceived as a rugged beauty rolling over 230 acres of lava hills, with the beautiful snowcapped mountains on one side and the roiling, furiously beautiful Pacific on the other—an extraordinary site, and an extraordinary golf course architect to meet the challenge it presented.

According to the publicity office of the Westin Mauna Kea, Robert Trent Jones Sr says, in remembering this challenge: 'It was one of our greatest opportunities. First of all, it was a lava wasteland. The site was so dry that only scattered cactus plants were growing there.'

Greens and fairways had to be hacked out of the solid lava rock, and, to enable the moon-like surface to support life, an elaborate automatic underground watering system was installed to pump more than a million gallons of water per day to fairways and greens—keeping the course in its prime condition all year round. Compensating for the coast's meager rainfall, this particular water supply system is unlike that used in any other golf course design in the world.

Soil also posed a problem because grass doesn't take root on lava. Jones Sr's solution was to create soil out of the lava itself! He brought in heavy construction machinery, equipped with special devices that he had invented himself, which crushed the brittle lava to a powdery consistency through repeated gradings and rollings. The rust-red-colored crushed lava was then spread over the course foundations, which had now been carved out of the same lava flow.

The same pulverization process was in turn used to make lime powder out of coral dredged from the nearby Kawaihae Harbor. A three-inch layer of this material was then spread over the lava soil, followed by a blanket of fertilizer. This was then carpeted with a new variety of hybrid Bermuda grass, which had all the fine qualities of Mainland golf course bent grass, but was suited to Hawaii's tropical climate. The bunkers themselves were filled with crushed coral.

Hundreds of coconut palms and other spreading and sometimes flowering trees—including rainbow shower, wili-wili, monkey pod and Chinese banyan were brought in to accent the landscaping, and to help anchor the topsoil to the lava base.

It was also a course that was designed to counteract scientific advancements in clubs and balls—improvements which enabled pros to hit the ball straighter and farther, and helped them to consistently score below par. Robert Trent Jones Sr intended to shake up the troops with his design. This is consistent with his philosophy, as stated by Westin Mauna Kea's press release: 'Every hole should be a demanding par and a comfortable bogey.'

Upon completing this course in December of 1964, Jones Sr described it as one of his crowning achievements. He had fashioned a course with an incredible panoramic sweep of sea and land, including snowcapped Mauna Kea itself, rugged lava beds and the blue Pacific, where golfers can view the whales that 'winter' just off the island of Hawaii's Kohala Coast.

Mauna Kea's undulating fairways, uphill holes, steep greens, doglegs, strategically placed bunkers and 120 sand traps make the course one of the most challenging in the world of golf. The *piece d'resistance*, however, is the course's incredible hole number three, where an inlet of the mighty Pacific Ocean forms the water hazard! This hole is rated as 'one of the Top 100 Holes in America' by *Golf Magazine*, and is considered by many to be one of Mauna Kea's most difficult holes. The challenge comes physically and mentally with a vengeance; the prospect of shooting 130 to 215 yards over surf ensures that.

The eleventh green, with a sheer drop of 100 feet to the ocean behind it, is part of another breathtaking hole; it measures 247 yards from the back tees—an almost unreach-

Seen *below* is an overview of the perilous third. With ocean updrafts and a 130 to 215 yard carry to the green, this hole is challenging, indeed. The Pacific Ocean breaks against the cliffs below as you tee off!

able distance when ocean breezes blow. Isao Aoki rates the eleventh hole as the hardest par three not over water. Hole number thirteen offers a breathtaking view of beautiful, awe-inspiring Mount Mauna Kea, which is snowcapped from December to June.

This masterwork was christened in royal style when, on 8 December 1964, a 'Big Three' golf tournament featuring Arnold Palmer, Jack Nicklaus and Gary Player took place there. Nicklaus, who won the match, gave the course perhaps the highest of all the very effusive praise that this course has gotten—he declared that it was 'more fun to play than any course I know.' After the course and hotel were opened to the public in July of 1965, Mauna Kea quickly became one of the world's leading golf meccas.

In 1968, Shell Oil Company's *Wonderful World of Golf*, which focused on the world's outstanding golf courses, filmed a segment at Mauna Kea. This television show featured a match between Peter Allis, Al Geiberger and the late Dan Sikes; Sikes won with a par 72.

The Westin Mauna Kea course has taken on a rich, mature patina in its quarter century of existence, and has been kept in top form under the careful supervision of Mauna Kea's golf course superintendent, Robert Itamoto. He has been at the course since the first rocks were scraped away for the greens.

The first notable changes made to the course were made by Robert Trent Jones Jr. It must have been a challenge indeed to work on his father's then-already legendary course. Yet if any man in the world were the one to modify Mauna Kea, it would be Bobby Jones. Due to complaints early on that the course was too difficult for players at the lower echelons of golf, Bobby Jones was contracted to make refinements in his father's design, which would provide fun, stimulating and challenging play for golfers at all levels. These refinements were made on holes two, three, six, eight, ten and fourteen, and involved softening the greens, thus increasing their playability.

During this four month project, the greens were entirely stripped and their rock bases were reshaped to provide an entirely different surface. In addition to this, some of the rock and brush adjacent to the course was cleared away.

When the revised course was opened in late 1975, the changes were greeted with enthusiasm. The following is a quote from Ben Neeley, then-head professional at Mid-Pacific Country Club on Oahu, whose team captured the annual Pro-Am tournament that year: 'It was a great golf course and it's still a great golf course....It's improved, but still it's the toughest in the state. Anyone who thinks the

changes have made this an easy course doesn't know golf.'

More subtle course refinements were made in 1983 with the re-establishment of 22 championship and alternate tees, which offer players a wider range of options and risk. JD Ebersberger and Bob Itamoto supervised these changes, which included the reinstallation of the original back tees, creation of some new tees and the realignment of other tees for better vision of the fairways. The black, championship tees total 7103 yards, the blue tees total 6781, the orange total 6455 and the white total 5659 yards. There are now a total of six tee positions on some holes, including the famous number three. According to JD Ebersberger, as quoted in the *Sunday Star-Bulletin & Advertiser* of 8 July 1984:

'The alternate tees offer a challenge to all types of players. We couldn't build the black tee on the third in its original position because the promontory there was washed away in a storm two years ago. But it is 215 yards across the ocean from the new black tee, and just as challenging as when Nicklaus, Palmer and Player played here.

'Sculpturing of the fairways has been carried out, allowing the grass to grow a little higher...This helps keep the balls in play. The fairways are Tif 328—around 60 yards wide in some areas, and narrow to 35 to 45 yards further out for long hitters. This gives a better challenge to both the high handicap country club players and the stronger players.'

Mauna Kea's fairways are of course a major consideration—nearly every one has elevated tees and greens of Tif 328, with rolling terrain between, adding 'character.' This also greatly adds beauty to a course in an already spectacular site. Mr Jones Sr designed the course so that the ocean would be visible from each green.

Quoted from the *Sunday Star-Bulletin & Advertiser*, JD Ebersberger says of Mauna Kea's par three eleventh hole: 'From the back tee, which is probably situated on the highest ground in the course, you can see Haleakala on Maui, Mauna Kea and the sea....No matter which way you turn, there is a spectacular view in front of you.'

Mauna Kea observed its 20th birthday with its two major yearly tournaments, a Pro Am in July, and an Invitational in early December.

So, as the product, essentially, of Robert Trent Jones Sr, and with important modifications by his brilliant son, Robert Trent Jones Jr, plus fine tuning by the able staff at Westin Mauna Kea, Mauna Kea was, is and will continue to be one of the world's truly great golf courses.

Hole	1	2	3	4	5	6	7	8	9	Out	
Black	400	390	215	420	580	350	210	534	433	3532	
Blue	387	360	210	410	560	350	188	515	408	3388	
Orange	372	330	180	396	514	333	178	510	380	3193	
Par	4	4	3	4	5	4	3	5	4	36	
Hole	**10**	**11**	**12**	**13**	**14**	**15**	**16**	**17**	**18**	**In**	**Total**
Black	353	247	385	414	393	204	415	550	428	3571	7103
Blue	480	208	385	335	393	204	410	550	428	3393	6781
Orange	475	198	375	332	383	191	394	534	380	3262	6455
Par	5	3	4	4	4	3	4	5	4	36	72

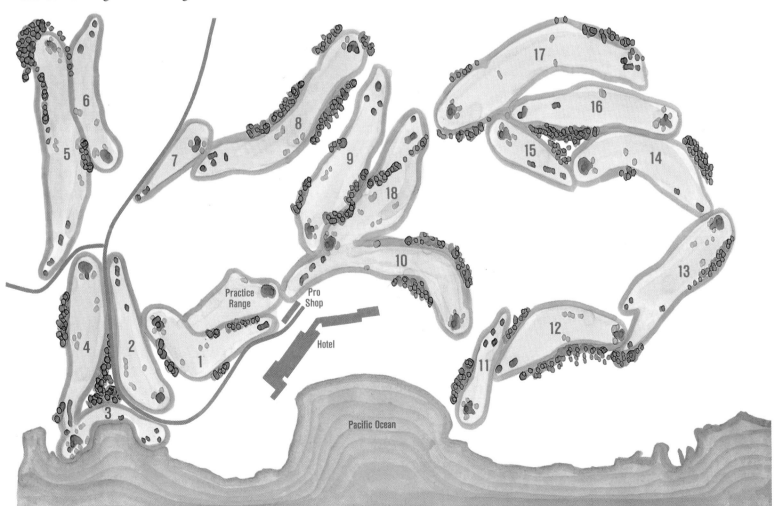

Meadow Springs Country Club Golf Course

Mandurah, Western Australia

One of the most recent courses designed by Robert Trent Jones Jr, this excellent young course is the centerpiece of a residential/resort complex which is located to the north of Mandurah, Western Australia's most popular holiday resort town. Mandurah is located just 43.5 miles South of Perth, and when the Perth-Bunbury Highway is constructed, that thoroughfare will increase public access to this development.

The Mandurah area is renowned for its vast inland waterways, majestic river system and miles of safe, sandy beaches. Bordering on the Indian Ocean, Mandurah is a paradise for water sports enthusiasts. The philosophy behind the development and golf course at Meadow Springs is to create maximum harmony with the magnificent natural environment and with the mellow life style that makes the region popular with both residents and visitors alike. Out of this milieu came the idea of building the Meadow Springs Golf Course and Resort Complex, which comprises a resort hotel, a holiday village, a commercial center, a retirement village and 4000 multidensity and single residential sites, all clustered around a magnificent golf course and country club.

Of Mr Jones' magnificent golf course, the Meadow Springs brochure speaks most eloquently, opening with a quote from Hugh Delehanty, taken from the *San Jose Mercury* of 7 April 1985: 'From the Pyramids to Pebble Beach, Robert Trent Jones Jr has built a reputation as the Frank Lloyd Wright of the links...What Frank Lloyd Wright did for architecture, Jones is doing for the game of golf, creating spectacular greens and fairways that not only play well, but also harmonize with the world around them.'

The brochure goes on to proclaim that 'The golf course at Meadow Springs is a Trent

At left, a golfer blasts out of a bunker on Meadow Springs' number one green. The golfer in the photo *above* is putting for the pin on the fourth green.

Jones (sic) masterpiece. Each of its 18 holes has its own distinctive personality. This 5793 meter (6335 yard), par 72 course is a picture of undulating verdant fairways, tantalizing bunkered greens and four sparkling lakes which have been added to the landscape to challenge amateur and professional alike. The intention was to create a unique and thoroughly enjoyable golf course. The idea has become a reality. As Robert Trent Jones Jr puts it: "In every sense, we feel we have captured fully, the unique potential of this splendid site, and have achieved a course that ranks among the best the world over."'

The course opened on 2 October 1987, with appropriate fanfare and celebrities, including Australian golfer Jack Newton, entertainer Barry Martin and the Premier of Western Australia, Mr Brian Burke. This course promises, with its spectacular setting and brilliant design, to be a treasure much sought by golfers the world over, and will truly be a pleasure for those who get to play golf in the land 'down under.' Following is a hole-by-hole description of this fine 18 hole layout.

Tree-lined hole one is a dogleg right with a large bunker on its 'knee.' The green is framed with large bunkers and trees on either side— essentially, the green exists in a 'hallway' of natural and man-made features. The second hole sometimes plays into the wind and has a tree-lined fairway with a narrow, well-trapped

green approach. It is a demanding dogleg left. Hole number three is short, but—with a tree-lined fairway and a sudden hook to the right at the green—demands your attention!

The fourth hole's heavy stands of acacia trees very well limn the boundaries of this playing surface. Tee shots carry over rough to an abbreviated fairway and a broad, shallow green. The green has a bunker incursing on its left approach, and a bunker at left behind; it's putting time! Hole five breaks right at a bunker and serpentines around the trees to a very interesting green indeed. Hole six drives to an open landing area with bunkers at right and trees to the left. The green is in a depression which is surrounded by large trees; two bunkers guard the approach on the left—this should be a very challenging hole.

Hole number seven is a great driving hole, and well explicates Mr Jones' 'great risks, great rewards' philosophy, with the incursing trap early on the right, which can be carried from the tees. The terrain is open but undulating, and the landing area is uphill from the tees. The green is guarded at right with several large, overhanging trees, and on the left by a Great White Bunker! The eighth is the first of four consecutive water holes, and demands a long tee shot over a lake for the valorous; others can play safe to the right. The green has massive bunkers all along its rear, so mind your distances.

The ninth's tees overlook the tip of a lake to an open, but undulating fairway having water at its right and a bunker at its left. The green is large and is bunkered right and left. Hole ten has water all along its right, bunkers on its left, and its green approach is pinched with opposing bunkers. Hole number eleven is short but very sweet! Tee shots are downhill, and can carry over a lake directly to the green, or can play over rough to a short fairway preceding the green, which itself has trees left, water all along its left front and one bunker at its rear.

The twelfth plays from a ridge line into a valley. The left-bending fairway has two bunkers on its outer 'elbow' and trees opposite these. Massive bunkers all along the left of the green create a tension with the many trees along the right. A gem! Hole thirteen's tees face a fairway with a large bunker pushing in from the right. Too far left, and the huge bunker there awaits you. The fairway plays over a ridge line and the green approach is well bunkered.

Hole number fifteen plays downhill to a clearing in the trees, which marks the beginning of a gently right-curving fairway having a 'gunsight' made of trees and a bunker-pinched green approach. The second shot, to the green, plays uphill. The green itself has trees behind. The sixteenth's back tee has a good way to travel to the abbreviated fairway/green setup on this hole. The contoured

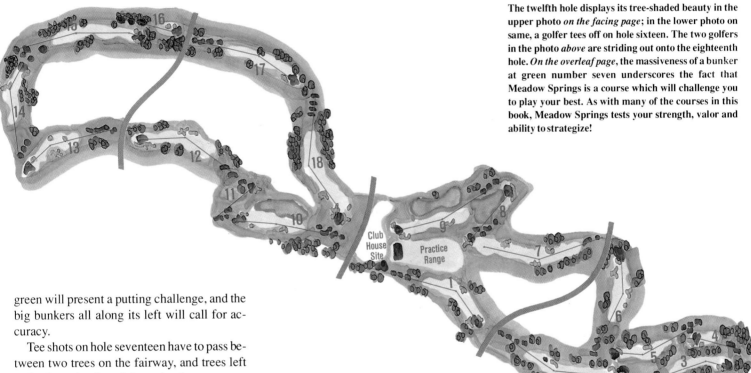

The twelfth hole displays its tree-shaded beauty in the upper photo *on the facing page*; in the lower photo on same, a golfer tees off on hole sixteen. The two golfers in the photo *above* are striding out onto the eighteenth hole. *On the overleaf page*, the massiveness of a bunker at green number seven underscores the fact that Meadow Springs is a course which will challenge you to play your best. As with many of the courses in this book, Meadow Springs tests your strength, valor and ability to strategize!

green will present a putting challenge, and the big bunkers all along its left will call for accuracy.

Tee shots on hole seventeen have to pass between two trees on the fairway, and trees left and a large bunker right make the green approach interesting. The green itself is elevated and is terraced into the side of a hill, so you should have your eyes open here! The eighteenth hole plays downhill through an alleyway of trees, then breaks to the left. A huge bunker cuts into the fairway's right side near the green, and the green approach itself cuts suddenly to the right, with an incursing bunker at its left, and massive bunkers on either side of the green. You can carry over the bunkers—if you dare! A great finishing hole for a tremendous 18 holes of golf.

The Meadow Springs course adds to the impressive roster of Robert Trent Jones Jr golf courses in Australia, which includes the Joondalup Country Club Estate course, the Cape Schanck Golf Club course and The National Golf Club course—all of which are superb, and represent the very best that Australian golfing has to offer.

Hole	1	2	3	4	5	6	7	8	9	Out	
Blue	395	535	340	185	360	390	530	190	430	3355	
White	365	485	310	160	330	360	505	160	400	3075	
Red	335	430	275	130	300	330	470	130	360	2760	
Par	4	5	4	3	4	4	5	3	4	36	
Hole	10	11	12	13	14	15	16	17	18	In	Total
Blue	400	180	415	370	350	490	195	410	485	3295	6650
White	350	160	365	330	330	450	160	365	455	2970	6045
Red	310	120	325	300	280	390	130	315	420	2590	5350
Par	4	3	4	4	4	5	3	4	5	36	72

Distances in meters

Mill Creek Golf and Country Club

Salado, Texas USA

'The stars at night
are big and bright
deep in the Heart of Texas...'

Mill Creek is a residential community in the small town of Salado, which is located between Waco and Austin, Texas. As has been recounted elsewhere, when asked where his new golf course in Texas was located, Robert Trent Jones Jr soon grew tired of describing in detail the exact location, and said, simply, 'In the heart of Texas.' which was, after all, very nearly the exact geographical truth.

Mr Jones then fancifully designed (what was then) the twelfth green of the then-unfinished course in the shape of a heart. Mill Creek's owners talked to Texas Governor William P Clements Jr, and when the opening ceremonies for the course were held in Oc-tober of 1980, a state official was on hand, with a signed declaration by the governor, that 'the number twelve green of Mill Creek Golf and Country Club is hereby designated THE HEART OF TEXAS for this occasion.'

Both the Mill Creek development and golf course are owned by a small partnership of three Central Texas residents. Schooling for

At left—a view of holes one (photo left) and ten. The 'Heart of Texas' green is shown *above*. The fifteenth green appears *below*, with hole seventeen beyond.

children of Mill Creek residents is provided by the Salado Independent School District. Also, the town of Salado has churches of nearly every denomination. The Mill Creek Club has fine dining, snack and bar facilities for both residents and visitors to its truly superb golf course.

This is indeed an interesting course, with wide open spaces and narrow undulant passages—there are situations to test every golfer's game. Some years ago, the course staff switched the front and back nines, making the famous twelfth green now the third green. The following is a hole-by-hole description.

Hole number one has a stream nearly all its length on the left, and the back tees must jump a wide stream to the fairway, which leads over undulating ground to a green

which is surrounded by four bunkers, and is separated from the fairway by another branch of the aforesaid stream. The second's tees face down a short fairway to a small green having two bunkers at its front. Hole three describes a dogleg right, with a voracious bunker just behind the 'knee.' The green is the famous 'Heart of Texas' green, since the front and back nines were switched some years ago. This green is protected at its point and at each of its lobes with sizable bunkers—one does not easily penetrate the Heart of Texas! The only thing this hole is missing are some yellow roses.

Players at hole number four tee off into the fork of a stream. The fairway forms a right angle bend, which coincides with another lacustrine fork, this time involving the

Above **is the fourth's fairway and green. The stream forks just to the left of this view, and the clubhouse can be seen through the trees in the background.** *On the upper facing page* **is a view of the seventh fairway, with Salado Creek flowing beside it.**

aforementioned stream and Salado Creek, to which the stream is itself a tributary. Landings on this fairway are risky, with stream everywhere left. Across the creek, then, is the green, with a bunker right.

Hole five is a serpentine with two bunkers on its first inside curve, and a bunker at right front of its green, while hole six is a very short hole, having a green with a bunker at left front. The seventh has Salado Creek to its right, and arcs gracefully to the left, with a bunker at midway just where incautious shots may fall short of breaching the arc. The green is a bit of

a surprise, as it's offset to the right at fairway's end, and has bunkers either side—watch out for that one on its left.

Hole eight gives golfers a good variety of shots—some tees must carry across Salado Creek, and the inner tees cross terra firma. Your shot across the creek could find the bunker on the fairway's left, then it's an approach to an irregularly-shaped green which is well-bunkered. At hole nine, you tee off over rough and then head down the fairway toward two large bunkers. Hopefully, your ball will stop short of these. Then it's a carry over Salado Creek to your right—to the second half of fairway and the green, which lie beyond the waves. A bunker lies where you may land, and the green itself is protected with bunkers right.

Golfers at the tenth hole tee off across

Salado Creek to a fairway with a strategically placed bunker at right, leading you to a green which is protected left and right with bunkers. Tee shots at hole eleven cross the tributary stream to a dogleg right fairway having bunkers on its inner 'knee,' and a heavily bunkered green. The twelfth has just a bit of fairway before one comes to the stream, and carries to the green, which is well-protected left and right, while hole thirteen plays down a long dogleg left with a bunker on its inner 'knee,' and then across Salado Creek to a very well bunkered green.

Hole number fourteen plays down a dogleg left, again with a bunker at the inner 'knee,' and with a pond riding its right to keep you on the straight and narrow, and then on to a triangular green, set 'chin' first, with bunkers on all sides. Play at the fifteenth begins down a fairway which bends to the right, having a bunker on the inside of the bend, and just as the curve of the fairway really gets going, there's a stream, across which is a miniscule chunk of fairway and a green protected directly on its approach with a bunker. The sixteenth is very short, and players here tee off across the stream to a green which has large bunkers right and left.

Hole number seventeen has an undulating fairway with a set of bunkers where they will attract any unwary shot. The green is well protected on its right and right front, directly in line with any approach shots on the subtly curving fairway. The eighteenth hole plays down a fairway with bunker left, then begins to wrap around a pond, with the green forming an incursion into same. With pond right and bunkers left and behind, it is a tight, dramatic end for eighteen holes of spectacular golf.

The Mill Creek course is a stroke of architectural genius, 'deep in the Heart of Texas!'

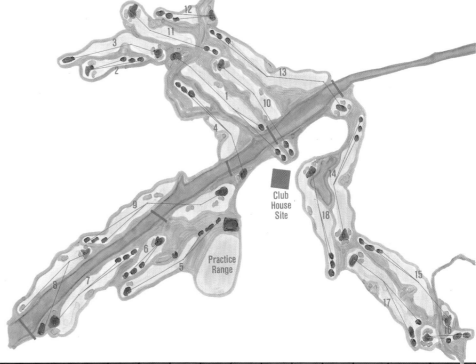

Hole	1	2	3	4	5	6	7	8	9	Out	
Blue	512	183	340	413	420	190	401	348	517	3324	
White	477	156	321	398	395	169	373	339	494	3122	
Red	368	136	289	372	361	143	340	278	449	2736	
Mens Par	5	3	4	4	4	3	4	4	5	36	
Ladies Par	5	3	4	5	4	3	4	4	5	37	
Hole	10	11	12	13	14	15	16	17	18	In	Total
Blue	398	346	182	556	411	392	132	376	369	3162	6486
White	364	324	160	536	395	363	109	338	341	2930	6052
Red	236	272	110	504	369	331	69	313	310	2514	5250
Mens Par	4	4	3	5	4	4	3	4	4	35	71
Ladies Par	4	4	3	6	5	4	3	4	4	37	74

The Links at Monarch Beach

Laguna Niguel, California USA

As quoted in *Golf Gazette* of 16 June 1985, Robert Trent Jones Jr says of this course, 'I see golf as 18 separate puzzles...and that's where the strategy comes in. You should stand on the tee, study the puzzle and decide then how you're going to solve that particular one.'

Situated near Laguna Niguel, which is 20 miles southwest of Santa Ana, the course is the only ocean layout between San Diego and Pebble Beach. Quoted in the same publication as the above, Mr Jones says that he put some extra effort into designing this one, '...after all, this may be the last ocean course ever built in the United States because of the lack of the available coastal land and the value of that land, along with increasing governmental restrictions.'

Mr Jones said—again, in *Golf Gazette*— 'We wanted to maximize the sheer beauty of the location...so we really moved to the Scottish tradition of almost letting the course lay itself out, following the coastline, or alongside the creek. That's why it will seem irrational to the golfer accustomed to American courses only. American courses are usually very rational—par 36 on the front, and back, all very rational. On the back nine you will find two par threes in a row, a real rarity in America, but that's what the lay of the land dictated.'

Seen *below* is the first of 18 separate puzzles on the course at Monarch Beach. We're looking across a massive bunker at the green, and the pond beyond.

The course changes with time of day, wind direction and pin placement—the course is actually several courses in one. It originally opened in 1983 as the Salt Creek Golf Course nine, and when the second nine holes were completed, the complete course opened in August 1984. Here, Mr Jones has added some of his own devices to classic linksland features, which are natural green dotted with sea grass and bunkers that take you by surprise.

To supervise this project, Mr Jones brought in one of his firm's top design associates, Gary Linn. The course is adjacent to the dramatic new Ritz-Carlton Hotel, which also is a part of this world class resort complex.

Chosen as *Golf's Gazette's* Course of the Month for June 1985, the Links is a course which players can play and play again without becoming tired of it—the course's dedicated staff, headed by the Links' capable golf director, is working to make it 'one of the finest in the world.' Following is a hole-by-hole course description.

Hole one features elevated tees, water on the right and a yawning bunker right in front of the green. If you're a good shot, the predominate tailwind will help you. The second hole features three fairway bunkers on the left, one on the right beside the fairway, one just behind the right of the green trees in a cul de sac behind the green. An elevated tee and a large green also predominate here.

Hole number three plays into the wind, and the approach to the green can be very interesting, as the two bunkers on its sides are dangerous. Hole four has a huge bunker on the fairway right, and two to the left, in the 'elbow.' Shaped like a porkchop, this hole curves to the left. The green and some water interlock on the right—a real challenge. At the fifth, Salt Creek winds down the left side, in concert with two bunkers—one imme-diately on the left of the green—cater-cornered from a bunker a little farther away from the green, on the right.

Hole six has a narrow fairway, and rangy tee shots cross Salt Creek, and the Creek borders the fairway on the left, balancing the bunkers on the right. Another creek shot can be played in a variety of ways: the green has bunkers front and back, plus trees back. Hole seven plays uphill, and is heavily bunkered—including four bunkers around the elevated green, and trees to the fairway left. The wind is against you. Hole eight's fairway is pinched, a third of the way up, with two bunkers; there is water on the left front of the green, and two bunkers on the back.

The ninth's fairway is lined right with bunkers, and one 'squeezer' on the right. It plays up to an elevated green sandwiched with bunkers. Good luck! Hole ten is an acute dogleg left. A lake is to the right, bunkers reside in the fairway's 'knee', and there is a

well-bunkered green; the wind is also a factor here. Hole number eleven is a dogleg left, with four bunkers and the Pacific Ocean on the right, natural sand and four bunkers left. It has a very tricky elevated green, and should be a highlight of the game.

Hole twelve has an elevated tee, a short fairway, and a green sandwiched sidewise with bunkers. It is a very scenic hole. The thirteenth's green is surrounded on three sides by bunkers and a lake, and Salt Creek cuts across the fairway—a water lover's delight. The elevated tees here are shielded on one side by trees. Hole fourteen plays uphill, and its green is bunkered on all of its triangular sides. Trees form one-half of a lopsided 'pinch' at about the midpoint of the fairway.

Hole number fifteen's green is bunkered beside and at left front: this bunker has to be jumped by tee shots, and its fellows are to the

right. Three fairway bunkers lay left, and two right. A very nice hole. Hole sixteen is a tricky, disjointed dogleg left with a well-bunkered fairway. The green is sandwiched with bunkers. Tee shots skim trees to the left. The seventeenth's tees face a fairway which describes a bend to the right. The green is semi-open from the front, with water on the other three sides, and with a bunker thrown in as well to the left front. A terrific hole!

The eighteenth hole's well-bunkered fairway bends to the left, with water guarding the 'shin' on the right just before the large green, which is very well bunkered. It is a great finish to an outstanding round of golf. This classically-influenced course should be a pleasure to those who are just becoming acquainted with it, just as it already is a true pleasure to those who know it—if such a wonderfully variegated course can ever truly be 'known.'

At above left, we have a distance shot of the green setup at hole seventeen, and hole sixteen is seen, from the green end, *on the facing page. Above* is the hole marker for seventeen, with a hole map from an overhead perspective. Compare this with the photo on page 100. *Overleaf:* A Pacific Ocean vista and the fifth green.

Hole	1	2	3	4	5	6	7	8	9	Out	
Champion	167	336	157	358	392	517	345	500	376	3148	
Mens	135	308	134	332	365	505	320	465	350	2914	
Ladies	106	272	111	295	337	488	300	430	316	2655	
Par	3	4	3	4	4	5	4	5	4	36	
Hole	10	11	12	13	14	15	16	17	18	In	Total
Champion	401	315	183	217	373	374	526	146	381	2911	6064
Mens	375	285	162	190	348	340	500	127	352	2682	5593
Ladies	340	253	130	160	307	300	462	90	323	2365	5020
Par	4	4	3	3	4	4	5	3	4	34	70

The National Golf and Country Club

Cape Schanck, Australia

In its own literature, the Club recalls Robert Trent Jones Jr's initial encounter with this site: 'When I first saw the land on which The National was to be constructed I instantly recognized the potential it held to design a truly great international course—one that could easily be ranked with the world's best.

'However, it was not until we had planned the course and cut the fairway lines that the full drama of The National became evident. We, as architects, had underestimated the full grandeur of this classic layout.

'It is an old saying that "great courses are not built, rather they develop." Not so in this case. From the day The National opens, it will be one of the world's foremost courses and time will only further enhance its ranking.'

The National is located adjacent to another of Robert Trent Jones Jr's great courses—the Cape Schanck Golf Club course—on Melbourne's Mornington Peninsula, near Cape Schanck.

Although critics felt that yet another golf club in the Melbourne region—already the home of several fine courses—would certainly fail, The National has proven successful beyond all expectations, and the course is slated to open this year.

Magnificent views of sights on the Peninsula, including beautiful Bass Strait, are availed to the golfer on this course—a beauty that will refresh golfers further while they engage in a refreshing and very challenging round of golf.

Five separate tee markers will be in place at each of The National's holes, as is the Robert Trent Jones Jr *modus operandi* of providing exciting, challenging play for a number of golfing levels. These tee markers are black, for championship play, blue for men's play, yellow for men's social play, red for women's championship play and white for women's play.

Following is a hole-by-hole description of the course. Hole one demands accuracy, and the green is protected by a cunningly-placed bunker and a tree. Hole two, a par three, features tee positions facing left over a wooded ravine to a large but treacherous green. The third curves gracefully to the right, and has a spectacular view. Changing elevations make this very interesting—it's a downhill drive to gradated fairway, at the top of which is the green. The fairway has six bunkers, to boot.

Hole four has a large, tricky putting surface and well-placed bunkers make this a 'long' par four. The fifth's a right, a left, and right again! This serpentine catches you with bunkers, and demands accuracy at every point. The green has a pinched mouth, a bunker and pine trees.

Hole	1	2	3	4	5	6	7	8	9	Out	
Black	344	139	473	403	521	371	308	198	390	3147	
Par	4	3	5	4	5	4	4	3	4	36	
Hole	10	11	12	13	14	15	16	17	18	In	Total
Black	358	168	511	337	342	420	390	165	475	3166	6313
Par	4	3	5	4	4	4	4	3	5	36	72

Distances in meters

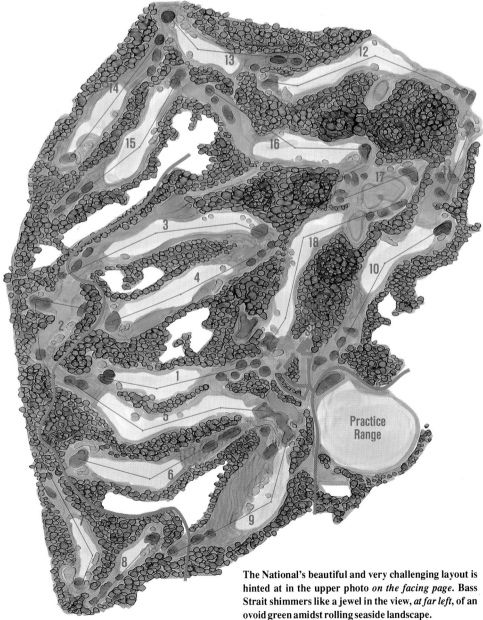

The National's beautiful and very challenging layout is hinted at in the upper photo *on the facing page*. **Bass Strait shimmers like a jewel in the view, *at far left*, of an ovoid green amidst rolling seaside landscape.**

Best of luck! Wide, gentle dogleg right hole six drives downhill to a green protected by two massive bunkers—an added feature is an island of tussock grass.

Hole seven is a delayed dogleg right—a fairly long drive with a bend at the end, and a tiny green protected by a stabilized sand dune. The eighth, another par three, is straightforward, with a severely pinched shot at the green. Five bunkers stand guard duty, and the green is large and sloping. A good, good hole. Hole number nine plays as a long, gentle dogleg left. Heavy bunkering on the left of the fairway, tall trees at either side of the green's mouth, and a bunker to the left make this a very nifty par four.

Hole ten is a dogleg right. You drive downhill into 'bunker heaven,' the golfer's demise—unless he's careful. A bunker waits on the right mouth of the green, and the tree on the right of the fairway, with the green bunkered behind as well, make this quite a hole. Tee shots at hole eleven must cross a deep ravine to the green, and a hidden bunker foils many shots to the left. The green slopes, to continue the fun. The twelfth is a dogleg left that almost repents before you reach the green. Just after the elbow, the fairway pinches in, asking you to shoot for the green at risk of hitting the large bunker at fairway's end, where the range shifts sharply to a 'peninsula' which aims toward the green; bunkers trail from right, right around the green. Good golfing!

Dogleg right hole thirteen demands a focused drive through very crafty bunkering. The final bunker behind the green will catch many a ball. Hole number fourteen features a clump of trees which inrupt on the fairway, and a bunker at left which cuts it two-thirds of the way down into a mere neck for the rest of the way—toward a supernally well-protected green. Great views here, and great golf.

The fifteenth's two big bunkers to the right could cheat you into aiming for the two big bunkers halfway down the fairway on the left. The green is protected by two bunkers left. Hole sixteen's tees face across a ravine where bunkers catch you short and long. Then you work uphill toward the large green past the two bunkers at fairway's end. Hole number seventeen is a long shot over water to a green protected by two bunkers and water at its very edge. A very thrilling par three. The eighteenth hole is a gentle serpentine on a fairway bunkered where it does good. A bunker cuts across the approach to the green, and a large bunker at left rear of the green take the golfer's attention away from Daryl Jackson's stunningly designed course clubhouse, which has at this point come into view. A great finish to a great 18 holes of golf.

At left: **With a fine, challenging course layout and natural beauty in abundance, the National offers an exciting round of golf for a variety of talents.**

Navatanee Golf Course

Bangkok, Thailand

Designed when Robert Trent Jones Jr was still in his early 30s, this course nevertheless bears his unmistakable signature and is considered to be one of the great courses in Asia, and beyond that, one of the great courses *in the world*. The whole course is dyked and is one of the few golf courses in the world in which Bermuda grass is used from tee to green. Like Mauna Kea, which was marked by the hand of both father and son, this is also one of a very, very few courses in the world which required a major engineering marvel to accomplish its existence and is the only course to have been created with the sole intent of having the World Cup Golf Championship played on it.

In 1969, avid golfer and entrepreneur Sukhum Navapan had the keen idea of hosting the world's greatest golfing tournament within Bangkok's perimeters. Sukhum just couldn't let the idea go, and he enlisted the help of close friend Andrew Eu, an executive in Hong Kong and himself an avid golfer who had played with Arnold Palmer and Jack Nicklaus in the Canada Cup Pro-Am in Tokyo in 1966.

As Chairman of the Fund Raising Committee of the Thailand Golf Association for nearly a decade, Sukhum was quite experienced in fund raising, and the many important connections he had made in those years among the

Far East's financial elite helped him greatly in his formidable task. Another great help was having the formidable talents of Robert Trent Jones Jr as his designer.

The story goes that, when Navapan took him out to see the site of the future course in 1969, they travelled by boat on one of Thailand's many klongs, or waterways. When they arrived at the site, after practically cruising through the verandas of the many pylon-borne houses that lined their way, they climbed a dyke, and beheld a landscape of rice paddies and dykes as far as the eye could see.

It required a vast effort to drain the land and to build a viable playing surface. It was a year

It's amazing that this began as a rice paddy! *Above*, part of the ninth and *at right*, the third at Navatanee.

before the road into the proposed golf course was built, even though the site is a scant 9.3 miles from downtown Bangkok. In the Robert Trent Jones Jr tradition, the native features of the course location have been incorporated as advantageously as possible into the course design itself. The extensive water hazards were formed from the old flooded fields and parts of klongs. Some form the series of moats in the monarchical Thai tradition that figure in play and 'guard the castle of the course, the clubhouse.'

Golf Digest acclaimed the course 'an engineering miracle.' Sukhum Navapan's dream came true—through much hard lobbying with his golfing friends and through the utter excellence of Robert Trent Jones Jr's course design. The 1975 World Cup was indeed played there and the new course put Southeast Asia on the world golfing map. Johnny Miller won the individual title, and he and Lou Graham won the team title for the United States. Many a pro bogeyed on the course's tough fifth and sixth holes (now the fourteenth and fifteenth holes since the club staff switched the front and back nines some time ago), and many a golfer has a similar tale of woe since the course was opened.

This course presents a wily challenge, as the forward tees are meant to provide a pleasant round of golf for players of modest talents. The back tees, however, represent a golfing challenge of rare proportion; the challenge, given the many water hazards of this course, is unique.

The following is a hole-by-hole description of this great course. Hole one has two nicely placed bunkers to the left, which could catch a short tee shot; the green is rather shallow, has a heavily bunkered front and bunkers at right and left rear. Players at the second hole tee off in the opposite direction, onto a fairway guarded with opposing bunkers at midpoint, and a green which is practically defended all along its front, right and left sides. Right rear and rear are open to the rough!

Hole number three has three well-spaced bunkers at left along the fairway, and a single bunker at the mouth of the fairway on the right, all of which will probably catch slices to the fairway. The oblong green is interestingly set at a left-tending cant, with cannily-set bunkers in the diagonal formed by its left side, on its leading curve at right and behind the diagonal formed by its right side. Go right, young man, or face the desert to the left! Hole four is very short, but demands accuracy: massive bunkers guard the green at front, and a pot bunker awaits the shot that 'threads the needle' formed by these behemoths, but goes too far.

Hole five begins the course's series of play incorporating the aforementioned moat. Those playing safe have to go far around, but the valorous will carry the neck of the moat near the tees. A road crosses the fairway early on, and a bunker at right awaits shots too far right. The water is to the left always, and the shape of the fairway keeps things interesting; the green has water on three sides, and heads into the moat. Approach is from the right, with

The arrangement *at left* is another view of the ninth hole. The green lies ahead, and the moat is to the right. Compare this with the map below and the view on page 109. Also see the text and map on page 113.

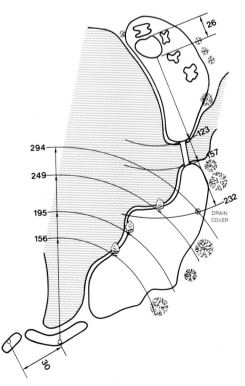

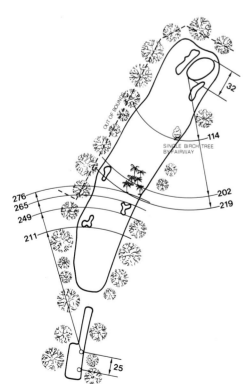

Seen *at the top of this page* is Navatanee's very beautiful hole eighteen. See also the chart *at left*, and the text and map on the facing page. *Directly above* is the sixteenth hole, looking toward the green.

bunkers right and left of the green, and many chances to sink your ball.

The sixth involves the moat in interesting ways—first on the left, then on the right. You tee off to a fairway which ends in water, then have a carry to the second half of fairway/green setup. This second half has water on the right, and a massive bunker across the approach to a green with water. Water everywhere else! Hole number seven is a long tee shot to a green which is bunkered front and back on both sides. Strength and accuracy are required here. Hole eight is subject to wind, and plays uphill. Bunkers all along the right may lead you to misjudge, and the bunker at the green on the left may focus your attention a bit more sharply.

The ninth features two carries (for the valiant) over the moat, and describes a giant arc to the left, effectively cradling the terminus of the moat. The back tee carries over one end of the moat, and the first bit of fairway provides ground for another water carry en route to the green, which has bunkers on its right approach and side, and water all along its left, and a bunker at rear. Not a hole to hook or slice!

The tenth is a breather, of sorts. With your back to the clubhouse, you tee off to a fairway which has two right-lying bunkers treacherously near your obvious line of flight. The green presents a narrow surface to the approach, widening out toward the rear, its three flanks well protected with bunkers. Hole eleven is a long par three, and—with its heavily contoured green having massive longitudinal bunkers right and left—will be a test indeed.

The twelfth tees face a fairway having water all along its right. Play right, and there's danger of the water, and a possible water carry from the fairway. Play left, and two bunkers strategically placed could help to pile points

onto your score. Hole number thirteen plays left, then right, then left, with bunkers guarding all the vital areas. Down near the green, the bunkering becomes intense, and the play is downhill. A well-earned par five. The fourteenth sets up an alley of bunkers on the fairway, and 'blinds' the alley with a bunker just before the green. Wear your glasses here, and be extra-sure of your distances!

Hole fifteen plays to a fairway having bunkers set near ball flight paths to the left. The green is a rolling, linksland-type green, and canniness is here essential! The sixteenth tends to the right, with a long bunker on the right which will figure prominently in play. Approach the green, and a large bunker dominates the approach from the right. Hole number seventeen carries over the moat from the back tees to a green which has water at

right and at right front, and bunkers left and behind. Neither too short nor too far with this one!

The eighteenth hole requires a very accurate tee shot, as the fairway presents another 'bunker alley' which is longer on the left than on the right—which would catch any late-hooking shots. Play is onto an oblong green having big bunkers right and left. A fine, clean finish for an exceptional 18 holes of golf.

Navatanee Golf Course measures 6906 yards from the championship tees, and its Bermuda Tifton covered fairways and greens are bordered by 62 kinds of trees and multitudes of flowers. Its pure, unsullied air will lift your spirits, and the impressive beauty of this magnificent course will calm your spirit. The friendliness of the Thai people is a balm to visitors, and this exotic country is well respresented in the lush, relaxing setting of the Navatanee Golf Course.

As originally set up, hole nine would have been the final hole, providing a truly smashing finish.

Hole	1	2	3	4	5	6	7	8	9	Out	
Championship	424	380	555	133	347	457	218	370	559	3443	
Medal	370	355	512	115	284	406	193	346	512	3093	
Ladies	330	311	446	108	236	349	141	299	468	2688	
Par	4	4	5	3	4	4	3	4	5	36	
Hole	10	11	12	13	14	15	16	17	18	In	Total
Championship	428	230	379	578	357	412	381	159	539	3463	6906
Medal	407	203	330	523	319	390	355	107	514	3148	6241
Ladies	363	153	282	476	262	342	301	82	455	2716	5404
Par	4	3	4	5	4	4	4	3	5	36	72

Oak Hills Country Club

Chiba Prefecture, Japan

Oak Hills Country Club is just one of several fine Robert Trent Jones Jr-designed golf courses in Japan, including the Shinwa Golf Group's great Golden Valley Golf Club, Cherry Hills and Pine Lake Courses.

The Coca-Cola Grand Slam is a yearly event here, with winners being Gene Littler in 1983 and 1987; Lee Elder in 1984 and 1986; and Miller Barber in 1985. The Lady Borden Cup is annually a featured year-end event at Oak Hills, for the best 30 players of the JLPGA tour. The World Championship/Nissan Cup was held here in 1984.

This is a beautiful, verdant course in which lakes, sandtraps and hillsides figure in the play. In addition to the fine playing qualities of this course, one can easily visualize the changing of the seasons here as a beautiful, haiku-like procession across and through the verdant greens and fairways of this challenging, meditative landscape:

> The oak tree stands
> Noble on the hill even in
> Cherry blossom time
> —Matsuo Basho (1644–1694)

The player at hole one tees off to a gently serpentine fairway having a bunker at left. The green is protected by two bunkers right and one left, and heads into the trees. Just beyond the trees to the left is a lake. Hole two plays with trees to the right, and tee shots have to carry over the inlet of a lake, carrying a good distance to a slender fairway which hooks to the right around a bunker to a green, the bulk of which hides behind this bunker, and which is also protected by a bunker at left. Trees lie dead ahead.

Tee shots at the third hole carry yards and yards to the fairway, which breaks to the right on a huge bunker, and has two outside bunkers guarding this 'knee' as well. The fairway then serpentines to roughly conform to the shape of a right-lying lake which also lines the well-bunkered green to its right. Hole number four plays to a wedge shaped green, the point of which faces the tees. A bunker in the flight path and a right-lying lake are hazards for the sliced or hooked ball, and big bunkers on the right and left of the green call for a good tee shot indeed, which, given the green's configuration, has to be right on the money. Too much power, and you're in the trees!

The fifth tees face a fairway which breaks to the right, and has a bunker and trees to the left and bunkers to the right. The green is surrounded with bunkers, and carrying the right front bunker is *de riguer* for a decent score. Hole number six has trees all along its right and heads into more trees. The tees are located in a cul de sac of trees, and most shots will tend left toward the massive fairway bunker at left or its compatriot just beyond. The green hides behind a bunker at left, and the bunker behind it will catch overpowered balls.

Hole seven describes a big arc which could just let your tee shots overshoot right into the bunkers early on the left. More bunkers on the left side keep the pressure on, and a bunker at

Oak Hills hosted the Nissan Cup in 1984, and some of the publicity for same is shown *on the facing page*. The photos in this section were taken during this tournament. Also, see the text on the facing page. *Above* is hole sixteen, in play. *Below* is a view of hole four; the tees are perched above the lake, and at photo right is the green.

right midway could catch the occasional, miscalculated carry over the rough there. The green has bunkers right, left and behind, and trees beyond that. Hole eight is a short, tricky tee shot to an irregularly shaped green having a bunker at left front, and situated in a cul de sac of trees. The back tee is in a pocket of trees as well.

The ninth hole has trees all along its left, and describes a dogleg right. Near the outside of the bend, a large bunker is set to swallow overshot balls, and the green approach is serrated by three long bunkers whose brothers guard the green's left rear and right rear. The tenth has a long, rolling fairway with a bunker right—and on towards the green, four bunkers at the right front, a very deep bunker at left rear, and trees dead ahead! Hole number eleven plays to an irregular, four-lobed green with four large bunkers surrounding. Trees provide a scenic surround here.

Hole twelve rather regally escorts you down a fairway with a 'royal guard' of two sets of opposing bunkers, to a kidney-bean shaped green having bunkers at its inner and outer bends. The thirteenth hole carries a long way over rough to a dogleg right fairway having four bunkers—and trees beyond—on its outer edge, a bunker and trees on its inner edge, and a big bunker dead center on the green approach. The green has a bunker inrupting from its left. Hole fourteen tees off over a pond to an irregular green having canny little bunkers all around. Beware the green! The fifteenth's tees

face a dogleg left which occupies a hallway of trees. At the extreme of its bend, a bunker lies in wait for overpowered tee shots. The green, set obliquely, has bunkers at left front and behind.

Hole sixteen is a 491 yard driver's delight. The back tee is situated far back in a hallway of trees, and features a long carry to the fairway, which has bunkers left and right—just in case mistakes are made. On toward the green, a small pot bunker on the fairway at left, and a large longitudinal bunker farther down on the right keep shots in line. The lake which cuts across the fairway in front of the green, represents a pretty good-sized carry. The arrowhead-shaped green has its base along the lake, a bunker at right and a bunker at extreme behind. It's a beautiful hole, with a stone bridge off to the right.

The seventeenth has a gently serpentine fairway with cater-cornered bunkers at the likely landing spot. Trees close by the left add

still more 'interest,' and the green, which is pinched by opposing bunkers, also has a bunker—and a panorama of trees—at rear. The eighteenth hole plays down a fairway having three bunkers and a gully at right, and trees and one bunker left, hidden in a curve just over the rise of the hill. The green hides its left edge behind the last aforementioned bunker left, and additionally cherishes another bunker set into its left side, and a bunker set into its rear edge. The fairway is rolling, and contoured, and at 407 yards, this hole provides a power and finesse test to end your round of golf. Ahead lies the parking complex and the clubhouse—where you may care to 'sip tea and reminisce' about the exceptional round of golf which you've just enjoyed.

Robert Trent Jones Jr makes a habit of creating golfing greatness out of various and sundry locales. His masterpieces are visible world wide. Robert Trent Jones Jr...the veritable *Hokusai* of Golf Course design.

Hole	1	2	3	4	5	6	7	8	9	Out	
Regular	406	400	493	201	374	398	569	167	384	3392	
Par	4	4	5	3	4	4	5	3	4	36	
Hole	10	11	12	13	14	15	16	17	18	In	Total
Regular	510	175	381	346	182	408	491	368	407	3268	6660
Par	5	3	4	4	3	4	5	4	4	36	72

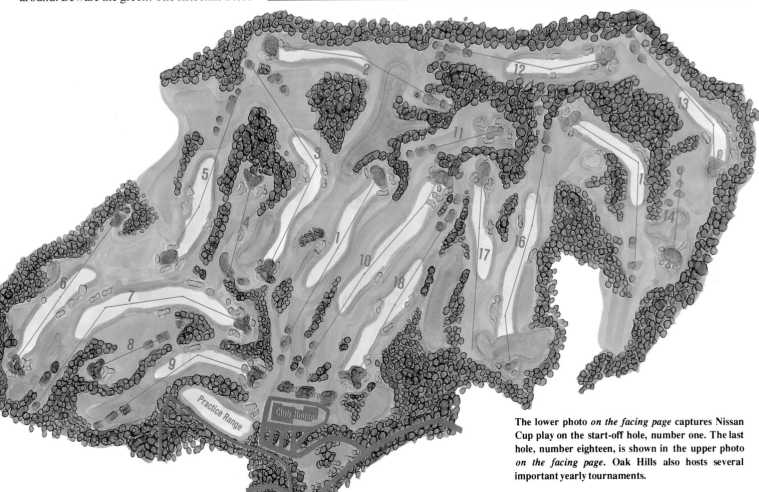

The lower photo *on the facing page* captures Nissan Cup play on the start-off hole, number one. The last hole, number eighteen, is shown in the upper photo *on the facing page*. Oak Hills also hosts several important yearly tournaments.

Pine Lake Golf Club

Hyogo Prefecture, Japan

Robert Trent Jones Jr designed the exquisite Pine Lake Golf Club course, which was honored to be the site of the Asian Qualifying Rounds for the 1985 World Cup and hosted the Mitsubishi Gallant Tournament in 1987. This course is sure to be the playing ground for many more distinguished golf events in the future.

In addition to Pine Lake, Robert Trent Jones Jr has designed two more courses for the Shinwa Golf Group—Cherry Hills and Golden Valley. These course designs are absolutely stunning. Pine Lake, in this instance, is a subtle blend of earth and water—a mystery in green that peacefully settles you into some of the finest golfing you have ever had. As with the magnificent course at Golden Valley, the Pine Lake Golf Club course takes you 'beyond'—to realms of concentration and contemplation that are not touched by the cares and worries of the everyday.

A worker of exquisite forms and textures is melded with a fine tactician in the person of Robert Trent Jones Jr. The pine Lake Golf Club course is a beautiful, serene and challenging 18 hole golf course. From the clubhouse—which is a copy of the Old Imperial Hotel in Tokyo—to the impeccable practice green, to the pristine lakes and rock-lined streams of this fabulous course, it is abundantly clear that the Pine Lake Golf Club course is a cut above most others.

Following is a short hole-by-hole description of this masterwork in green. From the back tees, hole one crosses a stream, and it's a fairly long flight to the fairway, which is bunkered left and right. The fairway then winds toward the right toward the green, which has a massive bunker at left front and at right rear, most probably coincident with the roll of the green. Trees, shrubs and flowers frame this entire hole. A beauty.

Tee shots at hole two pass through the woods toward a massive green having a large bunker set directly in front. Trees and flowers surround a valley over which, of course, your tee shot must pass! Hole number three is a dogleg right with two large bunkers on its outer bend. Past these is the lobe of a lake and a little sprinkling of flowers, and then the green, with lake left and a massive bunker right, just where an awkward fairway shot might find itself, and also where an unthinking shot to the green may wend its way.

The fourth tees off across a stream, with a lake inlet to the left of the tees. Tee shots pass close to undergrowth and trees which are to the right and meet the fairway just where it curves to the right, creating an opening to the bunker on the fairway's left, in a sort of 'the ground fell away from me' moment of suspense. From here, it's a shot to a triangular green, set 'chin first.' On either side is a bunker, the larger to the right—but don't discount that little one to the left. Trees and shrubs and flowers give this hole a mysterious

touch of nature, and grant it—even with the close proximity of a building complex—a sense of the unseen.

Hole five is a middling hop to the fairway or a slightly longer one to the green. It's risky business, though—the green and the fairway roughly form two equal halves of the letter 'C,' in this case, open to the left, and engulfing a huge bunker. Behind the green—to the right rear—is another bunker. Long dogleg left hole six's probable tee shots land near the end of the fairway, and have a bunker at right to look forward to, just as the fairway bends. From this bend, it's a shot to a tri-lobed green, having small bunkers at front and left and a large

Seen *below* is Pine Lake's hole number ten, where the fairway curves toward the green and is cut across by a rock-lined stream. *At right* is Pine Lake's clubhouse.

bunker at right. Trees and shrubs line the periphery of this hole. Golfers at the seventh tee off between trees and flowers to a fairway which bends quite a bit to the left; an inverted-triangle green has chin whiskers composed of bunkers right and left. Another delightfully woodsy hole.

Hole eight is framed by a variety of trees, flowers and shrubs to create the feel of a valley floor, a moment of seclusion. You tee off to a fairway which lies slightly to the right and

continues bending right. The fairway also slopes downhill toward the green, and contains a cunning little 'hook' at its beginning which embeds a bunker. From here, the downhill slope begins in earnest and leads you toward the yoke-shaped end of the fairway, which houses a bunker immediately in front of the green, which itself additionally has bunkers at left rear and all along its righthand side, and trees behind.

Trees encroach on hole number nine's tees

from the right. The fairway serpentines right then left, and then goes straight, having a stream on its right as its companion for approximately half its distance. Early on, a bunker at fairway right could catch an errant ball, and the grove of trees a bit farther on could catch a few, too. The two bunkers near fairway's end on the left endanger thoughtless 'general direction' shots, but the green, with bunkers right and left and flowers behind, is the thinking golfer's reward.

Shots from hole ten's flower-fringed back tee carry over a stream, and golfers at the next tee play around a clump of trees toward a complex, broken green which doglegs left. At the inner 'knee' of the fairway, which bends early on, is a large bunker. The fairway swings slightly left after this, and then heads back right—at the curve on the outside of the 'knee' is a very large bunker, and as the fairway heads for the green, a stream cuts it into two sections. Across the stream, the fairway fronts a large, irregular, almost oblong, green having bunkers at right and left and trees behind. This is a very woodsy hole, and again calls forth that sense of valley floor isolation—almost as if one is walking on a fine, old, mellow and mysterious estate. A real beauty.

While the others are 'landlocked' shots, hole eleven has one tee which crosses a stream to a fairway which is lined with stream on the right and with trees to the left; at its midpoint, the stream crosses the fairway and proceeds down the left—the fairway is at this point lined with trees on the right, and has a bunker which incurses two-thirds of the way down from the right. The stream again cuts across, this time separating fairway from green. The green now has stream right, and bunkers left, and trees behind.

The vistas at hole eighteen could make you want to live there. The scene *below* is ample proof of that—and of the fact that beauty and tranquility can both invigorate, and distract, almost any golfer.

Hole twelve is no mean feat of golfing. Shots from the back tees must carry over a ravine to an irregular, well-guarded fairway which is no larger than its green. Two bunkers strategically placed here make things very interesting. Surrounded by holes ten, eleven, twelve and fourteen, hole thirteen is a woodland beauty. The back tees again deal with trees, and the regular and front tees are, in addition, beautified with flowers. The fairway features a heavy bunker at immediate left, and a bunker between it and the tees will catch errant shots through the woods. The fairway rolls toward the green, which has large bunkers at left, front and right, and has trees behind.

The fourteenth is a subtle curve to the right, with a bunker across the fairway just in line with tee shots. The green is large and has a small army of bunkers on its right front, as well as flowers left at rear and trees elsewhere. A shallow dogleg left, hole fifteen has trees, shrubs and flowers on its left, and a stream beyond these. The fairway proceeds—with clumps of trees at right—to a green having a single bunker at right rear, and trees beyond this, as well as, of course, the stream to the left.

Hole sixteen's rearmost tee backs into a garden of flowers, and with the stream widening to a pond on the left, gives golfers pause to reflect. Trees on the right for the length of the hole keep things in line from that perspective, and tee shots find a rather short, chunky fairway which bends around the aforementioned pond. At the mouth of the irregularly shaped green, which tends left toward the water, there are two bunkers right and one left, all set for sand or water.

The seventeenth also has water its entire length as well. In addition, the rearmost tees must skirt trees which incurse from the left. The fairway is a serpentine which tends right, then toward the green, hooks slightly left again, around a pond to the left. At the outset of the fairway, three bunkers right could easily devour over-compensatory tee shots. There is also always the danger of water to the left, and the two bunkers on the right jawbone of the inverted-triangle green may keep you toward the water side, and the trees behind will keep things from going too far in that direction. Flowers at right rear add a light touch!

The eighteenth will make you want to go to the clubhouse and savor the memory of a magnificent round of golf. The scenery and the play will make your day without a doubt. With trees and flowers abounding, the tranquil beauty of this hole will balance the exquisite sense of challenge which Robert Trent Jones has designed into this course. It's stunning. The rearmost tee backs up to the pond which figured in hole seventeen. The pond at this point necks down to a stream which rides the first half of the fairway's left, then crosses over to become a lake to the second half's—and green's—right. Trees to the right and left of the tees keep shots straight to the fairly straightforward fairway, which has, counterbalancing the stream—trees at right. Now we come to water, and a shot across the mouth of the lake lands on the second half of fairway, en route to a green which broadens toward the rear and the flowers (which are sometimes hidden by grandstands that are periodically erected for important golfing events) there. The narrow chin of the green has a left-lying bunker. Trees, of course, have courted this second half entirely from the left. A truly memorable round of golf.

In the warmth, serenity and delight, there is a sense of the hand of Earthly genius imitating Heavenly moods. And in the sense of original, unspoiled Creation, there is a sense of beauty which arises rarely—in a far mountain retreat, or on the shores of a desert lake—that placidity, that calm...and that adventure.

Below far left is the eighteenth green during the **1987 Mitsubishi Gallant Tournament.** *Opposite photo,* **right to left: the practice green, the clubhouse and the tenth tees.** *Overleaf:* **The beautiful tenth green.**

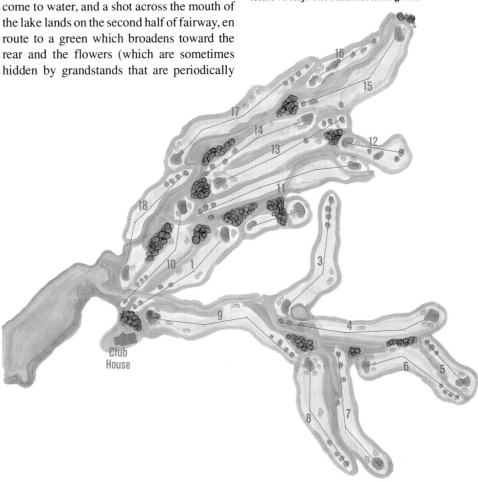

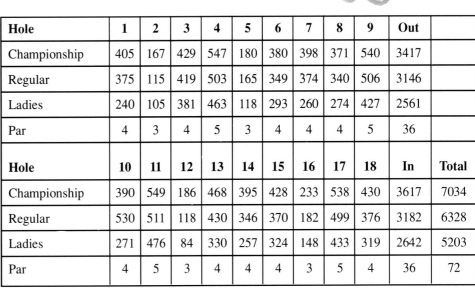

Hole	1	2	3	4	5	6	7	8	9	Out	
Championship	405	167	429	547	180	380	398	371	540	3417	
Regular	375	115	419	503	165	349	374	340	506	3146	
Ladies	240	105	381	463	118	293	260	274	427	2561	
Par	4	3	4	5	3	4	4	4	5	36	
Hole	**10**	**11**	**12**	**13**	**14**	**15**	**16**	**17**	**18**	**In**	**Total**
Championship	390	549	186	468	395	428	233	538	430	3617	7034
Regular	530	511	118	430	346	370	182	499	376	3182	6328
Ladies	271	476	84	330	257	324	148	433	319	2642	5203
Par	4	5	3	4	4	4	3	5	4	36	72

Poppy Hills Golf Course

Monterey Peninsula, California USA

Poppy Hills is 'One of Two More Jewels for Monterey,' according to Mark Soltau in the *San Francisco Examiner* of 18 July 1985. Indeed, the prospect of building a golf course on the far-famed and hallowed Monterey Peninsula would cause any course designer to feel the burden of his charge. Pebble Beach, Cypress Point and Spyglass Hill are there, infusing the area with an air of great golfing and imparting an atmosphere of great tradition.

Imagine, then, being the *only* golf course designer who has been chosen to design *two* courses on this, one of golfing's most sacred grounds.

Robert Trent Jones Jr is that man. His breathtaking collaboration with PGA Tour pro Tom Watson and former USGA President Frank 'Sandy' Tatum on The Links at Spanish Bay (opened in 1987) is a bold stroke indeed. But Poppy Hills would seem to portend The Links at Spanish Bay with favor. Opened in 1986, Poppy Hills already commands unusual respect for a young course.

Tour pros Sam Randolph, Bobby Clampett, Roger Maltbie, Janet Coles and Amy Alcott have played the course. Coles does much of her practicing at Poppy Hills and feels that it would be a fine course for an LPGA event, according to the *NCGA News*. Celebrities including Carmel Mayor Clint Eastwood, Fran Tarkenton, Daryl Lamonica, Bob Griese, Peter Ueberroth, Dave Righetti, Luis Tiant and legendary softball pitcher Eddie Feigner also have played the course.

Poppy Hills currently is the only course in the United States owned by an amateur golf association. The proud owner of the tough but very beautiful Poppy Hills course is the Northern California Golf Association. Its 168 acre, tree-lined site is in the Sun Ridge Area of Pebble Beach, and indeed, the NCGA has moved its headquarters there from the old site at Spyglass Hill.

The staff at Poppy Hills is aiming to make its services the best on the Peninsula. The restaurant can accomodate any group's needs with a standard menu that is first rate, serving breakfast and lunch regularly, and banquets on a limited basis. The Poppy Hills golf shop is fully equipped and features a broad array of apparel for golfing and other leisure time activities. Poppy Hills' resident pro Jack Guio,

an avid booster of the course, assumed his position on 1 March 1987 after serving in a similar capacity at Oak Ridge Golf Club in San Jose.

The following is a hole-by-hole description of the course. Hole number one is a long hole, arcing to the right along a deep creek. Tee

shots should just clear or be just left of the large bunker which awaits you at fairway right. Then it's a second toward an irregular green, which is well protected by bunkers on its left and right lobes, with an additional bunker out in front.

Hole number two is straightforward across

a deep ravine, but when the flag is placed on this two-tiered surface, it can make two clubs difference. Hole three bends to the left, and tee shots are immediately endangered by bunkers at fairway left, on the inner 'knee' of same, and bunkering right, on the 'kneecap.' Many of Mr Jones' signature 'turning mounds' are showcased here. Then, to the green, with bunkers left, left rear and right rear. The fourth is a double dogleg par five, highlighted by extensive bunkering on the second leg. The huge undulating green is the largest on the course.

Hole five is water for a man in the land of bunkers. The fairway bends slightly to the left, and things really get interesting near the end. A big bunker on the right is basically engulfed in the lake also at right, which dominates the latter fourth of the fairway and the right side of

In the photo *below*, we see Poppy Hills' tenth green, which is lined with Monterey pines, which are native to the Peninsula. The view *above*, of hole eighteen, hints at the subtlety of this layout.

the green. Overcorrect, and there are bunkers at left of the green. Watch the water, don't take a swim—watch the bunkers, the desert is not a nice place!

The par three sixth's tees play into a veritable explosion of bunkers; the long, narrow green is irregularly shaped and bunkers protect all the nooks and crannies. Good luck! Hole seven tees off on the left side of the lake, which is on your right. The fairway bends to the left and a bunker in its bend keeps things on course, and the bunkers left and behind the green also keep things interesting. The eighth is a tantalizing short par four with a sharp right dogleg which is bunkered well on its inner bend. It broadens deceptively between these bunkers, but don't be fooled. The green, which actually hangs off of the right cusp of the fairway, has a greeting smile which is composed of a large bunker all across its front. A test! To the lower left is a unique 'chipping bunker,' which is a Jones idiosyncracy.

Hole number nine is total class. With tees set in a 'Y' formation, what you have is essentially two (counting the 'legs' of the 'Y') dif-

In the view *at left*, the sixteenth green lies headfirst, with its fairway trailing up over the hill at photo right. A tree-lined fairway and massive bunkers stretch into the distance on the Poppy Hills fairway shown *above*. In the lower photo *on the facing page*, we have a view from just in front of the clubhouse of hole eighteen. See also the photo on page 127.

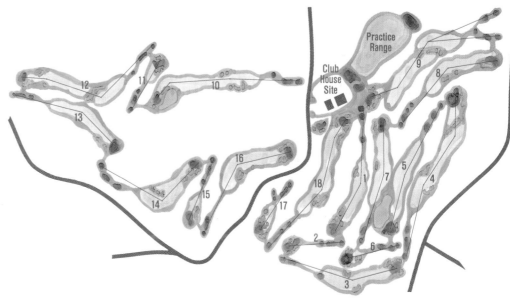

ferent holes here. The bare bones, though, is that you have a fairway which is broken into two sections, divided by extensive mounding and bunkering. The second shot calls for a decision—layup on the shelf fairway with a bunker at its tip, or go toward the green with a deep grass valley in front.

The tenth's tees play to a straight, narrow fairway which has a series of bunkers right and left to catch errant tee shots. A large pond guards the green, so the safe route is a layup shot to the right side, leaving a delicate pitch to a green which slopes away. Once on the green, take a look back down the hole—it's beautiful!

Hole eleven is a devilishly short hole. A straight away par three with a left sloping green protected left and right with bunkers.

The twelfth is a 90 degree dogleg right par five, and is broken completely across at the knee by a massive bunker. From there, it's a straight shot toward the narrowing end of the fairway, which is protected left and right with bunkers, and the ovoid green is protected on its entire left with a bunker. A slight bend to the

Hole	1	2	3	4	5	6	7	8	9	Out	
Blue	413	162	406	560	426	181	388	380	557	3473	
White	375	128	369	524	381	141	351	355	508	3132	
Par	4	3	4	5	4	3	4	4	5	36	
Hole	10	11	12	13	14	15	16	17	18	In	Total
Blue	510	214	531	393	417	210	439	163	500	3377	6850
White	467	174	502	368	392	175	409	126	474	3087	6219
Par	5	3	5	4	4	3	4	3	5	36	72

right, hole thirteen proves that great holes don't always need fairway bunkers, especially when the green is elevated, and heavily bunkered on the right.

Hole fourteen is a severe dogleg left, on which players tee off to a rather fat fairway. Just left of most tee shot landings, bunkers incurse deeply into the fairway, forming a *serious* trap. Approaching the green, the fairway fades to the left, leaving a gaping hole full of bunkers on the right.

The long par three fifteenth plays straight into a prevailing breeze to a large oblong green. A bunker for most of the way on the left will keep things honest, but if it doesn't, the large ridge mound in the middle of the green will.

Hole sixteen has the same sort of undulating borders that we have seen before in this course. It is a long dogleg right with a bunker inside of its 'knee' and an extreme bend on the outside. The fairway proceeds on to narrow severely toward the green, pinched in from either side by bunkers which also serve to protect the green at front right and left.

The seventeenth is short but intense. The five-lobed green is protected right, front and left rear, and bunkers to the left of the green keep all shots in jeopardy. A deep creek on the right of the green awaits the over-compensatory shot. A great buildup to the eighteenth!

The eighteenth is another double dogleg par five with a fairway which is cut into severely from the right with bunkers and a grass swale at the outset. Up toward the green end, the fairway bends around yet another bunker at right. The pear-shaped green is set on its side pointing to the right, with bunkers at left front and side, and at right front and rear. An interesting facet of this hole is that the left side of the fairway presents a smooth, even, 'nothing to hide' border which creates a marked contrast with the ruggedly undulating right border, which, of course, has a few bunkers among its irregular curves—and an ajoining riparian corridor. The hole is a subtle masterwork by one of the world's truly great golf course architects.

Robert Trent Jones Jr believes in providing challenging play for a wide range of golfing abilities, and he does so via the use of multiple tee locations, the most spectacular here having been those on the ninth hole. Still other interesting examples of tee placements can be found on the eighth, sixteenth and seventeenth holes.

This course tests all of a golfer's abilities in all facets of the game; the pacing of the holes is such that one would feel a sense of real accomplishment and the exhilaration of having played a challenging and very rewarding round of golf.

At right: **A bunker's-eye view of the eighteenth green, and the Poppy Hills clubhouse, just beyond.**

Princeville Makai Golf Course

Hanalei, Kauai, Hawaii USA

'If there's a finer place to build a golf course, I haven't seen it.' Thus said Robert Trent Jones Jr—as quoted by Princeville's own literature—before rolling up his sleeves to design the course that is thought to be among the most beautiful in all of Hawaii.

Comprising some 27 holes of unparalleled scenic beauty and marvellous playability, Princeville comprises three separate nines—the Ocean, Woods and Lakes courses. They meander through the incredible coastal scenery of the island of Kauai's northern shore, featuring ocean cliffs and verdant, impressive mountains. Princeville has been the site of LPGA Women's Kemper Open and the World Cup matches and soon, another 18 holes will be added, to make Princeville Hawaii's largest golf complex.

By combining any two of the aforestated nines, a golfer has a 6900 yard challenge from the back tees; 6200 yards from the middle tees; and 5500 yards from the ladies' tees. A hole-by-hole description of the course follows. Ocean one is a pretty straightforward drive to a large green bunkered heavily on the right, front and back. Also—watch for the bunker and tree at fairway midpoint.

Ocean two is, again, straighforward, with a 'pinch' of bunkers a third of the way home. A large bunker fronts the green, which also is bunkered to the right. Ocean three features a 100-foot drop from tee to flag which adds spice to this hole—as do the lake before the green, the tropical canyon behind, and the hillside of extremely high grass to the left. Many an experienced golfer—including pros—have made this little sweetheart into a two-digit experience. A very, very tricky hole.

Ocean four is a perilous, uphill drive into the wind. The green is protected by three bunkers, and the fairway is inrupted upon by a tree to the right, and a water hazard to the right of the tee. This is said to be the hardest of the Ocean nine. Ocean five's tee shots take you toward a bunker on fairway left; beyond this, trees. The left side of the fairway is dangerous. A helpful wind boosts shots on Ocean six, which gets you going toward an inlet of the Pacific Ocean. The well protected green has precisely that same inlet as a far hazard to its left rear—long shots here will overfly the tees of the seventh hole and may well provide entertainment for one of Hawaii's manta rays!

Shoehorned around the aforementioned inlet, Ocean seven has been compared to the truly great holes number three at Mauna Kea and sixteen at Cypress Point. Play from the championship and men's tees carries over the Pacific Ocean, and the upcurrents from this 160 foot ocean inlet cause interesting ball flight patterns. The green here is very large, and not what you might call easy. Ocean eight plays away from the ocean, and is bunkered before the green, with bunkers squeezing the fairway from the mid-point on. Though the green is protected to the left as well, this may be your chance for a birdie.

Ocean nine features another wasp-waisted fairway, with three bunkers for a corset. The green is bunkered right front, left front and behind, and is itself tiered. This is a fitting finish to this outstanding nine, and is a great prelude to one of Princeville's second nines—which could be, depending upon your choice, either the excellent Lakes nine or the great Woods nine. Let's go to the Woods nine for now, shall we?

Woods one features a long shot onto a fairway that will catch you on the right. If you evade that trap, it's onward to a very well-trapped green. Not easy, but tremendous fun. From the championship tee, Woods two is a tough dogleg left, which bends around a rough and the pines which are most generously distributed beyond and in front of the men's and ladies' tees. The green is narrow, and is trapped fore and aft. 'Careful sailing' or the 'deep six' here, on this rugged and exhilarating hole.

From the back tee, Woods three is a long shot to a fairway lined with eucalyptus (left) and pines (right). Get past these, and at the halfway point, there's a bottleneck of two opposed bunkers. Make it to the green shot, and your ball overflies a no man's land of bunkers to a narrow green. At its halfway point, Woods

Below is the beautiful Princeville Lakes hole six, with massive Mount Namolokama in the background. After you make the water carry at Lakes eight, the green *at right* is what you have to look forward to.

four's fairway bulges then shrinks, leaving you faced with a bunker on the suddenly-missing right, which is premonitive of the hidden lake just shortly beyond. This lake chomps all the way across—no hope of working your way around it; the little green, with bunkers beside, trees behind and lake in front, make this more a 'bogey haven' than a 'birdie nest!'

Woods five: Trees at left mouth of fairway—which is bunkered well on the left and bends to the left, toward the three-bunkered green which comprises two tiers. You play into the wind here.

Woods six is the toughest in the Woods. A well-placed bunker lies on the fairway's right, just as the fairway breaks right. A well-bunkered and tricky green and play into the wind make this a tactically-tuned hole and one which heartily challenges the golfer. Dogleg left Woods seven is tough out of the back tees; its fairway is bunkered right, and its 'slippery' green is bunkered front and left—making five traps in all.

Don't push too hard off the tees at Woods eight: a massive bunker cuts into the fairway at left. This is a beautiful bunker, actually—one-half acre of cool brightness from which two large lava rocks protrude—like a Zen garden. This hole looks out over Hanalei Bay, and its arrangement of trees make it extremely lovely. The fairway bends right around the bunker, then left again toward the green, which can be tricky. Very beautiful. Woods nine has a lake at left and trees to the right, which makes the tee shot dangerous for cuts. From the second shot, though, it's straight toward the green, protected on right, left and behind with bunkers. A possible birdie awaits the golfer here, as he finishes these amazing nine holes. Let's pretend at this point that we are actually in the *middle* of our game, and still have nine holes to go: onward, then, to the exciting Lakes nine!

Water lies by the left of Lakes one—a hidden lake is a danger for hooked tee shots, and an arm of a second lake cuts over in front of the green, which itself is protected at left and at rear with bunkers. In addition, trees one third of the way down the fairway on its left, and trees lining the fairway at right make this a very interesting hole.

Lakes two features straightforward play into the wind. A bunker at fairway left, and bunkers encroaching on the green approach from both sides make this challenging, and yet a birdie may be in hand here. Lakes three's championship and men's tees shoot through trees; a voracious valley lies to the left of the fairway; there are three bunkers tucking the fairway at its one-third and two-thirds way points on the downhill side. The green is trian-

With Hanalei Bay in the background, and beyond that, 2003-foot Mount Kulanalilia, the view from the Ocean six green (*at right*) is nothing short of riveting.

gular, and is bunkered on either side of its 'chin'—which faces the golfer. A toughie!

The beautiful vistas of Lakes four include the Pacific Ocean and Kilauea Lighthouse. The back tees shoot through the trees. A deep gulch runs in front and to the side, and the trade winds show their teeth here. There are bunkers on the left, front and right of the green. A challenge! An eagle is possible on Lakes five, but beware—the ocean's just an errant shot to the right. Tee off across a ravine, to an easily-hit fairway—watch out for the bunker right in your ball's flight path! The green is protected by two wide-set bunkers at left front and right front.

Lakes six has an incredible backdrop composed of Mount Namolokama and its several waterfalls. This hole is a dogleg right, long par four with a putt-resistant green. A bunker rests in the crook of the fairway's 'elbow' and the green is protected right, left and behind. Lakes seven's championship and men's tees play through the trees to get to the fairway. A large, hungry bunker to the right sucks at shots addressed to the green, which itself is tough to get a grip on. Deceptively hard, but a great deal of fun.

Lakes eight has trees to the right, trees to the left, and a fairway that depletes to the left in favor of a lake intruding from the right—just

before the green. Beware—the rear approach to this green is *not* preferable to dropping a shot in the lake—better to make it a short shot over the waters, to the green. A very neat par four!

Lakes nine is almost as good as the Ocean seven. Championship and men's tees play over a lake to get to the fairway; all players have to carry over another lake en route to the green. You can blast over the first lake, then jump across the second if you're very good—a bunker with greenery behind and a small gully awaits the overweening. Still, a shot along the lakes after the first jump will set up a good chip over the second lake to the small green,

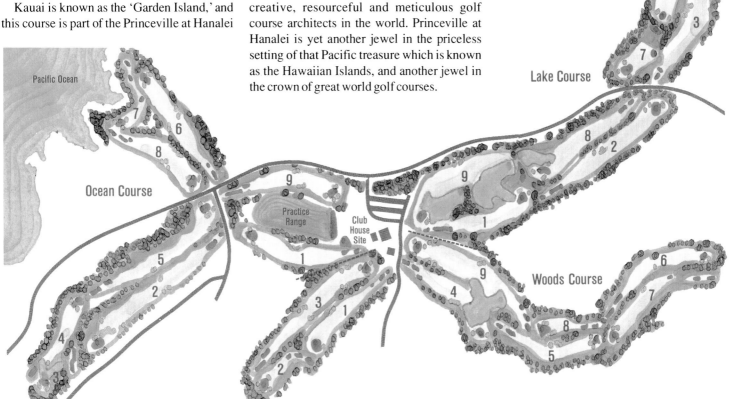

which is protected right and left with bunkers—the left bunker being in the line of any overshot ball. This is a great par five, and a great finish to a great nine holes—or it could be a great midpoint takeoff to either the Woods or the Ocean nine!

Kauai is known as the 'Garden Island,' and this course is part of the Princeville at Hanalei resort community, which is now being developed on 1000 acres of beautiful plateau meadowland overlooking the Pacific Ocean, Hanalei Bay and the mountains of the island. As is indicated by the 'Zen bunker' of Woods nine, Robert Trent Jones Jr is one of the most creative, resourceful and meticulous golf course architects in the world. Princeville at Hanalei is yet another jewel in the priceless setting of that Pacific treasure which is known as the Hawaiian Islands, and another jewel in the crown of great world golf courses.

Bunkers fore and aft and plenty of trees—the photo of the green *at left* is indeed a portrait of Princeville Woods two. Woods three, *below*, has everything—trees, ocean and an incredible view!

OCEAN COURSE										
Hole	1	2	3	4	5	6	7	8	9	Out
Blue	410	602	173	359	506	419	197	345	390	3401
White	388	559	130	316	493	388	141	287	356	3058
Red	348	537	130	264	448	345	102	275	317	2766
Par	4	5	3	4	5	4	3	4	4	36

WOODS COURSE										
Hole	1	2	3	4	5	6	7	8	9	Out
Blue	360	185	517	393	376	442	427	185	492	3377
White	336	170	480	362	345	416	382	144	463	3098
Red	284	137	441	317	335	356	333	132	392	2727
Par	4	3	5	4	4	4	4	3	5	36
Red Par (woods only)	4	3	5	5	4	4	4	3	5	37

LAKES COURSE										
Hole	1	2	3	4	5	6	7	8	9	Out
Blue	346	497	440	222	308	404	200	436	510	3363
White	342	463	406	182	276	337	177	382	453	3018
Red	316	425	328	132	252	320	93	330	416	2612
Par	4	5	4	3	4	4	3	4	5	36

SentryWorld Golf Course

Stevens Point, Wisconsin USA

Robert Trent Jones Jr incorporated over 300,000 geraniums and marigolds in this stunning masterpiece. He is quoted as describing it in SentryWorld's press kit as 'very possibly my Mona Lisa.'

Sentry Insurance is the corporation that developed SentryWorld. Its former chairman John Joanis, a 14-handicapper who played globally, conceived the idea of building a truly magnificent golf course, and then opening it to the public—which is an unusual and great idea in itself.

In 1984, SentryWorld was chosen as the best new public course in the United States by *Golf Digest*; rated as the best course in Wisconsin by *Golf Digest* in 1985; and was designated as one of the best 25 public courses in America by *Golf Digest* in 1984. In addition,

SentryWorld's famous 'flower hole' is shown *above*. As is shown *below*, cart paths wander through the many other flower gardens which also adorn this fine course.

USA Today asked the American Society of Golf Course Architects to compile a survey of the best designed courses in the United States in 1984, and SentryWorld was chosen as among the top three (designed after 1962) of the top 130 courses in the United States. This survey's criteria were natural beauty, design aesthetics, drama and subtlety, fairness and playability.

In 1985, Arnold Palmer, Jan Stephenson, Betsy King, Miller Barber, Bob Toski and Dave Marr were the featured players at the $50,000 Sentry Challenge Cup, hosted by SentryWorld. In 1986, this fabulous course was host to the USGA Ladies Public Links Championship.

Mr Jones carefully created this jewel of a course out of the native Wisconsin

countryside. Always taking care to meld his courses into a native environment, Mr Jones decided to do something a little different for the course's famed par three sixteenth hole: a concentration of 90,000 flowers literally creates an explosion of color on an already colorful course.

An interesting—and essential, in the minds of golfers—footnote is the various types of grass used on this course. The greens, tees and fairways were seeded with Penneagle Creeping Bentgrass—a hybrid which was developed by Doctor Joseph M Buich, professor of Turfgrass Science at Pennsylvania State University.

Roughs in sunshine areas were seeded with a mix of Adelphi Kentucky bluegrass, Barron Kentucky bluegrass, Negget Kentucky bluegrass and Pennlawn creeping red fescue. Roughs in shaded areas are seeded with Barron Kentucky bluegrass, Pennlawn creeping red fescue and Dawson creeping red fescue.

The following is a hole-by-hole description of this great public course. At hole one, players tee off to the fairway which lies, and continues curving, to their left—errant shots will find the bunkers to the right and to the left, which provide for a well-protected green. Hole number two is a slight curve to the right.

Above and below are further views of the sixteenth, which blazes beautifully with thousands of brilliant flowers. Don't be fooled, however—the flowers are most definitely a hazard, and this hole is tricky.

Again, a bunker catches the unwary—on the left perimeter of the fairway, just past the 'elbow'—and the approach to the green is pinched by two bunkers, with an additional bunker just to the right.

Tee shots on the third travel for a good distance over a stream which extends out from one of the course's ponds. Strong hitters chance landing in the bunker which lies directly in the well-placed ball's path, on the opposing side of the fairway. Then it's a fairly straight—but pinched on the approach—shot to a well-protected green; overshoot the green, and you're in the water—in the form of a narrow neck which connects the course's two ponds. Golfers at hole four can 'go for it' by carrying over an inlet of the pond, or they can play it safe by hitting for the right side of the well-protected green, so accuracy—no matter what route you take—is the key here.

The fifth bends around a pond, describing a near semi-circle to the left. A long shot onto the fairway is likely to land just where the fairway makes its first major bend, the outside 'elbow' of which is guarded by three bunkers—each attuned to the various tee placements. A bottleneck here forces shots to the left; just barely avoiding the rough to the left, and encourages a ball flight directly at the large bunkers situated just where the fairway makes its second major bend. From here, it's a shot to a well-bunkered green.

Hole number six shares its back tee with hole twelve. Hole six itself is straightforward, excepting that the tee shot must avoid the bottleneck with bunker, which is situated just where most tee shots will land comfortably, and another bunker diagonally across the fairway from it will catch inaccurate long shots. Then, it's a straight approach shot toward a green, which is well protected by two bunkers situated in the right hollow of said bottleneck.

The back tee of hole seven carries over a stream to the green, which is actually larger than the fairway. The fairway is massively bunkered on both sides and the green is bunkered in back—perhaps a good hole on which to forego the fairway altogether. Hole eight's a demanding tee shot, an immediate skew to the left with a bunker right, then a serpentine tending right with bunkers left—at least one shot has to pass over a bunker. At the end of the fairway is a rough—then a slender, hourglass-shaped green bunkered front and left.

The ninth has a fairway which is broken by a stream. After the stream, the fairway tends toward the left, with a subtle hook to the right as it approaches the green—of course, on the leading edge of the 'hook,' where it is likely to catch the unconsidered shot, is a large bunker.

At left: **SentryWorld is an excellent and highly respected course, and the sixteenth is certainly not all it has to offer, but let's have just one more look....**

Play is then right, across an extension of the same stream encountered previously, to a smallish, triangular green—the base of which faces the fairway, and the sloping sides of which are cut into by bunkers. It's a very dangerous green. Continuing on with this extraordinary course, hole ten describes a long arc to the left, dotted with bunkers leading to a triangular green whose 'chin' faces the fairway, and which is protected on three sides with bunkers.

Hole eleven is fairly straightforward, after a long tee shot onto the green, up until the fairway widens and doglegs left—at precisely which point Mr Jones has placed a bog to the left, extending from this 'elbow' up to and accompanying the left bunker which defends the green. The green itself is also bunkered right, and tapers in between the two bunkers. Any errant shots on this last stretch—dogleg left and green—are in serious trouble.

The front three tees of hole twelve have the option to carry over water, with the back tee carrying a long distance over same. The layout of this hole wraps the play around an inlet of one of the course's ponds. Combine a teeing off distance to the fairway with the fact that the fairway itself is no longer than this distance, and you have an interesting golf puzzle to solve—with a pinched approach to the green (which itself is protected by bunkers on both sides, and of course by the pond which lies to the left).

The thirteenth is a severe dogleg right, which, as it doglegs, slips in closer to the pond which lies to its left. A long carry from tees to fairway, with the line of flight head on toward

the bunkers in the dogleg's inner 'knee.' Over-correction will take you into the pond. Then, it's a drive toward the green, which lies, bunkered behind, at the end of a concave arc which curves away from the pond—shots had best be accurate here, or it's 'in the drink' for going left, and in the trap for going too long. An intriguing and very beautiful hole.

Hole fourteen combines a challenging tee shot to a fairway with a large pond on the right. Well-distanced shots are important here; and from this point, shots tending toward the right—which is the fairway tendency—will find the large bunker at right. At any rate, the green is secluded by its smallness and the armada of bunkers which surround it. Hole fifteen's straightforward fairway suddenly develops a case of the wobbles toward the green end. Neatly tucked into these wobbles are several hungry bunkers which will tempt you into going for a carry over onto the boot-shaped green, the heel of which is likely to let your ball kick off into the rough.

The sixteenth is the famous and fabulous 'flower hole'—perhaps the one hole in all of golfing that is likely to be known on sight by many non-golfers. The play on this hole is magnificent; the scenery, breathtaking. Tee off across a beautiful bed of flowers—which in effect is a water hazard—toward a short, narrow fairway which leads to a triangular green set with its chin buried in the fairway. Many golfers will go for the green immediately, though—and the green is trapped left and right, for short shots and long shots. In addition, another strand of flowers hungers to

A golfer makes it out of a bunker on one of SentryWorld's water holes, in the upper photo *on the facing page. At left*, late season mums bloom on the sixteenth.

mulch over-long tee shots. This is a very tricky hole, a delight to play and is visually an utter astonishment.

Hole number seventeen continues the pace with a long carry to a quick dogleg left, then down the fairway's 'shin' to small green trapped behind and protected at right by a small pond, which forces a bottleneck green approach, tending toward the left—a dangerous setup, as the green curves toward the right beyond the water.

The eighteenth hole is a marvellous finish to your round of golf. All but the innermost of the four tees have a long carry over a slender pond surrounded by rough to the fairway, which curves to the left and is bunkered at a likely place right. Bunkers dot the right side of this fairway, which leads toward a very

pinched approach to the green, which is bunkered right and left. Unsubtle shots will find the two right bunkers, as well as pot bunkers in back of the hole—these provide the ultimate challenge for a sand wedge shot. A great finishing hole, and more than enough reason to head for the clubhouse—which lies directly in your line of sight at this point—to celebrate an outstanding round of golf.

Add to this as complete and varied a practice range as one could imagine, and you have one of the finest courses in the United States—a course which has features found nowhere else in the world. Robert Trent Jones Jr has created a real gift to the public, under the auspices of the late John Joanis and Sentry Insurance. For golfers of all capabilities, Sentry-World is truly a 'Mona Lisa'...in Wisconsin.

Hole	1	2	3	4	5	6	7	8	9	Out	
Championship	417	409	399	177	513	407	196	357	501	3376	
Intermediate	382	375	371	140	492	372	152	331	469	3084	
Club	369	362	361	121	450	346	130	320	441	2900	
Forward	331	329	334	92	413	306	102	295	417	2619	
Par	4	4	4	3	5	4	3	4	5	36	
Hole	10	11	12	13	14	15	16	17	18	In	Total
Championship	391	533	216	389	509	448	166	406	417	3475	6851
Intermediate	380	492	183	363	475	398	135	370	406	3202	6286
Club	342	454	146	342	452	353	115	339	383	2926	5826
Forward	315	425	105	309	416	281	108	317	302	2578	5197
Par	4	5	3	4	5	4	3	4	4	36	72

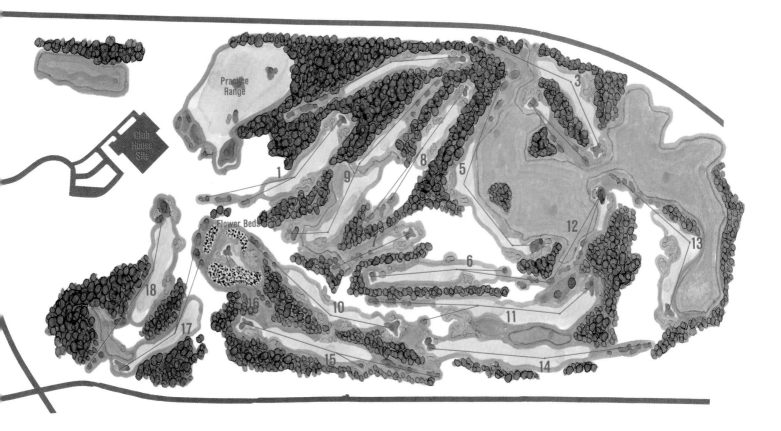

Silverado Country Club & Resort Golf Course

Napa, California USA

The history of this excellent golf course layout goes back into the mists of the nineteenth century. The Silverado Mansion was built in the 1870s by General John Franklin Miller, who had bought the major portion of the grounds that Silverado now occupies, to build a rather elegant ranch. The mansion incorporates Italian and French architecture, and it is rumored that the southwest section of the mansion's first story was actually built around—that is, incorporates into its structure—an old Spanish adobe hut that was rumored to bring good luck—or misfortune to the one who would dare destroy it.

To cite the more recent history of Silverado and its grounds, in October of 1953, Ben Harmon designed an 18 hole course for Pat Markovich, who decided to keep the name 'Silverado' and to apply it to his whole project due to the frequency of that name in the Napa area—it has historic roots going back to the earliest European settlers of the area, and to the silver mines of nineteenth century California. In 1955, the Silverado Golf Course opened for play, with Gene Littler, Johnny Dawson, Joe Spinola and Tony Celak in the first foursome to play the course.

Pat Markovich went on to other successful ventures, and the Westgate Factors partner-

ship took control of the club in 1966, and with that, the mansion which had been built by one of the property's original owners was remodeled, and—most importantly for our purposes here—Robert Trent Jones Jr redesigned the 18 hole course into two 18 hole courses that same year, which was also to mark his own stepping into the waters of independence from his father's firm; this is discussed in the introduction to this volume.

In the early 1970s, Amfac Resorts bought out Westgate and took control of the entire

The warm richness of the Napa Valley suffuses the view *below*, of the Silverado layout. With two courses to choose from, Silverado offers great golf.

resort and development. Amfac has constructed a series of condominiums and other structures on the property, but in keeping with their generally tasteful way of doing things, the whole is blended quite harmoniously. With exquiste dining facilities, a golf shop and other fine accomodations, the Silverado Country Club & Resort is the place to golf in the Napa Valley.

Artfully designed by Mr Jones, Silverado's two 18 hole courses offer tree-lined fairways, and cannily shaped greens and bunkers. The demanding South Course offers deceiving side-hill lies and over a dozen water crossings, and is 6632 yards from the back tees; the more forgiving North Course is 6896 yards from the back tees.

This fine layout is the recipient of honors and international acclaim. In *USA Today* of 11 April 1984, the American Society of Golf Course Architects listed Silverado North and South among their 130 best-designed courses in the US—the course was listed among those designed after 1962. Silverado North and South are also on the February 1987 *Golf Digest* list of Places to Play, a listing of fine golf courses around the world. Each year, 100,000 visitors use the Siverado facilities, and along with the members of Silverado Country Club, play 85,000 to 90,000 rounds of golf on the two championship courses.

The genius of the architect Robert Trent Jones Jr can only really be appreciated when one actually plays the course, but a hint may be granted by the following hole-by-hole description, starting with the Silverado North Course, which is considered to be the 'gentler' of the two 18s at Silverado.

Hole one tee shots cross a stream to a straight fairway lined with trees. The green is set obliquely, is wineskin-shaped and has bunkers at right, left and behind. Hole number two tee shots pass over two bunkers which pinch the front of the green. The green flares out behind these, and is set in a framework of trees. This hole is short but very interesting. Bending slightly to the left, hole three has a bunker at right. Its tricky green has semi-hidden bunkers left, right front and behind. Players at the fourth tee off past bunkers at right. A massive bunker is set into the front middle of the green. Tee shots at hole five carry over a stream, and the fairway swerves to the right immediately after—be accurate! Coming back on course, a bunker left, and later bunkers right, guard the curves as the fairway swerves left to a green which is bunkered all along its front.

The sixth plays to a fairway which has big bunkers on the left. Its green has bunkers at front left and right, and a bunker behind. Hole seven has a green which is practically devoured by bunkers. Hole number eight tee shots carry over a stream—be careful of that

bunker which is set in the middle of the fairway. Bunkers directly on the approach and to the right keep things hopping! The ninth hole is a dogleg right which culminates in a green having a bunker immediately at front and to the right, closer in to the green than as on hole eight.

Hole ten's tees back up to a pond and tee off down a rolling fairway. The green has a massive bunker all along its left side. Hole eleven has a long tee shot carry over a lake to a green which has a large bunker on its left side, and the lake to the right. The large fairway of hole twelve has a bunker to the left and immense bunkers all around its green. The thirteenth plays a variation on the same theme by varying the size and shape of the bunkers, and altering contours.

Hole number fourteen has a wedge-like bunker on the right and plays onto the apex of the inverted triangular green. Bunkers guard the 'point' at left and right. Hole fifteen tee shots carry over a lake and a bunker at right,

to an oval green that has two small bunkers strategically placed at rear. Two bunkers to the right of the tees await you on hole sixteen. The long fairway ends at a green with one bunker on the left approach, bunkers eating up its left, right and front, and a bunker at rear. Hole number seventeen is a dogleg left, with bunkers on its inner 'knee,' and very shortly thereafter, bunkers at the left, right and front of the green.

The eighteenth hole plays a long, nearly straight fairway with bunkers at right just where they'll do the most good. The front of the green is nearly occluded with bunkers left and right. This is a fine, satisfying finish to a superb round of golf. Now, perhaps it's time to test our mettle on the challenging Silverado South Course. This is the tougher 18 of the two courses at Silverado, and features a number of deceptive sidehill lies. It'll be up to you to play the course and find out what we mean. Meanwhile, the following is a general description of the great Silverado South course.

SILVERADO (North Course)											
Hole	1	2	3	4	5	6	7	8	9	Out	
Championship	436	195	405	382	536	435	208	375	528	3500	
Mens	404	150	348	371	512	405	186	323	493	3192	
Ladies	374	130	330	298	471	389	150	288	474	2904	
Par	4	3	4	4	5	4	3	4	5	36	
Hole	10	11	12	13	14	15	16	17	18	In	Total
Championship	418	183	362	420	400	195	525	357	536	3396	6896
Mens	381	122	348	400	375	176	500	336	521	3159	6351
Ladies	353	114	308	330	343	135	483	290	497	2853	5757
Par	4	3	4	4	4	3	5	4	5	36	72

SILVERADO (South Course)											
Hole	1	2	3	4	5	6	7	8	9	Out	
Championship	366	418	197	372	359	380	191	422	512	3217	
Mens	358	397	153	347	334	360	165	406	481	3001	
Ladies	354	369	116	329	312	369	142	360	434	2785	
Par	4	4	3	4	4	4	3	4	5	35	
Hole	10	11	12	13	14	15	16	17	18	In	Total
Championship	361	569	428	495	382	185	330	165	500	3415	6632
Mens	341	542	408	467	365	149	319	151	470	3212	6213
Ladies	324	500	385	445	321	125	258	113	463	2934	5719
Par	4	5	4	5	4	3	4	3	5	37	72

Tee shots on hole number one must carry over a broad stream to a fairway having two bunkers lying right. Also on the right are two bunkers leading up to and onto the green. Go straight, young man! Hole two has a right-bending fairway having bunkers in line with any incautious tee shots. The green has bunkers at front and rear right, and a monster bunker along its left side.

The third hole has a green with bunkers at four quadrants, while hole four plays down the fairway into the teeth of three bunkers left, near a suspiciously bunkerless green. Beware! A green with a mischievous grin composed of five bunkers set right out front of it awaits you at hole five. Time to carry! The sixth is a dogleg right, with a stream crossing the fairway at just the spot that will make your shot to the fully-bunkered green a real adventure. Hole number seven plays to a green with two bunkers in front. Don't let appearances deceive you! The eighth has a long, bunkerless fairway to an ovoid green with a bunker up front, in the middle.

The ninth hole bends gracefully to the left, with two bunkers left to catch carry shots which land midway. Then it's a carry over the tip of a lake to a green which has a bunker on the right side of its narrow chin. Hole ten is a dogleg right with a small bunker on the left at the halfway point. The green is fronted by bunkers left and right. Following this, hole eleven forms a massive arc to the left, with a lake dominating much of the inner curve. The green has one small bunker at right rear. Tee shots on hole twelve have a lake to the left which incurses on the fairway. The fairway curves right to a green having two bunkers at front and two bunkers at rear.

Hole thirteen has bunkers early on, to the left, and a stream to carry just before the narrow green, which has three bunkers strategically set along its left side. Dogleg right hole fourteen has opposing bunkers guarding its 'knee.' The green has two bunkers front and one behind—more than enough! Tee shots on the fifteenth must carry over the edge of a lake to a green having two bunkers cannily set behind. Short, and it could be sweet. Hole sixteen tees off to a gunsight of bunkers: two left, one right. The green is set behind two bunkers which are located on either side, and has a bunker at rear.

Players at hole seventeen tee off to a narrow green which has bunkers at right and left rear, and the truly challenging end is in sight—the eighteenth hole is a grand dogleg left, with a bunker on its outer 'knee.' The green is at the end of a long stretch of fairway, and its approach is occupied by the Sahara Desert. You'd better bring a camel!

The view *at left* presents the opening hole of the Silverado North course, which is considered to be gentler than the South. It's not exactly a pushover, though!

The Links at Spanish Bay

Pebble Beach, California USA

We are much indebted to the California Coastal Commission for certain information which they provided us on the development of this excellent course.

Opened in 1987, The Links at Spanish Bay golf course was built on some of golfing's most hallowed ground—the pebbled beaches of the Monterey Peninsula, not far from the Pebble Beach Golf Links, which is considered by many to be the premier golf course in the world. Adjacent to the Pebble Beach Golf Links, there is beautiful Spyglass Hill, designed by Robert Trent Jones Sr—ranked by *Golf Digest* as one of the top 40 courses in America—and in Monterey is the classic Del Monte Golf Course, the oldest course in continuous operation west of the Mississippi.

The Links at Spanish Bay was collaboratively designed by Robert Trent Jones Jr, world-famous professional golfer Tom Watson (winner of five British Opens), and former USGA president and renowned amateur golfer Frank 'Sandy' Tatum. Together, they formed a team which beat the very stiff competition—which included Jack Nicklaus and Arnold Palmer—who were vying to be the designers of this course.

Given the restrictions imposed upon the Monterey Peninsula by the California Coastal Commission, Spanish Bay is probably the final course that will be built here. With his nearby Poppy Hills course ranked among these crown jewels of the Monterey Peninsula, Spanish Bay makes Robert Trent Jones Jr the *only* designer to have *two* courses here on the Mount Olympus of golf.

Designing rights for this course were hotly contested because, as Hugh Delehanty stated in the *San Jose Mercury News* of 7 April 1985, '...it may be the last course in the United States built on a piece of true linksland, the rolling type of seaside landscape on which the game was born in Scotland. Being asked to build a links-style course in Pebble Beach, says [Robert Trent Jones Jr] is like "being commis-

sioned by the Pope to paint a section of the Sistine Chapel."'

The goal was this: to build the first and only true links-style course outside of the British Isles. This was to be an outstanding achievement, and to all current appearances, it certainly is. As Robert Trent Jones Jr says, quoted in an article by Ted Blofsky, in the *NCGA News* of July 1987: '...Spanish Bay will yield to good play and thinking; this course is totally Scotland.' Adds Tom Watson: 'We hope you can hear the bagpipes in the background when you play the links.'

The open arms of the golfing world were, for awhile, counterbalanced by opponents to the project, who claimed that the large resort hotel and condominium project which was part of the project would create additional traffic burdens for the area, and would create, during their construction, a serious nuisance to local residents.

The project is located near Asilomar State Beach, on a tract of land that was barren waste

Seen *below*, the first green at Spanish Bay, evidences seaside linksland terrain. The fourth, between dunes and in view of the Inn at Spanish Bay, is *at right*.

before the project began. Approximately 530,000 cubic yards of fresh sand were transported from two miles away by a special conveyor system, to replace that which was actually quarried from the site earlier in this century.

This, in combination with improved public access to the Del Monte Forest, can definitely be seen as a conservation-minded move. In a sense, it could be said that the golf course project financed and implemented the restoration of the area, which had been ravaged for its sand. Severe erosion would shortly have affected the coastline at this point, had not the developers restored this area to something approximating much of its original condition.

Mr Jones, along with Mr Watson, Mr Tatum and the Pebble Beach Company (developers for the project) saw the project as a positively transformative one, a restoration of the coastline to its former beauty, and the building of a recreational site that both golfers and non-golfers can enjoy.

The California Coastal Commission backed the plan initially, but complete approval was suspended for some time due to protests. A gamut of lawsuits—on the part of the cities

of Monterey, Pacific Grove and Carmel—had to be run. The opposition was vociferous, but the Spanish Bay project won out.

It was a very intense battle, and one that the golfing world will be glad was won. The Links at Spanish Bay hearken back to traditional golf. The civic-minded builders of the course graciously provided public access to Asilomar State Beach and a nearby state preserve. In addition, the Pebble Beach area in general is being made accessible to the general public via biking and walking trails that were built as part of the project. And further—this magnificent golf course is available to the public, though of course the housing development itself is private.

In addition, some 340 acres of Monterey cypress trees have been retained on the grounds of the Spanish Bay development. Natural habitats are being protected, and any rare flora that would be interfered with by the building of the course was transplanted to a location which was suitable to California Coastal Commission specifications. The dunes of the Asilomar beach area are distinguishable from those elsewhere on the Monterey Peninsula by their brilliant

white sand.

Likewise various species of fauna associated with the dunes had to be protected. All in all, a massive project, but one which has been successfully executed. Indeed, one is likely to encounter a wide spectrum of bird life—ranging from red-tailed hawks to red-winged blackbirds, while playing or even just strolling these links.

Truly, this is not only the building of a major golf course, but is also a major restoration project for the area. In keeping with Robert Trent Jones Jr's penchant for including native habitat in his courses, it could be said that nothing could have suited his very special talents better. It was, even so, a tough battle to get things rolling—and now, with many Coastal Commission conditions to have been met, one of the finest new golf courses in the world adds to the very substantial golfing glories of the Monterey Peninsula. Says Sandy Tatum, 'It's a great satisfaction to know we've made something useful and beautiful here.'

The Links at Spanish Bay include no gimmicks—just terrific golfing. The course measures 6820 yards and is rated at par 72. The fairways are rolling and narrow, and the roughs

at The Links include a stabilized sand dune 24 feet high on the ninth fairway. Pacific winds, and the well-known fog of the Monterey Peninsula form still other challenges at The Links. The course's large, undulating greens are a Robert Trent Jones Jr design signature, and an additional challenge. The majestic 100-foot Monterey pines of the Del Monte Forest line many of these holes, and form a beautiful and otherworldly frame for the playing surfaces of this great new golf course.

The eleventh green has, even this early on, added a new phrase to golfing's fond jargon of famous course features, such as the 'water hole' at Mauna Kea. At Spanish Bay, the talk already turns to the 'top hat green' at the eleventh hole. On the weekend of 16-17 January 1988, The Inn at Spanish Bay hosted the official grand opening for the resort and golf course complex. Among the guests were film star and mayor of the nearby city of Carmel Clint Eastwood, and film star and celebrity Sidney Poitier. Robert Trent Jones Jr was most noticeable among them, because the top hat that he wore was in the color of the celebrated 'top hat' green that he'd designed for The Links at Spanish Bay.

The view of the third hole, in the photo *on the facing page*, shows the daunting array of fairway bunkers one encounters early on. Looking at the photo *above*, of the seventh green, you can almost feel the ocean air!

Hole	1	2	3	4	5	6	7	8	9	Out	
Back	500	307	405	190	459	395	418	163	394	3231	
Middle	461	265	334	176	405	345	382	148	357	2873	
Forward	434	224	285	127	349	301	342	98	326	2486	
Par	5	4	4	3	4	4	4	3	4	35	
Hole	10	11	12	13	14	15	16	17	18	In	Total
Back	520	365	432	126	571	390	200	414	571	3589	6820
Middle	464	318	406	99	535	342	157	369	515	3205	6078
Forward	401	285	341	76	475	296	130	321	476	2801	5287
Par	5	4	4	3	5	4	3	4	5	37	72

13

12

11

10

Club House

6

14

5

7

9

4

18

1

Hotel

2

3

8

15

16

17

Spanish Bay

Pacific Ocean

Hole number one plays toward the ocean, with bunkers right and left off the fairway. Just before the green, a couple of fairway bunkers at left harmonize with the two bunkers on the left of the green to keep your shot tending right. The second hole plays inland, and the green is right under the Inn at Spanish Bay, which is perched on a hill overlooking the course.

There is a truly spectacular ocean view from the elevated championship tee at the third hole, which is a 405 yard par four, describing an extreme dogleg left which breaks at a series of interior bunkers and heads toward a contoured green, with the ocean in sight all the way. The short but tough fourth hole incurses sand dunes with its putting surfaces.

Hole five is a long dogleg that faces tee shots with three pot bunkers in a row set into the fairway. It doglegs right and heads toward a green which has a bunker at left front. The sixth has a contoured fairway having almost a

At left: The first green, as it appears from the eighteenth tees. The golfers *below* discuss a ball lost in the ninth's notorious block-long 'sand trap.' The thirteenth green is shown *at below right. Opposite:* The tenth green.

dozen bunkers sprinkled on and around it! All your golfing skills are called for on the approach to the oblong green.

The seventh's fairway has bunkers right, at the knee of the shallow angle it makes in breaking for the green. A hazard again must be overcome en route to the second stretch of fairway, which angles to the left and has a prominent bunker set into the green approach. If you look to the left of the green, you'll see the marsh which forms a hazard at the eighth.

Tee shots at hole number eight carry over a marsh. You can hear frogs, and you'll see plovers and redwing blackbirds who are nesting here. The contoured green will test your putting, and the wildlife will enchant—and distract—you. The ninth plays away from the marsh, and has a 24-foot sand hill all along its right, and fairway bunkers along the way—it demands the straight and narrow approach, and a good hand on the green!

Hole ten is a long, meandering double dogleg, with a bunker outside its first 'knee.' Toward the end of the fairway, three bunkers lie in line to the green approach, and a bunker to the right of the fairway, and another behind the broad, shallow green complete the chal-

lenge. The famous 'top hat' green at the 365 yard par four eleventh hole features a flattened hummock in its center, and the hole itself describes a dogleg right with strategically located traps.

Hole twelve has a straight-ahead fairway with a bunker left and a bunker right. The green is set sideways, with heavy bunkering at its right front and right. Tee shots at the very short thirteenth hole carry over a very deep ravine. Set end-on, its oblong green is bunkered right and left.

The fourteenth features tees which are essentially a series of buttes stepping down to the fairway. This entire hole is a long downhill toward the ocean, and is quite spectacular. Bunkers start at the left of the long, long fairway, and march across the fairway to the lower right end, and include a deep bunker directly in the middle of the fairway near the green approach. Directly on the right front of the narrow green is a pot bunker which will further add to the excitement here. Off to the left, in the triangle formed by the fourteenth green, the eighteenth green and the fifteenth's tees, is a conservation area in which redwing blackbirds are nesting.

You'll see the blackbirds near the tees of hole fifteen, as the aforementioned sanctuary is off to the left of the tees here. This hole is a dogleg right with a two-part fairway, which has bunkers on the right of its first half. The second half faces five bunkers set to the left half of the green, which is irregularly-shaped and curls around one of the bunkers. The sixteenth is a par three, 200 yard hole whose tees face an obliquely set, oblong green having numerous strategically-placed bunkers.

Hole seventeen plays along Spanish Bay Beach, and has the Pacific Ocean all along its right. The fairway consists of two parts, the first of which has a cluster of bunkers two layers deep on its right edge. The second part of the fairway has a single bunker at its right, and the kidney-shaped green has a bunker left.

The eighteenth hole plays also to a broken fairway, the second part of which branches into two prongs, and brings into mind Robert Frost's poem 'The Road Not Taken.' Talk about coming to a crossroads! The left 'prong' is precedede by a pot bunker, and the wine-flask shaped green is set narrow end first, to the left, with bunkers guarding it to the right. To the left of the green is the redwing blackbird sanctuary, and considerable charm—and distraction—will be availed to golfers during the final strokes of their round. This is an exciting hole, and an apt embodiment of Robert Trent Jones Jr's 'great risks, great rewards' philosophy.

This brilliant conclusion to 18 holes of spectacular golf can only make you want to return again and again to the greatness and challenge of this rare gem of a course. The

Links at Spanish Bay course has been planted, after much consideration, with fescue grass— the putting surfaces being a mix of bent grass and fescue. It was felt that this seeding would produce a surface that would be ideally resilient in, and tolerant of, the often very dry conditions of the Monterey, California region.

This grass treatment will enhance the qualities of ball movement which are necessary for the windy peninsula upon which the course lies—conditions which are very similar to those at classical Scottish oceanside linksland courses. Fescue is, after all, the very green that is to be found prominently on most Scottish courses.

The majority of the 18 holes of this course provide awesome Pacific Ocean views, and the closeness of that huge liquid body, its waves smashing grandly on the shore, will provide stimulus and distraction. This is a strategist's course, and calls for meditative, yet powerful and accurate golf. It should be very rewarding for those who are willing to take risks for the truly good shot.

The photo *at right* features the seventeenth hole, with Spanish Bay Beach and the Pacific Ocean along its right hand side. Clockwise from the left *in the photo below* are holes seventeen, fifteen, eighteen and one.

Spanish Trail Golf and Country Club

Las Vegas, Nevada USA

Decorated with sparkling ponds and babbling waterfalls, in full view of Nevada's spectacular Spring Mountains, Spanish Trail Golf and Country Club is located in close proximity to the city of Las Vegas, which has long been one of the leisure capitals of the western world. This excellent course is a host site for the annual Panasonic Invitational, which boasts the richest purse in PGA history.

Spanish Trail is destined to become one of the premier golf courses in America's great Southwest. Both the touring professional and the player of only modest ability will find this course a challenge and a pleasure. With a variety of tee setups, Mr Jones has assured a great game for golfers having a wide range of talent and experience.

Spanish Trail's 43,000 square foot clubhouse contains club rooms, card rooms, a dining room, a cocktail lounge with terrace, a spa, and a complete golf shop. The clubhouse is of stunning design and is fitting landmark for a truly fine Robert Trent Jones Jr course. Following is a brief hole-by-hole description of the first 18 holes in play. Nine new holes were subsequently constructed to bring the total of playing options to 27 holes.

Hole one forms a slight dogleg left, and plays along the side of a lake. Trees on the right and bunkers left emphasize accurate tee shots here. The green is well contoured, with a bunker in front, and your putting best is required.

Hole number two has the lake to its right, and tee shots will have to carry over the tip of same. The green is guarded on the left and in the back with deep bunkers. Hole three tees off between two town homes on the left and a gully to the right. Play is uphill to an elevated green which itself has two tiers: you hit the heights, in the best sense of the word.

The fourth's tees play to an area of the fairway which is surrounded by huge bunkers that make this the toughest par four on the course. The hole doglegs slightly to the left, and the undulating green is surrounded with bunkers as well. Hole five is straight on with bunkers on the left and right. This long par three was the 15th toughest scoring hole in the 1987 tour. The sixth rolls a bit, and the tee shot must be well directed or the bunkers right and left will devour it. The green is bunkered in front and

on the left, and a gully nearby could also lead your ball astray. Once you're on, look to be below the hole on this undulating, tough-putting green.

Hole seven's tees face across a gully and chance a left-lying fairway bunker. From here, there are three bunkers left which could cost the unthinking golfer a stroke or two, but the brave have to exercise finesse in getting to, and playing, the well-contoured green. Players at hole number eight tee off to a dogleg right with bunkers left and right. From here, it's through the needle's eye to a supernally well guarded green. A tricky little par four.

The ninth hole demands that you tee off straight over a gully toward a lake. Dips and rolls dominate the right side of the fairway, as does a deep gully to the left. Don't go too far,

and still you have to carry over the lake to the undulating green, which has bunkers at rear—in full view of the clubhouse! Hole ten has a gully left with bunkers and obstructions right. Two huge bunkers guard the tiered green. Getting there is half the battle on this long par four hole.

Water on the right and a deep bunker that encloses the putting surface add to the interest at hole eleven. Behind and below the green, waterfalls provide a pleasant distraction, but can sometimes make concentration difficult! The twelfth's tee shots must go straight down the line between bunkers right and left of the fairway. The heavily contoured green could spill your ball into the bunkers on the left and in back. Hole thirteen has a well-bunkered and contoured fairway that in turn points you

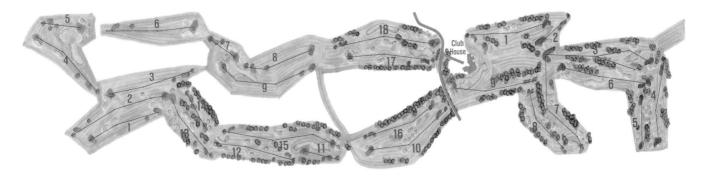

Hole	1	2	3	4	5	6	7	8	9	Out	
Yards	414	184	538	426	224	427	493	386	415	3507	
Par	4	3	5	4	3	4	5	4	4	36	
Hole	10	11	12	13	14	15	16	17	18	In	Total
Yards	463	192	405	359	218	567	431	422	496	3553	7060
Par	4	3	4	4	3	5	4	4	5	36	72

and mounding behind. The seventeenth's tee shots carry over a lake to the right and have to settle to the left of bunkers on the fairway. The narrow green is contoured on its right, and is guarded by bunkers on four sides. Hole eighteen features extensive bunkering, two lakes, and a babbling brook that runs through the middle of the fairway; accuracy is again the key here. This hole demands both strength and cunning. A subtly contoured green with water on the right provides a very tricky target here. This hole is the *piece de resistance* to an exciting 27 holes of golf.

toward a green which hides among mounds and bunkers. It's time for sharp shooting!

Hole number fourteen features a long shot to an elevated, contoured green with bunkers on the left and right. At 567 yards, hole fifteen is the longest hole on the course, with bunkers and two lakes—one along the fairway and one guarding the front of the green. The green has bunkers behind, so, not too hard here! Players at hole sixteen tee off to a dogleg left and a probable lie in bunkerland. The contoured green is elevated with a deep bunker in front,

Below is the ninth green, with the Spanish Trail clubhouse behind. Note the lake at photo right. Since this volume's first printing, a third nine has been completed to complement an already outstanding 18.

Springfield Golf Club

Gifu Prefecture, Japan

Springfield Golf Club is located near the municipality of Tajimi, which is renowned worldwide for its Noritake chinaware. At a spot of level ground in the hilly area just north of Tajimi, Robert Trent Jones Jr laid out this splendid new golf course, which includes several man-made lakes. Springfield Golf Club's clubhouse overlooks the entire course.

Flowers adorn each and every hole here. The flowers were chosen for their symbolic value, and seem especially appropriate in the premier land of flower arrangement.

The Springfield Golf Club is a first class golf club with a small membership of just under 1000. The course was opened on 1 May 1987, and plans are in the offing for a large international tournament in the near future. Gallery mounds for spectators have been built into the course.

The number one hole, like a good prologue, states the water theme which runs through most of this outstanding golf set up. Teeing off directly at a massive bunker on the fairway's right, we follow a gentle dogleg left. This leads to a green that is heavily bunkered on the inside of the curve it describes—in hooking left around a lake which has followed the fairway from the midpoint of same.

Hole two plays downhill to a contoured, obliquely-set fairway which is divided into two halves by a gully, the second half of which describes a serpentine toward a triangular

green having a bunker pinching the approach from the left. Hole number three arcs to the right around part of a lake—with the green gaining much in the way of protection by means of practically burrowing into the lake, with trees on its left and a massive bunker to its right rear, just in line with a tee shot from the back tee. Practically any tee shot here has to carry over the lake.

The fourth has a serpentine fairway with a bend right, and a bunker on the inside, and a bend left, and a bunker on the inside, and then the fairway narrows toward a green which wraps to the right around a nest of bunkers. A delight and a challenge. Hole five plays downhill over the flowers to the first part of a three part fairway. The jump from the first to the second part has the lobe of a lake to the left. Then this same lake must be carried in reaching the third part—which has two bunkers left to catch overzealous shots—and serpentines as it narrows to the green. The green approach

is pinched by a bunker at left front, and has bunkers at left and right rear. All the while, this last third has had the lake to the right.

Hole six drives straight on to a straight fairway which is contoured, and which hooks suddenly to the left for a green approach which is pinched by bunkers left and right. The seventh begins down a steep hill, again across the flowers and a lake to a green which is protected at right rear and at left rear with bunkers. Hole number eight plays uphill with a lake to the immediate right, and has to carry over a flower garden en route to a slight dogleg left, with bunkers right and left where errant shots may fall. The fairway then proceeds to an obliquely set green which points to the left, and shelters a large bunker on its inner side.

The ninth hole loses some altitude toward the green, teeing off to a fairway which curves around a hillock to the left, and then swings back to the right around a bunker. A stream

Seen *above* is the Springfield clubhouse, part of the ninth and the practice range. *Below* is the eleventh green and, across the lake from it, the tenth fairway.

The fifth green of this beautiful and very challenging course nestles beside a shimmering lake, as is shown in the photo *above*. The photo *below*, of the eighteenth fairway, hints further at Springfield's treasures—but for mood, you just can't beat the view down the fifth hole from the green, which is shown *at right*.

splits the fairway and it continues on, serpentining left and then right around clusters of bunkers to a proportionally small green, which is protected by bunkers at left front and by trees behind. At this point, while still charged from the exhilaration of playing nine such magnificent holes of golf, you may well want to avail yourself of the refreshments and amenities of the 'halfway house' near the fifth tee.

Hole ten is the beginning of a great nine holes 'going in.' This hole commences with flowers to the left and encounters a fairway which bends slightly to the right, with a bunker on its inside edge. A stream cuts the fairway off from the green, which has a yawning bunker to its left, slightly hidden by a 'mere nubbin' of fairway. Good golfing! The eleventh is a champion hole for the bold. The fairway and green wrap to the left around the lobe of a lake, and the green has a huge bunker right and right rear, and a small bunker to the extreme left. The fairway is close to the tees, but the real money is on carrying over the lake to the green—but, my oh my, does that look like a lot of water to your left!

Hole number twelve has a split dogleg right which loses altitude toward the green. Surrounded by greenery, there's not much chance to shoot awry here and still make a good score. That bunker in the pocket of the first half of fairway as you approach the split could surely undo the unthinking golfer. You have to carry rough to the second part of fairway, which necks down to a green set in such a way that only its end is attached to the faiway, and its chin reaches left, creating a cul de sac of fairway and green for a bunker lurking there. The thirteenth plays uphill from the back over a lake to a serpentine fairway having bunkers at right. The fairway narrows to a pinched green

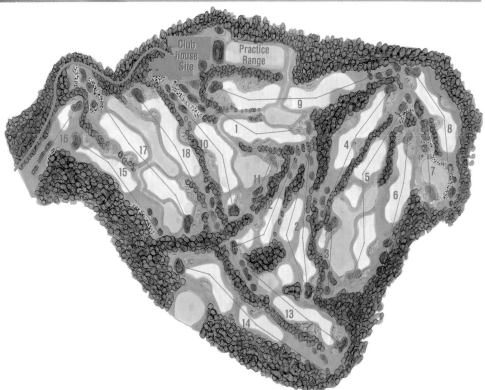

Hole	1	2	3	4	5	6	7	8	9	Out	
Blue	370	390	170	380	500	355	180	350	510	3205	
White	345	370	150	355	475	335	165	325	490	3010	
Red	305	330	100	320	440	290	110	255	435	2585	
Par	4	4	3	4	5	4	3	4	5	36	
Hole	10	11	12	13	14	15	16	17	18	In	Total
Blue	380	140	320	350	500	345	205	495	400	3135	6340
White	355	120	300	325	480	320	175	475	380	2930	5940
Red	310	95	260	285	440	285	135	405	310	2525	5110
Par	4	3	4	4	5	4	3	5	4	36	72

Distances in meters

approach that is heavily incursed by a huge bunker left and a small bunker at right. The bulk of the green 'chins' over the bunker left.

Hole fourteen goes into a slight valley, rises, plateaus and falls, only to rise again at the back of the green. You tee off to a fairway which has an incursive bunker at right—and then is split by rough, only to continue with a sharp bend to the right and then back left again, with a bunker on the inner curve. The fairway narrows to a green which has bunkers at right front and at rear. Downhill, on the left of this hole, is a lake which no doubt has swallowed many an errant ball. Hole number fifteen plays uphill with flowers and trees to the left of the tees, and lake and stream to the right. The fairway 'moseys' to the left, with a heavy bunker set just in line with most tee shots—so the overreaching will find the desert. The green hangs off the end of the left-tending fairway, itself an oblong headed right. In the juncture of these contradictory landforms is that old and well known acquaintance, Mr Bunker!

The sixteenth has flowers and trees on either side of the tees, for a truly festive (and straight and narrow) pre-penultimate hole. And a good setup for a good setup it is! Losing a few feet in altitude from back tee to green, it's a straight-on shot to a fairway which curves around to the left in an arc that is completed by a green curving to the right. On the inside of this arc is a bunker, and on the outside, ditto. A good, neat, challenging little hole.

Hole seventeen tee shots must carry over the flowers and the end of a lake to a bipartite fairway separated by a stream. The first half of the fairway has the lake always riding its left, and a semi-hidden bunker near its end on the right. The second half of fairway has the lake for one-third its length on the left, and the stream, and then a lake, on its right. Heavy bunkering completes the scheme on the left, and the fairway necks down to a green approach having a heavy bunker left, a bunker at left rear of the green, and the very present lake to the right. Be sharp, and a great reward is yours!

The eighteenth hole rises from tees to green. An incursive bunker right keeps a balance going with the lake at left. Suddenly, the fairway disappears on the left, and between you and the lake is a massive bunker; keep too far right, and the yawning bunker there will swallow your ball! Follow the fairway neck to the left, or carry the bunkers, for the pinched approach to the green features bunkers left and right, and the green is contoured with bunkers left and right. A truly grand finale for a wonderfully challenging 18 holes of golf.

The seventeenth green, with lake and bunkers, is shown *at left. Overleaf*: This greenward view from the eighteenth tees is almost as memorable as the hole itself.

Sugarloaf Golf Club

Carrabassett Valley, Maine USA

Robert Trent Jones Jr's Sugarloaf Golf Course was chosen as one of *Golf Digest's* best new courses of the year in 1987. The February 1987 issue of that magazine states that 'Sugarloaf provides a visual feast for the golfer. Several tees are elevated 50 feet above the fairway. The eleventh through fifteenth holes play along and over the South Bend of the Carrabassett River, a gurgling stream dotted with white rock. Our panelists gave it the highest numbers for aesthetics of any new course in all categories.'

The course is the product of a joint agreement between the town of Carrabassett Valley, developer Peter Webber and the Sugarloaf Mountain Corporation; specifically, this scenic layout is owned by the town of Carrabassett and is leased to Mountain Greenery, a joint venture between Sugarloaf Mountain Corporation and Peter Webber.

Initial discussions for the course were begun in the winter of 1983, and Robert Trent Jones Jr began work on the course the following spring. Over 100 workers were on the site at peak construction; to create the 100 acre course, 155,000 yards of fill, topsoil and beach sand were trucked in, and more than 4000 cords of wood were cleared.

The Sugarloaf brochure quotes Mr Webber on the philosophy behind the creation of Sugarloaf: 'The concept all along was that we had to have a great golf course. People won't travel here just to play any golf course, and that's why we had Bobby design ours. We had the best designer, the best site, and the result is absolutely spectacular.'

Each hole is closed off from the others by dint of the course's having been created from mature forestland—the trees are dense, and each hole has a very marked feeling of individuality. Yet the course does exist very strongly as a whole, so that the overall effect is very much like a Beethoven symphony; strength upon strength—a very spirited and exquisitely beautiful course. Robert Trent Jones Jr himself is quoted in the Sugarloaf brochure as saying 'Of all the golf courses I've designed, this is one of my favorites.'

The course has Penneagle Bentgrass on the tees and greens with combination bent grass on the fairways, and the course, despite being closed during the winter, is kept in absolutely first class condition. Its popularity is growing

On the facing page is a view of the fifteenth hole, alongside the Carrabassett River. *Above* is a photo taken near the dogleg on Sugarloaf's first hole.

very rapidly. Excellent facilities await golfers in Sugarloaf's 'Stay & Play' program: the beautiful Sugarloaf Mountain hotel is seven stories of comfortable accomodations at the base of Sugarloaf Mountain, and the Sugarloaf Inn—another hostelry which is affiliated with the program—is home to the fine cuisine of the restaurant known as The Seasons.

Three more fine restaurants lie within easy walking distance of the Sugarloaf Mountain Hotel—the Gladstone, specializing in gourmet veal dishes; the Truffle Hound, well known for its French cuisine; and Gepetto's, which provides meals with an American accent. Both the hotel and the inn have swimming pools and tennis courts, and regional activities include fishing in the pristine local streams and incredible rafting on the Kennebec and Dead Rivers.

In addition to Sugarloaf's acclaim in the February 1987 *Golf Digest*, that magazine and the magazines *Golf Traveler* and *The Golf Club* have published feature stories about this marvellous, mountainside course. Sugarloaf has also appeared on the covers of *Golf Traveler* and *The Golf Club*. Also, as of this writing, an article in *Golf* magazine on this fantastic course was in the planning stage.

Championship tees are 6902 yards total, and front tees are 5324 yards. At this point, the course appears to be a real 'comer,' and considering its almost unbelievably auspicious beginning, could well become a hallowed golfing legend.

Sugarloaf/USA's *News From the Mountain* of May 1987 quotes Robert Trent Jones Jr as saying—in an article authored by Chip Carey—'We tried to do something quite different for this part of the country in that it's a mountainous setting: It's a deep wilderness course, which is Eastern, and we used some of the third dimensions that are apparent in Western golf. The combination is unique in the whole country, where you have a wilderness course and occasionally a moose will come and add a little interest to the shot and each hole is virtually separated from each other....'

The course is very interesting both from a scenic and from a golfing point of view. This is an excellent golf course, a sure test of your skills that challenges and rewards with great generosity—which is not to be confused with unremittant ease, but is to be equated with the very best that golf has to offer for all levels of golfing skill. This course is truly 'a cut above...'

The following is a hole-by-hole description of this beautiful, white birch-and-river-adorned golf course. The holes start out playing downhill, and follow a big spiral around and up the hillside, for a variegated sense of play and a visually stunning variety. Hole one is a dogleg right with multiple bunkers just beyond the bend of a tree-lined fairway, and heads toward an obliquely-set green having bunkers left and right. Trees all around add beauty, and of course, something to stay away from!

The second hole is a double dogleg—first right and then left. Tee setups include a back tee with a stream which must be accounted for inrupting from the right and trees pinching in from the left—and a much more open tee setup which avoids the stream altogether. The first bit of fairway here arcs around to the right, and has the stream on its edge at right and trees left. From this fairway, you cross the stream to another bit of fairway which has a massive bunker lying in wait for overpowered shots, and has the stream at left for underpowered shots. Finesse here! This takes you to the left—and a green which is well-bunkered

right (especially) and left, with trees, of course, behind.

Hole three is a short, straight hole with almost equisized fairway and green, but having a bunker dangerously set in the slight notch cojoining the fairway and green. Trees at left, rear and right rear. Hole number four is a tree-lined, stretched-out dogleg left, with a small bunker incursing from the left almost immediately. The bend in the fairway may cause some overshooting to the right, into the trees, and the bunker left almost at the end of the fairway will keep shots dangerously right—three bunkers surround the green, and two lie rightward. The fifth is a dogleg right whose

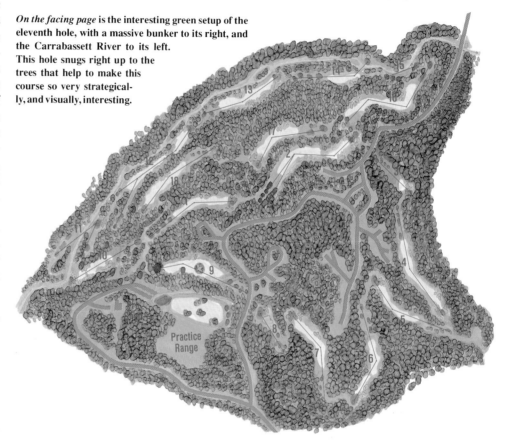

On the facing page is the interesting green setup of the eleventh hole, with a massive bunker to its right, and the Carrabassett River to its left. This hole snugs right up to the trees that help to make this course so very strategically, and visually, interesting.

back tee has a narrow passage around some trees leaning in from the right. Trees close on both sides here, and the green lies at the end of a narrow, recurving bit of fairway with large bunkers at right and left front. Trees and another bunker on the left and rough behind make this a challenge.

The sixth plays downhill to a landing area and doglegs right 90 degrees— then it goes sharply uphill over a series of bunkers. You've got to risk the bunkers, but it's worth it—for that green is a wonder, with the rolling Bigelow Mountains for a magnificent scenic backdrop. Hole number seven plays straight away on a dogleg right with a bunker

Hole	1	2	3	4	5	6	7	8	9	Out	
Championship	416	550	217	533	405	403	380	187	417	3508	
Regular	400	518	190	508	385	361	354	172	392	3284	
Club	366	487	169	456	361	338	327	150	364	3018	
Forward	333	463	155	396	328	307	308	120	339	2749	
Par	4	5	3	5	4	4	4	3	4	36	
Hole	10	11	12	13	14	15	16	17	18	In	Total
Championship	355	222	554	405	367	180	530	384	417	3394	6902
Regular	275	200	520	373	327	167	509	365	384	3119	6403
Club	255	176	505	360	291	133	455	353	367	2895	5913
Forward	222	151	443	320	250	110	437	305	337	2575	5324
Par	4	3	5	4	4	3	5	4	4	36	72

just beyond its bend, and plays up to a highly irregularly shaped green having trees close by and bunkers at right front and left rear. The eighth is a beautiful par three, and players here tee off to a green with a pond at its entire front, a bunker right, and trees at left and behind.

Hole number nine tee shots must carry across a stream—directly toward an 'X'-shaped bunker which is situated just where most shots would land on the fairway; a companion bunker lies to the right, just off the fairway: lay up or go for broke. The fairway tends left here, and to make it even more interesting, a tree incurses from the left just a bit farther on: accuracy is needed. Then it's a shot to a rolling green having a bunker on its left approach and trees at left, right and behind.

As quoted in the Sugarloaf brochure, Robert Trent Jones Jr describes hole ten in particular and the second nine, generally: 'Number ten starts from on high and plays up the throat of the Carrabassett River. Then the next series of holes plays down, over and around the river like a chain of diamonds—these are the sparkling holes.'

Indeed, hole ten tee shots have to pass through the trees straight toward a fairway with serpentine sides—in the convolutions are hidden three large bunkers, two left and one right. This heads into a green approach which is blocked directly with one frontal bunker, two bunkers left and one right, trees to the left and the Southern Carrabassett River slanting from right to rear. Absolutely great!

Hole eleven features tee choices similar to hole number two: three tees must carry the river to the green, and two tees shoot down a narrow hallway of trees with no river crossing. The green itself has a bunker at rear, a tumble downhill to the depths of the forest at right rear, a massive bunker all along its right and the river close on the left. With white birches in evidence, and the mountains in the distance behind, hole eleven is a glorious par three.

The twelfth plays down a narrow hallway of trees to a divided fairway, the first half of which tends to the right, leaving most shots headed for the grove of riverfront trees to the left—double jeopardy, trees and water. Shots too far right from here will find the bunker near the fairway break, which break is protected by three bunkers all across. The second half tends left, straight at the river, and the green is canted slightly left so that its left side is on the water. Bunkers left and right pinch the approach, and a grove of trees will swallow shots too far to the rear.

Hole number thirteen's fairway curves to the left along the river. Tee shots too far left could find the bunker which incurses from the

At right is a view down the tenth fairway from the tees. To reach the green, you'll have to carry the big bunker that the golfer in this photo confronts.

fairway's left, or the riverfront trees there, or the river itself; and shots too far right will find one of two bunkers on the fairway's right. The green approach is over a stream and is pinched by two bunkers at right. Hole fourteen drives straight at a fairway which has a bunker at right, just where unthought-out tee shots may find their way. From here, it's a sudden dogleg left between trees and across the river to a small green which is cannily bunkered rear for over-reaching shots, and has trees left and river all along its front and right.

Tee shots on the fifteenth have to carry across one of the river's meanders and a sand bar to a green having huge bunkers at its right, and a smaller bunker—and of course the river—at its left. The forest lies dead ahead. In the autumn, the foliage will easily outclass any other generally available distraction, as is the case with any hole on this course—the eastern autumn is, in a word, spectacular! Hole fifteen is an unforgettable par four.

Hole number sixteen forms a right-angle dogleg right which then repents itself into a more graceful dogleg left. On the inner 'knee' of the first dogleg, bunkers lie in wait, and at the end of the comparatively long stretch to the second big bend, bunkers await overreaching shots on the outer 'knee.' The green heads into an arboreal corner, with a bunker even deeper in to catch shots too strongly hit; the call is for accurate landing and restraint here. Hole seventeen is a dogleg left with a bunker early on, on the fairway's right. Then it's a drive to a green with two 'X' bunkers right out front, and a copse of trees on right, rear and left.

The eighteenth hole drives obliquely onto a fairway having a very deadly bunker set to the right, in perfect alignment with most tee shots. From here, it's a drive down a long fairway to an ovoid green which is canted to the left and has two bunkers left to protect that vulnerable side, and one bunker at right rear, to catch overflights from the left. Trees lie directly behind and to either side. A good, clean finish to an exciting and exquisitely beautiful 18 holes of golf.

This course demands every trick from the golfer's bag, and yet—with its multiple tees and tee placements—is geared to challenge any golfer's talent at his or her level of capability. Designed by a man whom many consider to be the best golf course designer in the world, Sugarloaf is sure to be a memorable course on anyone's docket of play.

We leave the summing up of this article to the designer himself, as quoted in the Sugarloaf literature: 'There are a lot of good golf courses in New England, but there's nothing that compares with this one.'

At left **is another view of hole ten, clearly showing Sugarloaf's mountain vistas, and the hillside behind the green—beyond which flows the Carrabassett River.**

Sunriver Resort North Course

Sunriver, Oregon USA

Robert Trent Jones Jr, has carved Sunriver North from the native Central Oregon land to provide a tranquil setting, combining the beautiful scenery of this glorious countryside with the challenge of a brilliantly designed golf course—one of the outstanding courses in the Northwest. The course was featured in a major article in *The Middle Tee, the Magazine of Northwest Golf*.

Nearly every hole is a dogleg in terms of play, and the many trees and stumps that dot this course will make the golfer's focus on accuracy a crucial one. More than 50 bunkers and several lakes combine with Mr Jones' 'enticement philosophy' (which involves presenting great rewards for great risks taken) to make this a challenging and extremely playable course.

As with many of Robert Trent Jones Jr's projects, the overall course is not necessarily long, but is long on play; the traditional Scottish values of strategy, accuracy and power control are featured and combined with new usage of hazards. This makes for much player interest and conscious involvement in each shot—unthinking shots will get you into trouble. A variety of tee placements makes the proper level of play available to every player. Completed in 1981, this course is a bright companion to Sunriver's older South course, which is a fine course in its own right. Following is a hole-by-hole description of the Robert Trent Jones Jr-designed Sunriver North Course.

Hole one is carved out amidst the trees. A long tee shot down the right side will allow you the opportunity to reach this par five in two. If not, an accurate layup shot will put you amidst—rather than within—the cluster of bunkers which front the elevated green. Hole number two has lodgepole pines along its right, and a bunker left at mid point. The lightly elevated green has bunkers left front and right, so don't stray. The third is short but demanding. The green has a large bunker left and traps at front and rear on the right. Play it smart, or you could make this a very long hole! Hole four has two 'gunsight' bunkers which assure your concentration on accuracy coming off the tees. The slightly elevated green has bunkers—two left, one right, which commit you to further 'sharpshooting.'

The fifth hole demands that your elevated

tee shot be on target, and the bunker at left could swallow errant shots. The green hides behind a natural lava mound on the right, and has a large bunker at left and a smaller bunker right. No matter what, the tendency is toward the bunker at left! Hole six plays to the left, and tee shots should carry the large rolling bunker that cuts into the fairway from the left. Bunkers wind around to the front from the left of the green; pines, lava rock and a bunker provide an interesting carry down the right side to the green. Hole number seven plays again to the left, and gives you a beautiful panoramic view of the mountains rising up toward Mount Bachelor, which looms skyward in the background. A bunker at right could catch tee shots without a will of their own; also, avoid the bunkers on the green's

right and to the left of the fairway beside the green by aiming straight at Mount Bachelor. You will, of course, want to stop short! Hole eight is short, but then again, the green heads into a lake, and has a bunker left. The bunker could be a hazard, or it could keep your ball from a watery grave. Play this one with eyes wide open.

The ninth hole has a lake on the right, which cuts into the fairway, and a bunker on the left which could force a carry over the lake; straight down the middle is the way to go. Bunkers at left and right frame the green, and the subtle, undulating putting surface there will make closeness to the pin a necessity. Hole number ten plays slightly to the left, with a lake wrapping the green on the back and right and right front. A carry could get you where you want to go, or in the water, or in the bunker at left rear. The two-tiered green will reveal the amount of putting practice you've had recently.

Hole eleven has a lake almost all the way along its right, and has a strategically-placed fairway bunker at left which may as well be 'all along' that side. The green features a bunker left—keeping up the pressure on that side—and is contoured so as to require short putts. Hole twelve breaks suddenly to the right after a pair of pinching bunkers on the fairway. The green has a large fronting bunker; also two bunkers guard the right and there's another at left rear, so shots to its cannily broken surface had better be on the mark.

The thirteenth has large rolling mounds on the left side of the fairway, and vast teeing areas which give a false sense of security. A

bunker right adds pressure to the 'squeeze play,' and a long shot may overcome this obstacle. The green has a subtly contoured surface and a bunker at right, as well.

Hole fourteen plays downhill to a deep, narrow green which is shaped around a bunker on its right side. Judgement of distance is the key. Lined with trees, hole fifteen has a 'hallway' formed by strategically-placed bunkers early on at right, and later at left, and a tricky right angle green having bunkers on both sides. A real test of golfing ability! The sixteenth hole tees off to a large, undulating green having bunkers at rear and at left.

Two trees guard the left side at the turning point of the fairway on hole seventeen: go too far left, a lake awaits you; go right, a lava outcropping must be carried. The large, three-tiered green has lake on the left of its narrow 'snout,' and bunkers on the right of same. No easy task, but immensely rewarding. The eighteenth hole is a dogleg left sandwiched by lakes. A big pine in the middle of the fairway increases the tension. You could carry the lake at left, but stop short of the bunker which fronts the green. The green has lakes and bunkers at left and right. It's on the mark or it's water and sand, and a beautiful hole any way you look at it.

The Sunriver Oregon Open Invitational PGA Tournament and the Oregon Invitational Pro-Am are yearly events on this great young course. Sunriver's 1987 Oregon Open Invitational was won by an amateur, Arizona State student Jim Strickland. Strickland praised the course, and added—as quoted in the *Sunriver Sun*; 'I had to play until my last shot. It was a good win for me, and I'm looking forward to coming back next year.'

Altogether, Sunriver North is a wonderful course to play, and its very pleasurable qualities are a fitting tribute to its designer, the brilliant Robert Trent Jones Jr. Fairways lined with pines, beautifully sculptured bunkers, glorious mountain views, natural rock outcroppings and native shrubbery, plus several cunningly designed lakes give the North Course at Sunriver an unforgettable beauty.

Hole	1	2	3	4	5	6	7	8	9	Out	
Blue	506	414	149	372	397	530	392	183	438	3381	
White	486	389	131	340	372	493	360	143	404	3118	
Gold	426	357	117	328	320	441	341	116	347	2793	
Par	5	4	3	4	4	5	4	3	4	36	
Hole	10	11	12	13	14	15	16	17	18	In	Total
Blue	550	387	398	394	188	543	168	398	416	3442	6823
White	512	357	352	355	148	510	140	345	371	3090	6208
Gold	456	304	293	323	115	427	116	282	308	2624	5417
Par	5	4	4	4	3	5	3	4	4	36	72

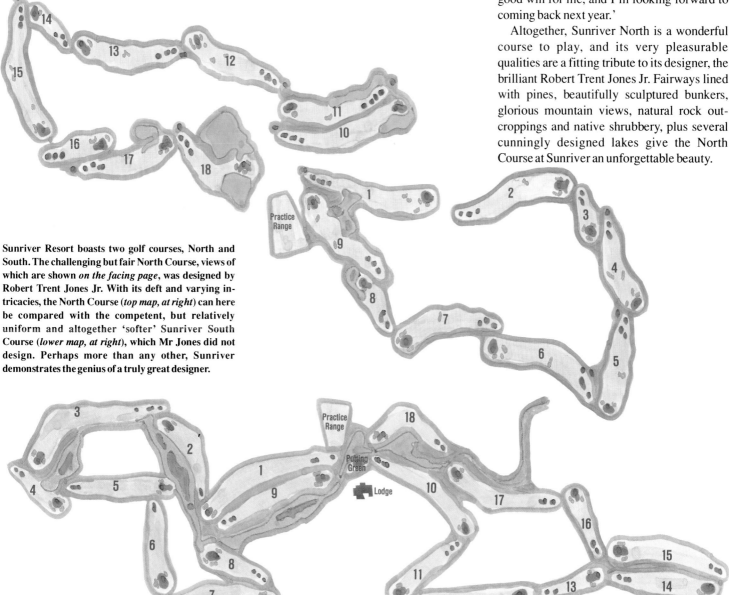

Sunriver Resort boasts two golf courses, North and South. The challenging but fair North Course, views of which are shown *on the facing page*, was designed by Robert Trent Jones Jr. With its deft and varying intricacies, the North Course (*top map, at right*) can here be compared with the competent, but relatively uniform and altogether 'softer' Sunriver South Course (*lower map, at right*), which Mr Jones did not design. Perhaps more than any other, Sunriver demonstrates the genius of a truly great designer.

Sun Valley Golf Course

Sun Valley, Idaho USA

Redesigned from 1978-80 by Robert Trent Jones Jr, this course is a rugged beauty which will provide any golfer with a challenging and rewarding round of golf. The course's origins go back to 1938, when the first nine holes were designed and built by William Bell, one of the leading golf architects of his day. In 1962, George von Elm, a former golfing champion, designed and was in the process of building Sun Valley's second nine when he died during the construction work.

In 1978, the famous Sun Valley Resort underwent major renovation work, and now provides the same legendary luxury with a renovated efficiency. The Resort's fine restaurants offer everything from Sunday brunch to Maine lobster to Italian cuisine and the finest steak. The Sun Valley Resort also offers such 'on the go' specialties as outdoor barbecues and cafeteria service. This winter/ski resort, summer/golf retreat has achieved a renown paralleled by few establishments. Opportunities for virtually every summer recreation surround the quaint walking village of Sun Valley.

In the same year that the Resort underwent renovation, Robert Trent Jones Jr was called upon to upgrade the golf course here. Finished in 1980, the result was, and is, a masterpiece; beautiful, sparkling Trail Creek, a trout stream of great renown, winds in and through the course. In the summer, when the course is open, swans, geese, ducks and other wildlife call the course home—adding yet another unique touch to this rapturously lovely course. At

par 72, Sun Valley is no pushover, and yet any golfer can find a challenging, rewarding game here, thanks to the varying tee placements. A hole-by-hole description follows.

Tee shots on hole number one must carry over a stream to a straight fairway which culminates in a green having trees incursing from the left and bunkers at right. Hole two's back tees have to carry over Trail Creek (front tees feature a radically different, altogether less risky approach) to a fairway which describes a segmented dogleg left, which is lined on the left with trees—this setup could make your tee shot a 'shaver' over there. From the bend, it's a short distance to the second stream carry of the hole, to a 'mere smidgin' of fairway leading to a green with bunkers at left front, which squeeze access toward the trees to the right of and behind the green.

The third features a fairly lengthy carry over rough to a green which is fronted by the creek. It has a deep line bunker running from left front to rear, and trees behind.

The back tees of hole four carry the creek and some yards of rough before encountering the first section of the fairway—a bit of playing surface which precedes the main fairway, itself long, rolling and, for the most part, lined with trees. The green has bunkers from front to rear on the left, trees on the right, and rough and a grove of trees at rear. It should be mentioned at this point that holes four, six and seven feature an apparent carryover from the previous architects; a bit of fairway im-

Hole	1	2	3	4	5	6	7	8	9	Out	
Blue	360	428	160	559	101	415	278	397	545	3243	
White	348	412	133	465	96	388	246	382	508	2978	
Red	290	279	115	389	81	317	227	346	442	2486	
Par	4	4	3	5	3	4	4	4	5	36	
Red Par	4	4	3	5	3	4	4	4	5	36	
Hole	10	11	12	13	14	15	16	17	18	In	Total
Blue	374	291	382	407	490	244	525	197	412	3322	6565
White	361	313	367	400	450	180	508	133	367	3079	6057
Red	348	249	351	350	413	135	470	112	327	2755	5241
Par	4	4	4	4	5	3	5	3	4	36	72
Red Par	4	4	5	4	5	3	5	3	4	37	73

On the facing page, sun-dappled Trail Creek wends its way along and through the Sun Valley Golf Course. The rugged splendor of this fine resort course is most visible in the photograph *at the top of this page*, which depicts a green setting that practically exudes fresh mountain air.

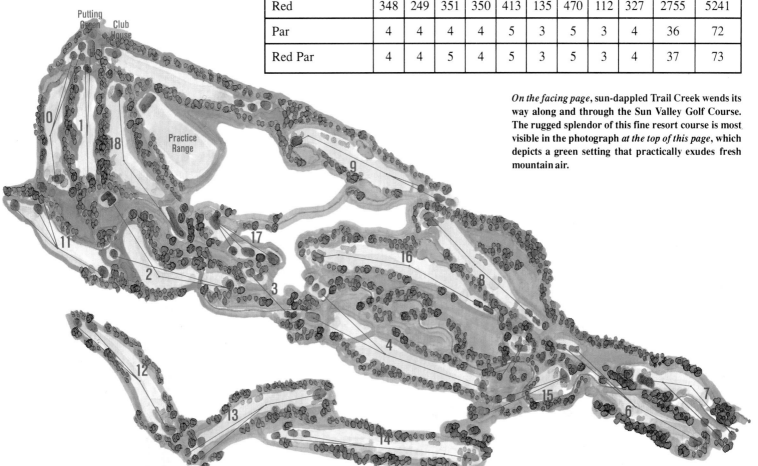

mediately preceding the stream carries, presumably for the edification of those who wish to play such carries 'safe.'

Hole number five's tees face across a creek to a green bunkered at left front and at rear, with a downhill roll to a clump of trees at right front, and the same to the rear. Hole six tees face across the creek to a fairly straighforward fairway having a bunker on its right— amongst the trees there, just where aberrant tee shots might land. Then it's rolling play to a green which is bunkered right to right rear, having trees right and rear and rough and trees left.

Hole number seven tees play across the creek to a fairway curving slightly left and set almost side-on to the tees. This fairway plays to a green bunkered heavily right, which has to its left a small bunker, trees and the stream itself, not necessarily in that order! Golfers at the eighth tee off straight up the fairway— which has bunkers right at the one-fourth and halfway points, trees most of the way and a bunker halfway on the left, to keep your drive 'honest.' On the left, the trees give way to a lake a slight distance off the fairway, which stretches onward toward the green. The green itself is bunkered heavily on the right, at rear and at left rear. At left front is a depression full of rough, and, downhill a short way is the lake.

Hole nine has a fairway with three massive bunkers far down on the left, hooks sharply to the left, and has bunkers just beyond this bend—on the right of the green to be exact. These will catch incautious shots. The green, in addition to the aforementioned bunkering, has a lake all along its left, and rough and trees ahead. Play at the tenth starts with a stream carry and trees virtually scraping in from the left, leading to a tree-lined fairway which endangers your shot with a 'crimp' of rough lying left halfway down. This precedes a green which is heavily bunkered from right front to left rear along the front, and has trees and rough at rear.

The front tees of hole eleven have it easy, teeing off actually on the fairway itself, but the back tee must 'shoot the chute,' carrying a stream while at the same time negotiating a narrow, oblique, tree-lined passageway over same to a fairway which tends left. The green has trees at left and a bunker at right front. Hole twelve plays down a tree-lined fairway which curves to the right, and suddenly gives way at the left to massive bunkers which actually front the green, such a deep incursion onto the fairway do they make. Trees at left, right and behind the green complete this test of accuracy. The back tee of hole thirteen faces between trees to a fairway which curves gently to the right, and has heavy bunkering at its 'apex.' Lined with trees, it's then a drive

The combination of variable terrain, stream and trees shown *at left* adds a special dimension to Sun Valley.

toward a green which is heavily bunkered left and right, with rough dead ahead.

The fourteenth drives straight down a tree-lined fairway with an incursion of trees at right, likely to 'shave your shot.' A bunker farther on at left will keep you from overcorrecting for the trees, and the green is bunkered, bunkered everywhere but rear, where still more trees keep a silent—thank goodness—watch. The golfer at hole number fifteen tees off over Trail Creek, and the back tee has, additionally, a narrow 'door' in a wall of trees en route to the creek and the fairway to deal with. The fairway itself is short, and the approach to the green is guarded by bunkers left and right. The green has the creek to its right rear, and trees at rear.

Hole sixteen's fairway curves left. It has a lake early on at right, trees right and a bunker right near fairway's end. The green heads into trees, and is bunkered at rear and at

Well-kept greens at Sun Valley: wooded (*at left*) or open (*above*), the vistas are exciting. The course is part of the Sun Valley Resort complex.

right and left. The seventeenth tees off across a pond to a shallow green having bunkers at rear and at left rear, and a stream at right. Trees are a backdrop to everything here.

Play at the eighteenth hole begins with a stream carry to a tree-lined fairway which bends to the right, and has a bunker just at the outer bend, where incautious tee shots could quite possibly find it. Then it's straight down the fairway to a green which is bunkered at right and left rear, with rough beyond. Hole eighteen is an exhilarating finish to a truly championship quality round of golf.

The splendor beheld today at the Sun Valley Golf Course is brought to you courtesy of the genius of Robert Trent Jones Jr, with all due respect to the designers who set their hands to this course before him.

Waikoloa Beach Golf Club Resort Course

Waikoloa, Hawaii USA

This is the second of golf architecture genius Robert Trent Jones Jr's fine courses on the 'big island' of Hawaii, the other being the upland course known as the Waikoloa Village Golf Club. Located in close proximity to the Sheraton Hotel, the largest hotel in the area, the fabulous Waikoloa Beach Golf Club Resort Course offers the best in golfing and the best in Hawaiian history that the big island has to offer. Ancient burial caves, petroglyph fields, historic fishing villages and lava formations are all part of the Waikoloa Beach championship layout. Ancient Hawaiian royalty used this area for sport and relaxation; Robert Trent Jones Jr has honored that tradition by building a truly regal recreational golf course here, in the playground of the ancient kings.

It is hard to grasp, but the Waikoloa Beach course is as different from Waikoloa Village as it would be if only one of these courses were built in Hawaii, and the other in Switzerland! Waikoloa Beach differs from its upland brother in that Waikoloa Beach features a sprawling linksland pattern which has its origins in the time-honored seaside courses of Scotland; like them, Waikoloa Beach is subject to the variegated weather that one associates with any seaside locale.

On the other hand, Waikoloa Village is built on mountainous terrain, and bears the compacted, highly variegated geomorphological layout of such other mountain courses as Mr Jones' exquisite Sugarloaf Country Club Course in Maine's Carrabassett Valley. In addition, Waikoloa Village exists in what is actually a high desert climate, which is the result of winds descending from Kohala Mountain. These winds create a constant, mostly sunny, low-humidity atmosphere which is unique in all the islands of Hawaii. In general, mountain courses demand an underpinning of rock riprap to forestall erosion. Judicious gardening is also in order; plants and trees help to anchor soil to unstable surfaces, by virtue of their root systems.

Beach courses such as Waikoloa Beach also benefit from prudent plantings, as the typically sandy, shifting beach surface would other-

wise undo all attempts to create a permanent layout: roots make marvellous anchors! In the case of Waikoloa Beach, a special circumstance was the existence on the site of a massive lava flow—out of which the course literally had to be carved. Wind is a factor in any locale which is exposed to the elements; mountain sides or beaches are much more likely to feel the effects of wind than such protected locales as valleys, for instance. In this, both beach and mountain courses have a

Below is the fourth green—with lava wall and lake. Compare this with Waikoloa Village six on page 184.

similarity. For further information on the Waikoloa Village course, please refer to the course discussion which follows this one.

The Waikoloa Beach course was completed in 1981, and tournaments thus far hosted include, among others, the American Airlines Golf Classic for 1983 and 1984; the Pan American Worldwide Friendship Golf Tournament for 1983; the Amaretto di Saronno National Ladies Club Championship for 1984; and the Steve Garvey Billfish/Golf Tournament for 1985 and 86. In the championship layout, Mr Jones has incorporated, in addition

to the historic features aforementioned, 76 sand traps, three lakes, tight fairways and lava beds bordering every hole.

The greens vary in size, and wind is definitely a factor—which has, of course, been accounted for in Robert Trent Jones Jr's intricate design. The par three fourth hole is an example of the tough short holes one has to master in this course: fronted by a lake, backed by three bunkers and framed by a 60-foot wall of black lava, this hole exists in a serene setting that will make the necessary concentration difficult. Be on your toes, but figuratively, *figuratively*—be at your best stance here, be alert! Following is a hole-by-hole description of this fine golf course.

Hole one's fairway tends left, and has opposing bunkers at its halfway point—a needle's eye to thread en route to the green, which lies at an angle, with bunkers at its right and left. Hole number two describes an arc to the left, with a fairway bunker far down on the right, making positioning a real strategy for the left-lying green which seems far away, on the other side of the lake which now confronts you. Carry the lake, and the bunker at rear of the green could swallow an overpowered shot. Hole three tends slightly left, and the bunker dead center on the fairway will make blitheness impossible. Beyond this, the front of the green is open, but everywhere else is Bunkerland!

The fourth exemplifies the true beauty of this course—couched in an obsidian-black lava bed, fronted by a lake and backed by three bunkers, the green is like a rare, mythic gem made all but unavailable by the dangers that surround it—only the true of heart may attempt it! Carry the lake on your teeing off, don't overpower and keep it on the mark—the gem is yours! There are lava flows in abundance here, as well as famous historical sites, such as the burial caves near the driving range. In a sense, the hole four 'gem' is a microcosm of the very beautiful, and priceless course!

Hole number five is lined with small trees, and its fairway is bunkered well on the left, and its green is bunkered well on the right—contouring is the word here. Hole six is very intense. Trees inrupting from the right, and a lake all across, and 'greeting' bunkers right and left guard the tee approach to the fairway, ensuring that your tee shot has to bear left, and must carry the lake and the bunker left en route to a narrow green which is bunkered right, left and at front. The seventh's various tee placements all carry over a sizeable lake to a green which is bunkered right and left, and is backed by rough and trees.

The fairway at hole eight has a broad central bunker, and a bunker guarding each of its irregular curves. The green is well protected everywhere but at its back. The ninth hole is a dogleg right with a broad bunker set at a right

angle to the bend on the right, and a broad opposing bunker having a companion a little farther on, to the left. An additional bunker boldly inrupts on the fairway farther on, near left center, and a bunker right guards the approach to a green which is basically surrounded by bunkers.

Hole ten curves gently right, with trees along its 'belly.' The triangular green is small and is bunkered on all sides. Hole number eleven plays short to a narrow green which is protected right and left with bunkers. Dogleg left hole twelve has opposing bunkers strategically placed at the bend, and has trees a little beyond, on the left, to ensure your being squeezed right on the fairway—which rapidly narrows to the left. The bota-shaped green presents a tiny tip which peeks out from among its bunkers.

Hole thirteen's fairway is pinched at the two-thirds point with opposing bunkers. The two-lobed green presents its smaller lobe, guarded with a bunker at left front. The fourteenth is a dogleg left, with a bunker just this side of the inner 'knee,' which may tempt you toward that bunker at right on the 'kneecap.' Bunkers right and left guard fairway's end, and that one on the right could cause trouble for approaches to the right-lying green (itself

protected at right and at rear). Hole fifteen's a long, gentle sweep to the right, and bunkers on its right will tend to keep things left. The green is virtually surrounded with bunkers.

The player at hole number sixteen tees off to a widening green having trees left, and one bunker at the two-thirds point on the right. The green has bunkers at right and left front.

The seventeenth has a short fairway and an irregular triangle green which is set baseforemost at an angle, with bunkers on each side—the rearward bunkers being the larger. The eighteenth hole describes a broad arc left, having trees at left, a broad bunker set in the 'belly' of the fairway, and a narrow green squeezed between bunkers at left and right. This hole is a marvellous test of accuracy, and an altogether satisfying conclusion to a superb 18 holes of excellent golfing.

The black lava flows which are evident everywhere on this course remind one of times long gone past—when islanders believed that the volcano goddess Pele both protected and punished them with these 'rivers of fire.' Later legends of European saints and mystics abound and echo through the mountains clefts, and drift along the sands of Waikoloa. Hawaiian royalty once played here, and given half a chance, they'd surely do it again.

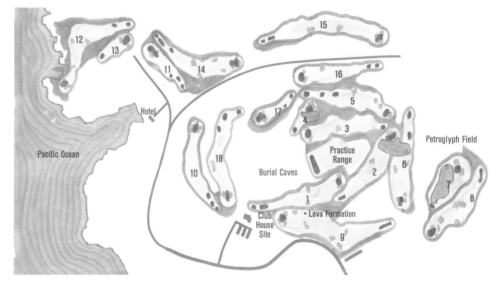

WAIKOLOA BEACH GOLF CLUB RESORT COURSE											
Hole	1	2	3	4	5	6	7	8	9	Out	
Blue	417	384	354	126	389	387	201	374	539	3171	
White	381	358	319	115	315	343	172	361	510	2874	
Par	4	4	4	3	4	4	3	4	5	35	
Hole	10	11	12	13	14	15	16	17	18	In	Total
Blue	411	187	492	185	441	579	362	171	410	3238	6409
White	366	179	466	161	400	530	322	146	366	2936	5810
Par	4	3	5	3	4	5	4	3	4	35	70

The Waikoloa Village Golf Club

Waikoloa, Hawaii USA

Waikoloa Village Golf Club lies just 900 feet up the western slopes of 14,000-foot Mauna Kea, the tallest mountain on 'the big island' of Hawaii. The course is located in a high desert, due to the winds descending from Kohala Mountain to the northeast. These winds create a pleasant, low-humidity atmosphere with lots of sunshine, and as such, it is unique for a Hawaiian golf course locale.

Completed in 1972, the course has aged very well, and features two small lakes and well bunkered greens. This 18 hole championship course is owned and operated by the Waikoloa Village Association, but predominate use is by people other than owners of lots in the Waikoloa Village development, which surrounds the course.

The Waikoloa Village pro shop, complete with driving range accomodations, was completed in 1987, and a bar and restaurant are located nearby. Special golfing packages include accomodations in course-side cottages, many of which are equipped with their own swimming pools, and 'downhill,' of course, are some of Hawaii's finest beaches.

Robert Trent Jones Jr designed this fabulous golf course for the Waikoloa Village Golf Club, and it is endowed with many of the exciting features which have come to be associated with Mr Jones' course designs. The club symbol is the bright red wiliwili flower, a beautiful and historical indigenous plant which can be seen in proximity to the course at certain times of the year. A hole-by-hole description of the Waikoloa Village Golf Club course follows.

Hole one lies right of the driving range and follows a dogleg left pattern. The fairway has a small bunker in its inner 'knee,' and drives onward to a green which has two bunkers at right front on its approach and a bunker left. Hole number two plays opposite, and to a dogleg left having bunkers at its inner and outer 'knee.' The green is tightly bunkered front, at left and right. The back tees of hole three must carry the length of a peanut-shaped lake to an uneven but nearly round green which is cannily bunkered rear—at the apex of the delta formed by all tee shots (the forward tees risk this bunker as well)—and at right front. At left front, should you become too secure, is the lake.

The fourth plays into a dogleg right with a bunker on its inner 'knee,' which bunker may well capture the shots of those who too incautiously try to reduce their score by shortcutting this hole. The fairway drives on toward a green having bunkers directly in front and along the left, which bunkers work in concert with the particular cant of the green to make for a cautious approach. Hole five tends to the left toward a green which is bunkered at rear and across its front. Hole number six features a radical crescent bend to the right, which has most tees carrying rough to a slanted green that is bunkered right and left and fronted with rough.

Behind is rough as well, and the approximate 'heart shape' of this green could prove to be deceptive, depth-wise, for the unwary golfer. Hole seven features a dogleg right with bunkers on either side providing pivots—and hazards—for the bend. A bunker very far out on the right could even catch errant green shots on hole six! The second stretch takes you toward a treacherous bunker left, very close to the green—and a bunker right at the front of the green. The eighth is a dogleg right having a bunker on its inner bend, and drives toward a green which is bunkered right. The ninth hole drives straight up a narrow fairway which has a tricky bunker left early on, and a trio of ball-catching bunkers left near the green, which it-

This mountain course offers challenge, sunshine and awesome vistas; the view *below*, of hole six, can only hint at the superb quality of its high desert atmosphere.

self also has a bunker all along its right hand side, and rough at rear.

The second nine is an excellent, challenging and most appropriate 'in' to the already exciting 'out' of the first nine. Hole number ten describes a deep dogleg left with bunkers 'riding shotgun' at the bend. Approach is to a green set just so that long shots will find the bunker at rear, and cuts will probably result in a stint at the left front bunker. The eleventh has a straight, rolling fairway with a treacherous stretch at midpoint, where bunkers at far right could take you into the land of extra strokes. The two-lobed green is heavily bunkered along its left approach and at its right front—a sharpshooter's hole.

Hole twelve features three widely different tee locations—all aiming toward a green which has a right lying bunker that dominates the approach, and a small bunker at extreme left for 'insurance.' The thirteenth has a fairway which bends left, having a series of bunkers at the apex of said bend, and a small 'spoiler' bunker on the inside for shots that run too far left. The green is virtually bunkered all around. Hole number fourteen is a dogleg left with a bunker on its inner 'knee,' where short cuts had better not be short shots. The fairway

bends a little more tightly toward the green end, and features a cunningly set bunker at the right there. The green is bunkered very dominantly on the right front and right, and sports a large bunker at left.

Hole fifteen heads down a caveman's-club shaped fairway toward the thick end, and at about the two-thirds point, opposing bunkers threaten, and shots will tend to the left of the green and the bunker lying *there*. Shots carrying over the bunker at right may find the bunker which lies at the right front of the green. The player at hole number sixteen tees off to a contoured green which is bunkered at front, right and left, and has rough at rear, while hole seventeen plays down a rolling

fairway to a lozenge-shaped green set at a cant to the right, with bunkers on its underlying left side, and a large bunker on its exposed right hand side. This calls for accuracy.

The eighteenth hole is a sweet ending indeed for this round of golf. The dogleg left fairway has opposing bunkers at its 'knee,' and plays from there down toward a lake, which must be carried to the green. The green has one bunker rear—in line with water-carry shots—and of course has the lake front downhill at right, left and front. A sweetheart, and a true reward for good golfing! The Waikoloa Village Golf Club course is yet another natural canvas in the extensive, worldwide gallery of Robert Trent Jones Jr's original masterpieces.

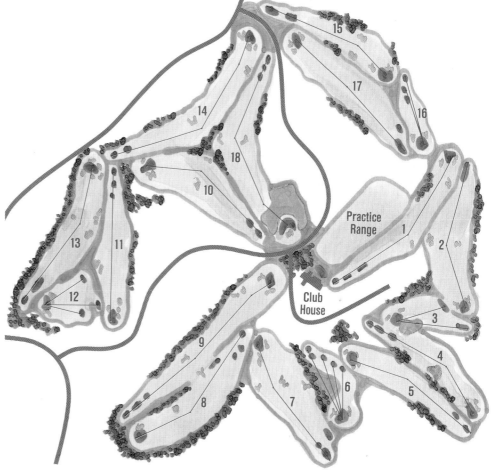

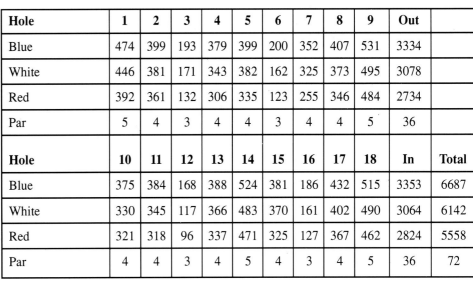

Hole	1	2	3	4	5	6	7	8	9	Out	
Blue	474	399	193	379	399	200	352	407	531	3334	
White	446	381	171	343	382	162	325	373	495	3078	
Red	392	361	132	306	335	123	255	346	484	2734	
Par	5	4	3	4	4	3	4	4	5	36	
Hole	10	11	12	13	14	15	16	17	18	In	Total
Blue	375	384	168	388	524	381	186	432	515	3353	6687
White	330	345	117	366	483	370	161	402	490	3064	6142
Red	321	318	96	337	471	325	127	367	462	2824	5558
Par	4	4	3	4	5	4	3	4	5	36	72

Wild Coast Country Club Golf Course

Transkei, South Africa

Robert Trent Jones Jr's beautiful course qualifies as the best in South Africa. Nestled just inside the Transkei border—about two hours' drive down the South Coast Road from Durban—is the Wild Coast Sun Hotel, Casino & Country Club. Though the hotel is fully equipped and offers elegant service, the most striking element in this compound is the fabulous golf course, which exists in the minds of many of the golfers who have played it as the word 'Magic'!

Sculptured out of natural hilly, undulant terrain, it creates for golfers an ever-changing variety of exquisite Indian Ocean coastal beauty. The course is situated in a conservation area and has been designed to harmonize with its surroundings—which is, of course, a characteristic of Mr Jones' course designs.

In 1987, Wild Coast was host to its fifth Golf Classic, the Yellow Pages Skins tournament—the biggest Skins tournament ever held in South Africa—with special guest pros Nick Faldo, Bernhard Langer, Curtis Strange and Lanny Wadkins.

Something of the beauty of this magnificent course can be imparted in words. Standing on the first tee, a gentle, almost still, lagoon forms the backdrop which leads onto a virginal hillside abloom with tropical trees which are sihouetted against the sea and sky. This is not an uncommon view on the front nine, and golfers may chance to see whales spouting just off the coast, and ships passing serenely by.

The back nine moves inland, and the contours here frame visions of hidden valleys, tree-filled gorges and gently rippling lakes which are incorporated into the play of each hole. As was mentioned above, Robert Trent Jones Jr has here designed a course which both *involves itself with*, and *incorporates into its challenges*, the natural wonders and beauty with which its venue is endowed.

Following is a hole-by-hole account of this unusual and highly playable course. The wind from the ocean becomes a factor on some days; on other days, the limpid stillness causes attention to flag in favor of simply savoring one's surroundings—a challenge, and what a pleasurable challenge it is! The following is a hole-by-hole description of this course.

Hole one plays down toward Thompson's Lagoon in a dogleg left. The fairway is squeezed between two opposing bunkers, and an overhanging tree at left. The green is bunkered left and at rear, and has the lagoon at rear and all along its right side. The second hole plays away from the lagoon to a sharply right-curving fairway which leans out from a bunker on its inner curve. The narrow green has two bunkers right, and one bunker left. Hole number three plays onto the narrow end of a fairway which is pinched between opposing bunkers. The fairway widens after this—a watercourse follows the right side at this point—only to pinch down again near the green. This time the bunkers lie right, and the fairway is at this point a narrow neck which leads to the triangular green, which itself is bunkered on all three sides.

Hole four plays toward the sea, to a small, roughly triangular green having bunkers at left and at right front. A slope guards all along the right. The fifth plays along the crest of a high dune, and is comprised of a fairway—having three mounds on its right hand leading edge—which curves gently left to a rounded, triangular green having bunkers at right and at left front. A slope lies to the right and the rear. Hole number six plays downhill onto an abbreviated fairway, or more directly, onto its actually larger green, which widens toward the rear after its two bunkers each at right front and left front. A slope guards the rear, and could lead errant balls to the depths of the nearby Umtamvuna River.

The seventh has a long, serpentine fairway having three bunkers hidden in the folds along its left side, and having one bunker strategical-

ly placed on the right. A pinched approach leads to a green having three bunkers at rear and right rear, and a large bunker left. Hole eight's back tees carry a lake, which lies left, to a contoured green having a massive bunker at right. Short but deadly! The ninth has a dogleg left having a mass of bunkering on its inner 'knee,' and a green which is basically surrounded with bunkers.

The tenth features a right-tending fairway which has two side-by-side bunkers just in line with any straight tee shot, and is lined along its right side with a series of bunkers which are likely to cause consideration on any shots to the right of the green. The green has a bunker at front right and another, 'outrider' bunker amongst the trees at right. Golfers at hole eleven tee off to a very nearly equisized fairway/green combination wherein the fairway has a massive bunker on its left, and the green is backed by a slope all around to the bunkers on its left front and right front. The ball had better stop where you see it must!

Hole number twelve is a water carry off the tee, involving part of the large, spike-shaped lake which also involves hole eighteen. You then must thread the 'needle's eye' which is posed by the right-lying bunkers, encountered early on the fairway, and the left-lying bunkers

The view *below* shows Wild Coast's first green as it abuts Thompson's Lagoon. Hole one is the beginning of a varied and challenging round of golf. In the photo *above*, we see hole twelve as it winds up and around toward the green. Note the lake edge in the foreground; the lake figures in play from the back tees.

which guard the green approach. The contoured green could mislead you to the bunker at left rear, or the general rough at rear. The fairway is lined with trees and a watercourse at left.

The thirteenth is as sweet, scary and ingenuous as any hole you're ever likely to play. Pouring into a tree-lined gorge is a beautiful, robust natural waterfall. This natural marvel is a natural *challenge* for many golfers, as hole thirteen demands that you tee off over said (cavernous-seeming, I might add) gorge to a green which is large enough—but is seemingly small with the hefty bunker at its back. This bunker is calculated to gather in all overpowered shots; of course, all underpowered shots will find rest far from the worries of the game at the bottom of the gorge!

Hole fourteen's fairway bends to the right, and has a bunker designed to keep tee shots to the right on the fairway. Watch out for the water hazards which cut across the fairway at the one-third way point. Beyond these is a small garden to the left, and the green—which has a large bunker at left front. Hole number fifteen has a welcoming committee on the fairway, composed of a large bunker stretching across, and two opposing large bunkers and a smaller pot bunker a tad farther up on the right. This precurses a roughly heart-shaped green having a bunker at right front and at left front. The sixteenth plays into a valley. Its fairway describes a slow arc around to the left, with two ponds on its inner curve and a bunker right to keep things even, and a lake guarding the entire right half of the green. How wet was my valley!

The player at hole seventeen has to tee off across a tree-lined ravine to a broadside fairway having a green which is accessible from the tees, but which is protected from them by bunkers at left and right on its green-facing side. Short shots find the ravine or the bunkers, long shots find the slope to the rear. Hit it on the lip or sink the ship! At the eighteenth hole, play commences with a carry across the foot of the spike-shaped lake that we visited on hole twelve. The fairway rides the high ground, and has two pinching, opposing bunkers early on—make that tee shot down the middle! From here, no less than four bunkers stagger across the fairway in quick succession on the slope to the green, which itself is set fortress-like—bracketed by a massive bunker at left, a bunker at right front and another at right rear.

It's a short trip to the clubhouse from this grand, grand finale. The Wild Coast Country Club Course is a masterpiece—on the edge of the Indian Ocean.

Hole	1	2	3	4	5	6	7	8	9	Out	
Championship	368	335	500	112	387	182	512	171	366	2933	
Club	363	305	472	102	362	161	477	143	340	2725	
Casino	324	280	449	83	337	142	442	108	315	2480	
Par	4	4	5	3	4	3	5	3	4	35	
Hole	10	11	12	13	14	15	16	17	18	In	Total
Championship	353	189	457	175	400	374	515	160	346	2969	5902
Club	338	163	437	150	372	350	492	141	323	2766	5491
Casino	295	140	388	131	320	309	449	138	286	2456	4936
Par	4	3	5	3	4	4	5	3	4	35	70

Distances in meters

The sixteenth hole is absolutely splendid—and terrifically challenging—with lots of water, as is shown *on the upper facing page. On the lower facing page* is the fairway and green setup of hole eighteen.

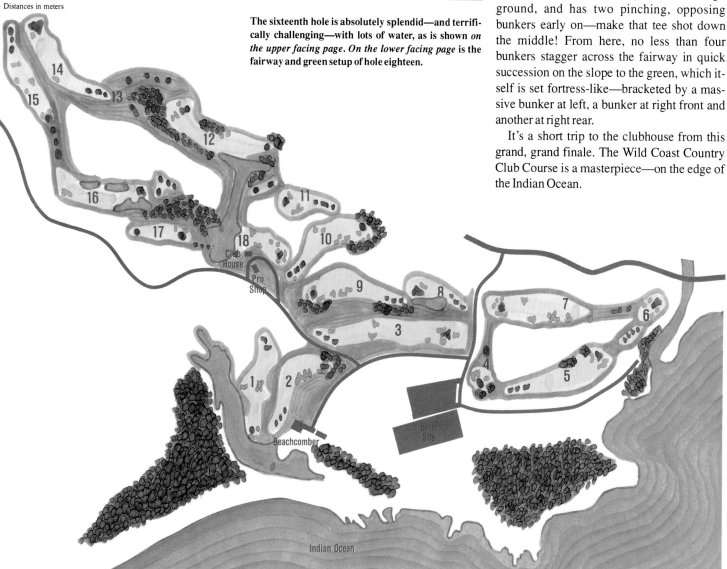

INDEX

Overleaf: **A classic shot of Poppy Hills' great hole eighteen in play.**

Acknowledgements

We wish to thank the people, including those whose names follow, without whom this book would not have been possible: Mr Terry Brandson, Consul and Director of Public Affairs at the Australian Consulate-General; Mr Gary Holloway of the California Coastal Commission; the Japanese Golf Association; the Shinwa Golf Group; our researchers Ms Pamela Berkman and Ms Julie Hawkins; Mr Phillip Mok, for his invaluable assistance in Hong Kong; and Mr TPC Street, Publisher and Managing Director of Courseguide Publications Limited.

We also wish to thank Barbara Miller of the Arrowhead Golf Club; Dennis Kalkowsky of Bodega Harbour Golf Course; the publicists at the California Golf Club; Dave, the course director at Cochiti Golf Course; Anne Mosler of Coto de Caza; Bertie To, Jr of Discovery Bay Golf Club; Linda Cooper and Steve Davidson of Edinburgh, USA; Jill Wood, Marlene Daily and Jeff Stuery of Elkhorn at Sun Valley; Mr Gross of the Eugene Country Club; Norby Wilson of Forest Meadows Resort; Don Price of Glencoe Golf and Country Club; the publicity staff at Glendora Country Club; the public relations department at Golden Valley Golf Club; Karen Olson of Grand Teton Lodge Company, and Herbert Cerwin at Cerwin & Peck Consultants, the public relations firm for Jackson Hole Country Club; Mike Brown and David Day of Joondalup Golf Course; Bob Jafee of the Keystone Ranch Golf Course; Charles Ortega of Kiahuna Golf Club; Nick Lombardo and Joan Hafner of

Laguna Seca Golf Ranch; Bill Hall of Lake Ridge Golf Course; George Foster of Le Triomphe Golf Club; Patti Cook & Associates; and Pat Searight of Mill Creek Country Club.

We also express our gratitude to the publicity staff at Meadow Springs Golf Course; Carl Marino and Gary Boelzner of the Links at Monarch Beach; Henry Cussell of the National Golf Club of Australia; the publicists of Navatanee Golf Course; Masanoa Inui of Oak Hills Country Club; Kay Mahan of Oxbow Country Club; Cathy Kreis and Mac Hunter of Princeville Makai Golf Course; Joan Elchepp of SentryWorld Golf Course; Kirk Candland of Silverado Country Club; the publicity department of Spanish Trail Country Club; the public relations department of Springfield Golf Club; Floyd Bashant of Sugarloaf Golf Club; Sue Demuth of Sunriver Resort Golf Course; Shannon Besoyan at Sun Valley Resort Golf Course; Dennis Rose of Waikoloa Beach Golf Club Resort; Harry Rorman of the Club at Waikoloa Village Golf Club; and Sherri Dene and Margaret Lossl of Wild Coast Country Club.

We would also like to acknowledge Joann Tarantino and Jamie Warren of the Pebble Beach Company, as well as Kathleen O'Brien and Jon Bomers of Thomas Cook Travel for hosting a wonderful on-site orientation to the Links at Spanish Bay.

Finally, we'd like to thank Mr Pat Sullivan, golf writer for the San Francisco Chronicle, for lending his technical expertise to the project, and for reviewing the manuscript.